*To th Raven Foundation —*
*Let us create peace, and*
*create th future, together !*

*Bob Kehler*

*Courage Grows Strong at the Wound*
First Edition

© Robert C. Koehler

First published by Xenos Press in 2010.

Xenos Press
6166 N. Sheridan, 18C
Chicago, IL 60660

ISBN: 978-0-557-71754-5

T3-BHM-246

Typeset in 9pt Palatino Linotype
By Outsider Editorial Services

Book Design by Interloper Designs

Cover Image by Nancy Ohanian

To my late wife, Barbara
To my daughter, Alison
With love

# *Courage Grows Strong at the Wound*

## Table of Contents

# Foreword

*By Marianne Williamson*

In his legendary poem "The Second Coming," poet William Butler Yeats describes a time that feels eerily like our own:

> TURNING and turning in the widening gyre
> The falcon cannot hear the falconer;
> Things fall apart; the centre cannot hold;
> Mere anarchy is loosed upon the world,
> The blood-dimmed tide is loosed, and everywhere
> The ceremony of innocence is drowned;
> The best lack all conviction, while the worst
> Are full of passionate intensity.

I think of that stanza whenever I'm reading an essay by Bob Koehler; at a time when so many of the best lack conviction and many of the worst are full of passionate intensity, Bob is one of the best *and* he's full of passionate intensity. When an issue arises on our contemporary horizon, I often ask myself, "I wonder what Koehler thinks." When his essays arrive in my inbox, I always make sure to read them. I look to him for a mix of things: his searing intelligence, his brilliant insight and his passionate heart.

Koehler makes you look at things you'd rather not look at; he refuses to pussyfoot around painful facts, yet he always articulates the moral point to which they lead. And that's what makes Koehler important. He doesn't shy away from the stark realities of our time, yet neither does he shy away from putting them in a spiritual context. And it is just such a voice that the world needs now. The current trend of anesthetizing ourselves in one way or another so as not to have to look at what too often is happening around us is a potentially tragic shirking of our responsibility as citizens of the world. But when facts are just thrown at us, harsh and with no context for either compassion or understanding, then of course the mind shuts down. That is the role of the public thinker: to help us put all the pieces together. And no one does that better than Bob Koehler.

Koehler's points are made with a combination of journalistic acumen and spiritual precision. He takes you by the brain and will not let you go to sleep, will not let you shut down, will not let you look away – and yet, in the same essay – will not let you lose hope, and will not let you stop believing in the spirit of goodness that lies within us. Koehler has his finger on something more important than the pulse of this moment; he has his finger on the pulse of love. He looks with searing clarity at what's happening, and with equally searing clarity at what's still possible *despite* what is happening. He sees through the veils of institutional, political and ideological obfuscation, while tenderly invoking our most beautiful potential. I don't know how he does it, but I deeply admire his skill.

Koehler's mind is amazing and he has the literary skills to match. Simply reading this book, both your mind and your heart will be expanded. You won't see the world quite the same after reading it, so in a very real way the world won't *be* the same. Koehler is one of those extraordinary souls who makes you think a bit differently *about* the world — and thus he changes it, one essay at a time.

INTRODUCTION

# DO YOU BELIEVE
# IN THEM YET?

*confined expectations. I could only write a column I believed in and such a column is not one that would be content to spend its life in QuikPublish.*

    *Another worry they expressed was how I would handle working with an editor who is also a colleague, like I had to reassure them I wouldn't … what? Talk back? Argue my case? Go postal? It was like they sensed in giving me this column, they'd be unleashing … Ego Man? Unreasonable-hope-exuding writer from hell?*

    *I kept my cool. I said, "Look, there's a certain amount of gunpowder involved in the creative process …" and proceeded to, oh, I dunno, state the truth, I guess. Make 'em see that the box they were trying to put me into was just a bit ridiculous. I gave myself a little breathing room.*

Somehow the column survived my intense emotions and sense of bubbling destiny about it. I did manage to write the samples and get the seal of approval from my bosses to begin writing weekly commentary for QuikPublish. This would, of course, be on the side, in addition to my editing work, and compensated at the rate of other QP contributors. The final challenge was thinking up a name for the column. I devoted several days to the task.

*Sept. 12, 1999*

*On Thursday, I just started writing down name after name after name on pages in a legal pad. Restless Angels, Wet Gloves, Sanity's Muzzle, Breast Pocket, Amber Waves, Next of Kin … 129 in all before I found my winner … Drum Beat, Matter of Course, Vacant Lots, Subway Walls, Still at Large, Brake Lights, Motion Detector … Naked Bacon (!) …*

*On Friday morning I actually snapped awake sometime after 5 in a fever sweat of possible names, some of which were starting to feel so-o-o-o close: Center of Gravity, Grace Notes … oh yeah, I like, I like. There was also Vanishing Point, Sea Change, Trouble Sleeping, Grappling Hook. And then I was on the el reading Theodore Roszak and all his talk about shamans and mysteries and I scribbled down first Common Mysteries, then Common Awe and finally, No. 129, Common Wonders.*

So Common Wonders it became, the name a challenge to left-brain journalism. My sources would be the tripwires of daily life, every last one of which was also an opening, a glimpse, as I stumbled, beyond the gated community of our collective certainties. I was inspired by the dancing plastic bag scene in the movie *American Beauty*, which came out shortly before the column launched. What could be more emblematic of our throwaway culture than plastic grocery bags, strewn across lawns, snagged in tree branches, slowly shredding but incapable of breaking down and returning to the earth? But here's one of them caught in an urban mini-whirlwind, a free spirit, "like a little kid begging me to play with it," as the young man in the movie put it.

"That's the day I realized there was this entire life behind things, and this incredibly benevolent force that wanted me to know there was no reason to be afraid, ever."

I sat in solidarity with that idea every week as I wrote, summoning, as best I could, this benevolent force to animate my words as it had animated the plastic bag. This was the "wonders" half of my column. The "common" half, however, proved to be more complicated than dancing litter. "Common" also included politics, current events, the daily bread of trouble.

*July 9*

*The latest issue of Extra (July-August) reports an amazing bit of dialogue from Howard Stern's radio show of April 21. It begins with a young male caller who, the article said, "described how he got off of watching Littleton girls run out of Columbine High with 'their boobs bouncing ... turning me on.'"*

*To which Stern responded: "There were some really good-looking girls running out with their hands over their heads. Did those kids try to have sex with any of the good-looking girls? They didn't even do that? At least if you're going to kill yourself and kill all the kids, why wouldn't you have some sex? If I was going to kill some people, I'd take them out with sex."*

*The article's author, Jennifer L. Pozner, goes on to note that the criticisms Stern received in the mainstream media amounted to praising him with faint damnation — calling his commentary "hurtful," "out of bounds" and "insensitive" — rather than calling it pro-rape.*

"Our world faces a crisis as yet unperceived by those possessing the power to make great decisions for good and evil. The unleashed power of the atom has changed everything save our modes of thinking, and thus we drift toward unparalleled catastrophe." — Albert Einstein

Common Wonders, then. Common Outrage. Common Despair. I wanted to get back into the column-writing game in order to be part of the national conversation, to push at our modes of thinking, to push at the void, to push at the disconnect permeating this conversation. But how? What could I say? The damage that resulted from the coarse national exaltation of the immature ego was ongoing and lasting, yet begged for something more than censure.

I had to write, somehow, about what had happened in my life — my wife's death — yet move beyond that to a world at war with itself (and this was two years before the war on terror officially launched in the wake of 9/11). So that became the unstated goal of the new column: nothing less than to resacralize the national discourse on life and death. And where a single column might fall short or contain only a hint of the wholeness and complexity this

Garden of Eden) to the day's news and our relationship with our planet. I understood this in a brief flash, as I held the planet's future in my arms."

Finally, **Part Seven** pushes the book outward again, giving us glimpses of some of the people who are building a culture of peace, sometimes in the process losing their lives. This section has the same name as the book itself, "Courage Grows Strong at the Wound" ("Virescit Vulnere Virtus"), which is the motto of Scotland's Stewart Clan. I heard it used several years ago in a seminar on forgiveness and felt instantly permeated by its wisdom. Instead of striking back at what has hurt us, we must learn and grow from it. Indeed, this is what we do in the course of growing up. Childhood traumas become the sources of adult wisdom and courage. The book's final point is that humanity as a whole must become conscious of this truth and reorganize itself around it, in the process weaning itself from its infantilizing addiction to violence. Everything that precedes the final word of the manuscript stands as the definition of that word.

## Acknowledgments

I would like to acknowledge, with gratitude, Tracy Clark, my editor these past dozen years, who saved me more times than I can count; my friend Leigh Hanlon, who designed and tirelessly maintained my website; and Eve Becker and Fred Schecker, who took a risk and gave the column the go-ahead in 1999. In addition, I am indebted to Nancy Ohanian for her beautiful cover drawing.

# PART ONE

## LOVE AND GRIEF

## HAUNTED HOUSE

When my wife died, I spent my first month of mourning disentangling the house from its ghosts and clutter.

I was suddenly appalled at what a wreck the place was. Even under ordinary circumstances, we had fought a losing battle against miscellany. We shoved stuff into corners; chaos bestrewed itself with an easy shrug across every available surface of our lives. After a year of cancer — with such urgent matters as pain management, constipation relief and a quest for miracles claiming every moment of our attention — all order in the house was shattered.

I set to the task of cleaning and reorganizing more out of numb instinct than reawakened guilt. I needed a challenge and this one was Herculean. But even more than that, I sensed that putting myself back together was somehow connected to putting the house back together.

I was at Barbara's bedside when she died. I held her hand and watched her suffering dissolve in the last hour of her life; her ragged breathing grew calm and the pain furrows on her face loosened. A sudden cloudburst out the window caused me to glance up. When I looked back, her breathing had stopped. That was it. Death came as a gift of peace.

Despite its reputation, death, it turns out, is kind.

It helps to know this. It helps to know the only suffering, after the fact, is yours, the survivor's; the only sharp edges are around the hole in your own life. But this can be endured, even welcomed. If there had been no great love, the ache would be small. So to me, grief in its intensity, the broken tear ducts — the downpour that came, for instance, when my daughter placed Mother's Day presents, bubble bath, talcum powder, in Barbara's still arms — is love all at once, love no longer paid out slowly, over the life of a marriage, but here now with the force of gravity. After death, love is a falling into her absence, not her presence. And that's what grief is.

And cleaning the house my wife no longer lived in was a continuation of this, a falling in love all over again — a falling in love with the worn and familiar. As I began disturbing the settled dust, crawling around in three stories and 15 years of married life, I soon realized that everything I touched — this tumble of old letters and frayed linen, castaway toys and defunct appliances — was charged with Barbara's absence. I wasn't merely restoring order to a house, I was freeing the past, setting its genies scampering.

Basement storage. Cardboard box crammed with travel brochures and misfolded maps, the moldy remnants of trips spanning two decades. Out tumble Missouri and the Berkshires and Urquart Castle and Kettle Moraine State Park.

Kitchen. That overflowing bookcase by the basement stairs. Spillage of old Weight Watcher pamphlets, never-used cookbooks, unwanted small appliances (gift Cuisinart that mysteriously alarmed Barbara, still secured in its Styrofoam packaging).

Upstairs linen closet. Baby blanket. Light blues and pinks, worn through in spots, numerous stains, the batting lumped in one corner.

Oh, the shards and accumulated scraps of a marriage, stashed and forgotten, compressed into layers. Now it's all luminous, each thing as it is surprised loose from hiding bearing witness to what once was. In the language of life, these are metaphors, compressions of meaning almost too large for the heart to bear.

And Alison's tattered blankie is the most powerful of all, as I hold it against my face and know too much about loneliness. I fold it and remember what it was like to surrender everything for love.

*November 1999*

## WHO'S THIS, DAD?

Other than the planet Pluto, maybe — which moves into a new astrological sign every 20 or so years — the main force that shapes generations is the music.

Once you're old enough to realize you're different from your parents, you turn on the radio and suddenly an electric guitar's turbulent chords drill you to the soul, a wailing voice stabs you with the truth about love and, most of all, the beat gets loose inside you, presses against every cell in your body.

What happens on the radio — on the right stations, anyway — is way cooler, way more urgent, than what happens almost anywhere else and swims through everything else, swims through every spare moment with your friends, swims through your solitude, your study time and your thoughts.

And, incredibly, your parents know nothing about it. They couldn't tell *Limp Bizkit* from the *Goo Goo Dolls* or *Garbage* from *The Flys*.

That caps it. Music sweeps you past your parents as they stare open-mouthed. One of the red-letter moments of growing up is realizing you're smarter than they are.

I remember how much smarter I was than my own parents, up to, oh, the age of 25 or thereabouts. The illusion served a purpose; it let me start making my own decisions and fall on my face a few times all on my own. Thanks, Mom, thanks, Dad, for all your patience.

Now that I have a 13-year-old daughter — now that irony takes a bite out of my soul pretty much every day — I show how good-naturedly I can go along with the human condition by allowing her to tutor me in current pop music.

It's a game we play in the car — "Who's this, Dad?" she'll say continually during our journey, as Lit or Blur or Smash Mouth obliterates the silence — but often it doesn't seem like a game. It gets far too serious. No hints, she solemnly informed me at one point, as though my constant wheedling for assistance had finally worn her patience thin. Another time she made a rule of not divulging the name of the artist till the song was over, to prevent me from giving up after one half-hearted try.

Through it all I've been the very model of the impenetrable schoolboy, the hopeless dullard straining to remember his lesson. An hour after I've been informed, "Duh, Pearl Jam, Dad," and I've responded, "Yeah, Pearl Jam, definitely," the same song will air again and I'll swear I've never heard it in my life.

I've finally figured out why this is so. Whereas a given song will command 100 percent of Alison's attention and be the most important event of that particular moment, I, with my spinning mind (thoughts about traffic, the bills, my career, what's for dinner, the leak in the ceiling, dental plan, antifreeze level, the Big Bang, etc.) give at best 1 percent of my attention to the same song, so it may take me 100 listenings just to remember it, let alone connect it to an artist.

Musically speaking, my day has come and gone. I like my daughter's music well enough, but it has no chance of transforming me at the roots, the way Dylan did, or the Beatles, or, heck, The Crystals, Del Shannon. The edge of my life has moved elsewhere, out to the land beyond mortgages and 401(k)s and financial security, out there where the body breaks down and courage sits waiting for the long night.

But sometimes I get it right. Sometimes my heart makes space for a song and I remember it. Sometimes my daughter even concedes that I'm cool — once, memorably, "scarily cool." Such an assessment, from a 13-year-old, carries a lot of weight. It offsets a thousand "dorks."

*October 1999*

*Update: Pluto's status as a planet was rescinded by the International Astronomical Union in 2006. Reclassified a "dwarf planet," it's still out there in the Kuiper Belt, orbiting the sun. The IAU ruling leaves it unclear whether I need to rewrite my lead paragraph. Taking a fleeting stand against impermanence, I've left it as is.*

## THE BEATING OF TWO HEARTS

She was wearing her heart not exactly on her sleeve — well, it was on her wrist.

I hadn't expected something so revealing at the food court at the local mall: a chance encounter with a friend's mother, the ticking of two hearts, the nature of love.

The level of depth Lanny showed me, amid the plastic forks and spoons and plates of shrimp fried rice, was as deep as a bullet wound. She did so quite unintentionally, but without embarrassment or guardedness.

I was with my wife and daughter, she with her two granddaughters. The moment was no more than this: My wife took the kids to get ice cream and Lanny and I sat casually talking. All of a sudden I noticed she was wearing two wristwatches (on the same wrist) — a small delicate lady's watch with gold chain and a masculine, leather-bound one. When I asked her about it, she said, "Oh, this one's Al's ..." And a look of love and pain swept across her face. Her husband had died about 10 months earlier.

"My watch always runs fast," she said. "Al's is accurate."

"Oh," I blurted and looked down at my dinner tray. There seemed to be nothing more to say, so we sat in silence until the kids returned, squealing and sticky. End of mall moment: Love endureth.

This was before I lost my own wife to cancer.

Today, such a disclosure as Lanny's would not tip my social balance into the awkward zone. I'd be better able to meet the sudden, dizzying openness in her eyes as she looked up at me. I wouldn't have looked away. I would have tolerated this momentary flush of closeness.

When you lose a spouse, you become aware that so much more is going on at any given moment of your life than you can ever acknowledge, let alone appreciate. Knowing this is not a virtue, it's simply unavoidable. All the while they were married, Al and Lanny were in orbit around each other, influencing, modifying, steadying one another. Mostly this happens in silence, without show. They were part of each other, joined at the hip, joined at each ache and uncertainty. It's just how it is.

Not long ago, I popped briefly into a large, multipurpose building in search of a schedule of cultural events. At that very moment, the theater in the building opened its doors for intermission and I suddenly found myself surrounded by the audience, who stood in small knots — mostly as couples — talking and laughing. I was hardly prepared for the effect this had on me. A sense of loneliness took my breath away and I missed my wife so much I had to grasp the handrail as I left the building.

Intermissions, carpeted lobbies, folded playbills, $3 cups of Sprite, phone calls to the babysitter — what a part of my life these had all been! Just silently standing around. Maybe disclosing, "I think I'll use the restroom." A spouse knows these things about you, knows the routine intimacies of your life. You can't possibly understand how much you'll miss this.

But my loss is at once its own gain, in the realm of awareness. It's called wisdom and it's a comfort, even when it hurts. It pushes back the edges of tolerance, makes you a bigger person — lets you live, certainly, with less impatience about the content of life. That's just the side show. Something, a

elemental conviction that being part of a couple is worth it, is perhaps the highest thing we seek, despite the impermanence of the arrangement.

And it is across the heart of this conviction that the noise of the TV scratches on a lonely night that precedes a day of promise.

*May 2000*

## FATHER KNOWS BEST

So my daughter tells me on Wednesday that the essays are due on Friday if she wants to apply for a $7,500 scholarship, and soon enough we're both tangled in a knot about it. Perhaps a dozen separate strands of our lives had wound themselves around this parenting challenge.

If this had been an old-fashioned sitcom — "Father Knows Best," to pick one at random — you can be sure, by the end of the episode, those essays would have been written. By the end of this episode, the one without the laugh track, ambiguity ruled and I could only try to loosen the knot strand by strand:

1. *The money.* We ain't rich, dear. If there's money dangling from a tree branch, reach up and pick it, right? In other words, I was pumped. Alison, on the other hand, has never in her 13 5/6 years felt the sting of want; the cash was a vague abstraction to her, which as far as she knew would have no impact on where she went to college four years hence.

2. *Character.* Of course you have to apply — beyond the cash lurks the principle. It haunted me, dweller as I am in the land of parental peer pressure. You can't let your child blow off a challenge like this, can you? This is about how the kid's gonna turn out. Will she go after life or wait for it to come to her? I saw the seams of her future undo themselves if she failed to give this the old college, or at least the old elementary school, try.

3. *The Writer Within.* The requirements were perfunctory: two essays. Discuss three personality traits that impact on your academic achievement. Discuss your career goals. OK, this is the sort of cod liver oil schools are always making kids swallow, and Alison was gagging. But, by gosh, I'm a writer; I know something about tapping the inner resources, transcending fuddy-duddy assignments and speaking from the heart. You can always write. How I wanted her to know what I know.

4. *Single parenthood.* The biggest rub of all. Surely my late wife would have wanted Alison to apply for the scholarship. Surely the two of us together could have exerted the necessary pressure. The most solemn vow I've ever made was that Alison not face a diminished life for having lost her mother. Would I be mocking that vow by letting her slide away from a challenge of this magnitude?

So, groan, there was plenty of parental freight in my voice as I discussed the matter, even on Wednesday, when I was affecting nonchalance and gently ruminating on her personality traits. "You like children, you're sensitive to others. And, yeah, remember when you broke your arm but went to your ballet recital anyway?"

"What kind of personality trait is that?"

"Well, I think they call that heart. You've got heart."

She grimaced. "Heart? Yucchh." And then: "I don't see what any of this has to do with school."

Now it's Thursday and she won't talk to me about it at all. I plant myself in front of her, desperate, groping for words. "I don't care what you do," I finally say, condensing my anxiety into a sort of battlefront triage, "but we have to have a real conversation."

And she breaks into tears, wails that she doesn't feel she deserves the scholarship, she has friends who need it more than she does, she doesn't want to compete against them. And I flash on the kid as a second-grader, lost in kickball because her pals are on the other team. "I don't want to beat them. They're my friends!"

And all the fight leaves me. I sit cross-legged on the floor, holding in my heart the precious jewel of an honest answer. "It's your decision," I say. Well, of course it is.

May she get all she deserves anyway.

July 2000

## FAMILY OF TWO

"Uh, what's there to talk about?" Alison asked, drumming her fingers on the picnic table, raking her eyes around the little square at the center of camp as though in quest of subject matter.

This was Fourth of July weekend; the place was crawling with parents, up here to visit their kids at the midpoint of Session A of art-and-music camp. I was content just to watch the crowds on this perfect evening, but she couldn't relax. Her restlessness pressed against me. "Shouldn't we be talking about something?" She really sounded desperate.

If we didn't keep the words flowing between us, then ... what?

Alison's panic, of course, triggers mine. A lot of stuff unnerves me about single fatherhood. I'd have been unnerved by female adolescence in any case; all my equanimity can disappear into its messy mysteries. But for two years now it's been just the two of us, groping for a way to carry on without a mom buffering us.

I suffer great pangs of inadequacy in my role, never more so than here at Interlochen, where I'm surrounded by high-powered moms who never run out of conversation topics and instructional messages for their teen-age daughters. When I'd brought Alison up here two weeks earlier, I didn't really feel at ease with myself until she informed me, as she emptied out her duffel and set up her bunk, that she'd left her pillows at the motel — 17 miles away. I acted put out but was secretly relieved I had something to do besides schmooze with the other parents (which my late wife would have done effusively).

And when I returned with the pillows, I was sent immediately on another errand. Turns out she also needed an extension cord and deodorant. Not just any old brand, but, specifically: Secret, gel solid, shower fresh. She wrote it down for me.

Her instructions were so technical, it was as though I'd been dispatched for a jet engine part. I was dazzled that my baby had penetrated life to such a depth of discrimination — and, once again, comfortable in the role of Traditional Dad, remotely tying up his family's loose ends.

But now, on my midterm visit, there was no escape from family togetherness. At home, Alison and I never struggle for conversation, but that's because we each have our own rooms; most of the time, we live in parallel universes. Here on this gorgeous summer night in northern Michigan, however, it was just the two of us at a single picnic table, smiling awkwardly, wishing one another well, grasping at straws.

As I looked out at the passing parade, I suddenly realized the reason for Alison's discomfort. Almost every knickers-clad camper was in a crowd — Mom, Dad and generally a younger sibling or two. The invading families engulfed their respective campers; you could see it happening: The teen, often with a petulant look, would fold back into the family unit. The parents talked nonstop and, generally, parented around her. The kid had little to do except reoccupy her reserved space.

But for Alison, there was no parent-generated force field that existed independent of her participation. There was just me, a single pole in the relationship. Nothing really started happening — nothing turned us into a family — until she held up the other end of the relationship. And so she was trying to do.

"Let's go for a walk," I said. In motion, our creativity loosened and our discomfort dissipated. We invented the Jelly Belly game: You had to close your eyes and guess the flavor of the jellybean the other person handed to you. Bubble gum is pale pink; root beer, light brown; strawberry cheesecake, speckled white; pina colada, pinkish orange…

We played for more than an hour, Dad and Daughter, family of two, improvising our duet until that night's concert started.

*August 2000*

## TERRIER AND RAT

*Note from the future: Amazingly, neither of us had a cell phone then.*

You want insight into psychology, try tracing a concept to its physical origins — "worry," for instance. One definition is: "to shake or pull at with the teeth," as in "a terrier worrying a rat."

When we worry, we play both the terrier and the rat, sinking anguished teeth into our own psychic necks. Who hasn't tormented himself like this? Is doing so ever necessary, or is it just a bad habit, like biting one's nails? When has the body English of our fretting consciousness ever affected an outcome?

Someone once suggested that, if it weren't for worry, the life we're leading right now, whatever it amounts to, would be close to ideal. This is because worry projects us into the near future — the engine trouble that develops half an hour into the flight — and we "live," helplessly, in the scenario that hasn't occurred rather than in the present moment. Part of the art of living well is simply to relax, look out the window, eat the peanuts, enjoy the flight.

So, fine. I heel my personal terrier whenever I hear him growl. Down, boy! I take a deep breath, look around the room, reinhabit my interior space: Life is good. Even when things go wrong, it's good, so long as I deal with the difficulty when it occurs and avoid wrestling with its phantom beforehand. I've gotten the knack of this over the years — except in one circumstance … when it's not myself I'm worried about, but my kid. As a parent, I'm sheer dog bait.

All I can do is lick my wounds and dig for whatever lesson lies concealed in last Friday's comedy of missed connections. Alison, who's 14, is full of eager new independence. It's another of those delicate ages; and, as when the child begins crossing the street by herself, the parent must let go of her hand.

In the last year, I've begun ceding a big chunk of the city to Alison, as she has mastered Chicago's transit system. She gets to school and back on her own, and many of her far-flung friends are now accessible by train. She can also get downtown and back.

On Friday (a no-school day), she and I picked up an out-of-town friend at 2, at a hotel near where I work. Then I left them to hang out and revel in their freedom; the plan was, get to my office by 5 and come home with me, or call me before 5 if you decide to head home on your own.

I didn't hear from them again for almost six hours. She tried to call at 5 (I later learned), but it took her 20 minutes to find a pay phone, by which time I was impatiently waiting for her in the lobby. I finally left at 5:30, thinking they'd already gone home. My flawed assumption was that they were tied to my timetable and sense of urgency, and that 5 o'clock was a hinge time, as though no one, not even teen-agers with pocket cash, would want to stay downtown later than that.

So when they weren't at the house, or on train after train emptying passengers at our stop, I began to unravel. By 7, the situation pitched over the edge of plausibility. No benign scenario could keep them away from home this long. My child was incommunicado — dare I say missing? — in a city suddenly as enormous as the ocean.

And thus began the terrier's low, menacing growl — the bared fangs, the pounce. Worry was my only reality. I sat on the couch in the darkening living room and set about the business of slowly eating myself alive. The day ebbed, the clock ticked. 7:15, 7:20, 7:30, 7:40 ...

Doorbell's shattering *ring-g-g-g-g!*

And then, before I even fully grasp that my world has shifted again, I behold two wide-eyed, giggling 14-year-olds on my front porch, purses slung over their shoulders. "Hi, Dad." " Hi, Mr. Koehler."

One father, suddenly himself again; no dogs, no rats, just joy beyond measure, rushing into the void. The "self" is a temporary arrangement — I know this now — to be swept aside every time worry wells from the depths of parental love.

*November 2000*

## HEART OF A BOY

The pitcher, a lefty, spinning to dodge a furious line drive up the middle, throws his glove out behind him and spears the ball. INCREDIBLE! HE CAUGHT IT!

The second baseman dives to his right, snags the tortuous, twisting shot in the hole, then from a sitting position in the outfield grass — his back to the infield — flips the ball blindly over his head to the shortstop, who steps on second base. UNBELIEVABLE! A DOUBLE PLAY!

Pirouettes of sweat. Gazelles in spikes. The tape was called "Great Catches of the Year," a montage of spectacular diamond robberies: outfielders pulling sure home runs out of the stands, catchers tumbling down the dugout steps with the ball in their mitt, infielders uncoiled to their full lengths as they stop bullets. Poetry with grass stains, written in body language.

My friend Malcolm (fellow connoisseur of life — we've been comparing notes once a week by phone for years) happened upon the film as he flipped to ESPN in an idle moment. He couldn't pull his eyes away. One great play after another after another, each overlaid with an announcer's urgent commentary. HE'S GOING BACK, BACK ... HE'S GOT IT!!!!

"Watching so many in a row," Malcolm said, "allowed me to go back and be 14, to whatever age it was when the greatest thing in the world was making an impossible catch ... and then to wonder, is there anything I value like this now?

"And of course the answer is — family."

Now there's a leap. Certainly I could remember being 14, 13, 12, and the thrill of getting dirty, of diving in the dust for a line drive or running under the arc of a towering fly ball, of being connected to the ball in such a compelling way I'd have done anything to reach it. I remember crashing into a row of bicycles once — gouging knees, shins, forearms — but, ta tum, making the catch, waving my glove triumphantly at my teammates, the ball stuck in the webbing (the pain to come later).

The heart of a boy! Yes, a boy values great catches — he values bravery and heroism, longs to be the one to make the spectacular contortion, the blood sacrifice. This is the essence, the very boundary of boyhood. As a boy pursues The Great Catch, he feels the man inside him — the person he's becoming — stretch out his legs and urge him on.

The beauty of boyhood, at least when I look back on it, is the simple clarity of its values. There hasn't been any big disappointment yet to complicate objectives. So when Malcolm talked about searching his life after watching "Great Catches of the Year" and deciding he values family the way he once valued baseball, I paused, caught on reality.

Before my wife died, there was indeed a serious vein of boyhood, of baseball-loving eagerness and zest to play, running through my husband-daddy role. But since her death two and a half years ago, and the beginning of my new life as single father/mother to a teen-age daughter, the stands have grown quiet and the boy, I fear, has gotten lost.

I'm legging it out (pant, gasp), determined to deliver this beautiful, skeptical, eyeball-rolling 14-year-old, to ... herself, to responsible, decision-making adulthood. But there's almost no camaraderie or esprit de corps left in this role, any of the things that feed a boy's heart. Mostly there's dialogue like this:

"Here's your salad, Alison."

"What's your problem, Dad?"

I live with this and do my job. The motivation to sustain a family is the deepest and most enduring of my life. But is the boy really gone for good? Since talking to Malcolm, I've been aware at times of a small, eager voice in the background, murmuring, when I do something right as a parent, "INCREDIBLE!!!"

*December 2000*

## SACRED SPACE

Life's elemental transitions — birth, death — have more pull on me than ever as I age. When they touch my life, they open up a sense of sacred space that aligns my every cell in prayerful awe. Not only that, the two events often dovetail with an eerie coincidence that leaves me mulling their connectedness.

When my wife died (how hard it is to believe it's been two and a half years now), the "mystical" event that left a door ajar in my consciousness involved a 5-year-old girl, the daughter of a friend of ours who had been extremely fond of Barbara. I happened to mention to Becky's mom, as I relayed the sad news, that Barbara died at the very moment a sudden rainstorm broke.

"I remember that storm," she said. "We were in the car and Becky said, 'Oh, someone's having a baby.' Then she frowned. 'I think Barbara's having a baby.'"

I don't know why she would have felt or said such a thing, but I believe her words were blurted in innocent wonder as something passed across her heart; and it strains credulity far more for me to dismiss as "happenstance or whatever" that Becky uttered Barbara's name at the moment of her death, than to accept the possibility of a linkage between Becky and Barbara, or her spirit, at some level of reality beyond the naked eye.

But it's the child's choice of words — "I think Barbara's having a baby" — that utterly rewrites my definition of death. I've let go of the empirical skepticism I once settled for, that death is simply the big sleep, the cul-de-sac of existence. When death touches your life, when it ceases to be an abstraction, its particulars present too many clues to the contrary.

Fast-forward to a few days ago. My tech-savvy niece, Carmen, e-mails me the first "photo" (i.e., the ultrasound printout) of her in utero baby, at about seven weeks along. Joyous confirmation of a long-sought pregnancy! But it was the lab date on the printout, when I eventually noticed it, that really opened my heart and stamped the event: miracle.

It was dated Nov. 17, the one-year anniversary of a day no one in my family will forget — the day Carmen's father, who'd been battling cancer for five years, collapsed on his kitchen floor in respiratory distress and was rushed to ER. He died the next morning — his 53rd birthday — but Nov. 17 was the day of his death watch, the day his wife and daughters gathered at his bedside, held his hand and said their final goodbyes.

So that date, now attaching itself indelibly to Carmen's pregnancy as well, stirs the soul with a sense of eternal renewal.

About 11 p.m. on that day a year ago, Carmen recalled, she had a memorable last moment of eye contact and communion with her dad. She and her husband had already been trying for a year to conceive, and her period was enticingly overdue. "He was kind of floating in and out of consciousness. I said, 'Dad, I might be pregnant' — and he opened his eyes."

It was as though he'd blessed her, and his grandchild, with his awareness. Indeed, I believe this is so. Small matter the actual pregnancy was a year delayed — it comes bearing Grandpa's imprint, the pressure of his hand in his daughter's, his wide-open eyes. He returned to earth long enough to share the wondrous moment with her.

There are those who say that death is another type of birth, into the next level of being. I know only that it is something more than the flat cessation of existence, the terminus of striving, the last, bitter irony. In my experience, death has not rendered anyone's life "meaningless," but just the opposite — revealed it to be extraordinary.

A loved one's death may shatter us, but I believe at the deepest level the connection remains unbroken. In sacred space, all life is connected. The dead go away, but manage not to leave us.

*December 2000*

## THE GAME CLOSET

A widower's house contains rooms that open into the next dimension. They may seem unremarkable, other than being a mess (most likely) — but walk in the wrong way, with the intent to clean, for example, and you'd better be prepared to engage more than just clutter.

I thought by now I'd dealt with all such rooms in my own abode, but on a day off last week, I stumbled into one. I was looking for my daughter's camera. The urgency here was that the roll of film in it contained pictures documenting her science fair project, which was due on Monday; in other words, this was code red: A good grade was at stake. Single Dad to the rescue.

The camera refused to be anyplace obvious, like this drawer or that — somewhere I might have stashed it while straightening. Slowly it dawned on me I'd have to take on, gulp, the game closet, a narrow room off the downstairs study bursting with disorder and memories. There was no reason for the camera to be in there, amid old art supplies and perilously stacked boxes of

surprised me was the weight of the box. I let loose an involuntary "whoa" as I hefted it, and felt a tug along the length of both arms. I'll bet it weighed seven pounds, maybe eight … about as much, it later occurred to me, as a newborn.

On a day frothy with the joy of new life, I took custody of my wife's ashes.

I have survived three years of grief mostly by defying the traditional framework of bereavement, beginning with the term "laying the body to rest." The image of a corpse sleeping makes me shudder. It's part of the "buried alive" syndrome I've observed at some funerals, where the officiator shovels platitudes about death atop the departed instead of allowing us to feel and cry publicly over the jagged edges of our loss.

What matters is the life the person has lived, and comfort is to be found in celebrating that life, not seeing it dispatched to some generic hereafter as quickly as possible.

And making too much of the body — the vacated shell — has always seemed to me the height of profanity to that truth. So I was hardly prepared for the complexity of emotions that accompanied my tardy assumption of custody of Barbara's ashes, on this day that I was about to become a great uncle.

How real it felt — that was the surprise. After three years of savoring Barbara's spirit, of subsisting on nothing but memories and photographs, here I was, carrying upstairs, to temporary storage in a little-used closet, something with weight and substance: not a memento or possession, but her, or what used to be her. There was a simple, direct link between the contents of this box and the body my daughter and I embraced moments after Barbara died, in bed, at home, on a rainy afternoon when lilacs were blooming.

Last time I saw the body, wrapped in a blue-sheet shroud, two hospice workers were porting it downstairs. They had to remove it out the back door because the city had just repaved the sidewalk in front of our house and the cement was still wet.

That distant moment came back full force — the immediacy of losing Barbara, of saying goodbye, of holding my daughter and crying. I felt all that in the weight of the box that tugged at my forearms, as though the mystery of life and death could be reduced to seven pounds of ash. As I carried the box upstairs, I felt like a pallbearer.

That evening my niece gave birth to a son, and my attention leapt to the cry of life and the rapt awe a newborn inspires. But what symmetry there is, I thought, to the transitions on either end of life.

I don't believe in rebirth, exactly, but I understand the impulse to believe in it, if only because, every year, winter yields to spring. Those who leave us keep on nourishing us. It's all part of the same miracle.

*July 2001*

**INTIMATE WITNESS**

"You smell like Cheerios."

This accurate (no doubt) but faintly derisive observation, delivered to me by my daughter as we headed off to the grocery store on a Sunday morning, almost passed by me without notice. So I smell like a popular breakfast cereal — what's one more glancing half-insult in the crucible of our little family of two? Cause for a shrug. Before I left the house, I'd shoveled several handfuls of O's into my mouth. The box was sitting on the kitchen table and I just reached in.

And my daughter caught me in my unguarded boyishness. Teens specialize in being shocked by their parents' humanity. They find ways to hold it against us. But that's life. I winced and started the car.

Understand, I love my daughter beyond measure and take bottomless pride in who she is: A-student, friendly, talented, beloved by the parents of virtually all her buddies as the most respectful young person they know, a "good influence." How can you top this? In life's long pull, I ask for little except to be allowed to keep going, to keep protecting her until she outgrows her need for me. This is the parental mandate; I'm locked into it. Being appreciated isn't the point.

Respect, sure, that's kind of a big deal, but had she just been disrespectful? In my style of parenting — I've always been one of those playful, groan-eliciting, fooling-around dads, preferring to be a parody of authority rather than Authority Itself — disrespect is almost an invited guest. The rolled eyeballs. The "oh, Dad!" of disbelief that I would call waffles "warfles," for instance, or demonstrate Monty Python's Ministry of Silly Walks in public. In a lot of ways I just plain ask for it; I know this about myself. So what if it hurts a little to be told I smell like Cheerios?

Here's the problem. Our family of two — that dense nucleus — is being wrenched open. The old man, three and a half years a widower, is dating again — well, let's be frank. I'm falling in love, ready or not. Melanie, a hazel-eyed dazzler with a smile like the sunrise (musician, writer, lover of poetry), has slid into my heart. This is not something that happens politely. At my age, under my circumstances, it's a little like invasive surgery.

I don't mean this negatively. I couldn't feel luckier. It's just that nothing about this is simple. The most casual of family evenings — sitting around my living room, say, watching a video — can turn into a night of brittle tension. Nobody knows what anyone else is thinking, or dares ask. Three sets of eyes stay glued to the tube.

Still, no matter how hard I may try to keep the smiley-face of my relationship with Alison intact — oh, we're great pals, and look at that grade point average — Melanie is behind the façade now, trying to find her way into both our lives. She's an intimate witness to the stains and trouble spots, an outsider looking on with occasional disbelief at how father and daughter really get along.

"What's the deal with Alison criticizing the way you eat?" she wanted to know the other day, referring to … well, I didn't even remember the incident, but I went into a protective crouch, defending a flank I didn't know I had. That's how teenagers are, I explained, lamely.

A day later I was given the withering judgment that I smelled like Cheerios. The tone of the verdict was: "God, Dad, you made me notice you this morning." Alison then turned on the radio and disappeared into the music.

As I say, I almost let this one go. About a mile up the road, however, I pulled the car over, turned off the radio and said, "That hurt my feelings."

She looked up startled. This too is part of the art of parenting: defining the edge of respect, not with anger but with honesty. In the radioless silence we sat with our emotions. "I'm sorry," she said. That was sufficient.

*November 2001*

## SHARED ISOLATION

Joys bursts upon the oddest occasions. How tied it is to feeling needed.

My teenager. I entered the house the other day and she was on the telephone, in tears. When she saw me, she said, "Here he is now," and handed me the phone.

I've been raising her on my own for three and a half years. It's a job that's often shrouded in fog; all that's visible sometimes are those two burning adolescent cat eyes, boring into my soul. Who is she? I'll throw a dinner on the stove — green beans and pizza. Oh, you're tired of that now? Then I don't know what to make. And there's that look of sullen resentment, because I can't read her mind, because I can't know what she herself doesn't.

E.L. Doctorow proffered a fascinatingly cynical definition of love in his novel *Loon Lake*: shared isolation, he called it. He wasn't referring to fathers and daughters, but he could have been. Here we are alone in this somber house, with its carpet stains and messy bathroom. There's no magic about what happens here. Shoes kicked off next to the stairway stay there until (unless) someone picks them up. Junk mail piles up all week on the old sewing machine that functions, in shocking underutilization, as a catch-all table in the foyer.

This is life without a scriptwriter or set designer. It's life without Mom. It just goes on and on — a civil arrangement, triumphantly functional. She's growing up; I keep myself on the margins of this process. If I want to enter her room, I have to endure a look of such withering suspicion I do so only when absolutely necessary, taking in its exotic, adolescent strangeness (the word "chaos," for instance, ornately lettered, taped to the base of her desk lamp) when I do. Dad as trespasser.

This is our shared isolation — a temporary normalcy held in place by unseen forces and tensions. We live in it but look beyond it, to the future. It's not exactly how I thought it would be after Barbara's death, but it's OK. I'm used to the arrangement.

So when the tension collapses and we're thrown, floundering, into the present moment with each other, the mutual recognition — oh my God, this is how you feel? this is who you are? — jolts like electrical current.

The phone she handed me was damp with her tears. She fled to her room and I said, "Hello?"

The voice on the other end, a woman's, was startled and confused. "Oh my God, I'm so sorry I called," she said.

It took me a while to piece it all together. The woman was an old friend of my late wife's, calling on impulse to see how Barbara was doing. It was one of those startling failures of the grapevine — she had never heard the news of Barbara's death.

Alison thought it was a telemarketer. "Is your mother there?" This happens all the time. Her well-rehearsed exit strategy is to say Mom's not home, but the caller explained who she was and Alison was forced to deliver the bad news, which was suddenly shocking all over again: "Actually, my mom passed away." And her emotional flooring simply gave.

I talked for a while to the friend — it was someone I had never met — then went up to Alison's room and crossed its threshold. Something gave in me as well as I did so, a rush of sympathy that transcended reticence. She was still crying. I began rubbing her back. "I didn't realize I was so fragile," she said.

I heard myself reassure her, over and over. "It's OK to be fragile. It's better than not being able to feel." She allowed me to console her and rub her back — this complex child, my live-in mystery. "It's OK, it's OK."

This can't be joy I felt, not in the midst of such sorrow. But it filled me as though it were.

*November 2001*

## LOST PUNCH LINE

The joke went off like a small explosion. "What do you get when you cross Ted Kaczynski with Monica Lewinsky?"

In this season of grief, with a national tragedy still too-fresh in our minds, with war as a background noise, with loss and renewal crisscrossing our hearts like strands of DNA, I find myself thinking about the sense of humor of the gods.

After my wife died, my lot, for better or for worse, was to grieve in the midst of instant single-fatherhood, the whoopsy-daisy and fumbling desperation of after-school logistics and late-night stomachaches. I had never been the point person on this stuff; that was Mom's world. I had to start paying the bills again and return the household to a patched-together normalcy. I also had to learn how to be nurturing and sensitive, and poke around for inroads into my child's psyche.

The best I could do was mourn on the run. I had little time for reverie, for dwelling on my own loss. Barbara's death became a vaguely sensed absence, a shadow somewhere beyond the realm of duty and responsibility. It took a smart-aleck afternoon DJ on Alison's favorite radio station, and a car full of preteen girls, to put it back into the center of my life.

I had taken two days off work for Alison's birthday party. Day 1 began early in the morning, with rounding up the invitees at their far-flung places of residence and driving them 30 miles to Great America, where they would spend the day on their own. (Was this safe? I was assured they could handle it.) If all went well, they would meet me at the front gate in seven hours and I'd whisk them home for dinner, cake and an overnight.

I spent my seven hours of off-time fretting, of course, that I'd set myself up for disaster. This was a humongous amusement park, the size of a small city. They were sure to get lost, if not ... abducted? Swallowed up by the earth? What kind of judgment did these girls have?

My heart leapt for joy when I spotted them at the assigned location. I didn't care that they barely acknowledged my existence as they filed into the car; I was whistling to myself, practically, on the ride home, surrounded by their chatter and laughter, their innocence. How protective I felt, how self-pleased. I was pulling this thing off.

Then the radio stopped blaring rock music I didn't recognize and the DJ told his joke. This was in the middle of the impeachment hearings and Monica was big. So were cigars. So was oral sex. "Yo, Chicagoland, here's a new one. What do you get when you cross Ted Kaczynski and Monica Lewinsky? A dynamite ..."

What? Did he really say that? I listened in helpless amazement, a dumbstruck fuddy-duddy not believing you could tell a dirty joke on the air.

The car filled with silence.

Then one of the girls said: "What did he say? A dynamite what?"

A second girl answered, nonchalantly, "Blowjob."

"Oh."

The music came back on. The chatter resumed. Life went on. No one missed a beat, except me.

I can still feel the sputter frozen on my lips, taste the incredulity I swallowed back down like a chunk of lard. In that first moment, it seemed as though a stick of dynamite had been hurled into innocence itself, but when, upon recovering a modicum of poise, I was able to look around and ascertain that nothing, absolutely nothing, had changed – no 12-year-old tears, no looks of horror, no cascade of questions – I realized the only innocence that got shattered was my own. The girls were cool. They ... well, who knows what they knew, but apparently it was enough. Their pseudo-sophistication was unruffled.

And slowly, as I sped south on I-94 into the city, it dawned on me that something memorably preposterous had just occurred, a parenting milestone. And I wanted to laugh about it, laugh until it hurt, but I couldn't do so without relating the story to Barbara, the only person on earth who would instantaneously appreciate every nuance, including – she would have seen it as I told the story – the chagrin dripping off my face like custard pie.

This went beyond missing her. Here was grief, full bore, special delivery. Grief was the silence when there should have been laughter, spreading across her face, bursting from her lungs. No one else had such a laugh, or took such keen delight in upset apple carts and bawdily confounded expectations. Without it, I was stuck in the void of an undelivered punch line.

*December 2001*


## IS THE UNIVERSE KIND?

The wife of a man in the support group I belonged to for six months when my wife had cancer — the group was for spouses and other caregivers — had a shocking reaction to her own diagnosis: absolute refusal to acknowledge it. The man was beside himself. "She should do something, shouldn't she?"

We're supposed to wage war on cancer, not ignore it. War is our all-purpose metaphor for handling trouble. Choosing to whistle Dixie instead — to blow off doctor's appointments, clean the house, shrug, smile, look away — was reckless behavior, clinically out of touch, or so I might have thought had I been a little less steeped, at that point, in the futility of a great deal of cancer treatment. By then I'd heard more than one person in my group cry despairingly about her spouse's ordeal: "He doesn't have cancer, he has chemo!"

I could see her point of view, in other words. I could understand being more wary of the treatment than the disease, which — say what you want about it — was hers. Once you turned yourself over to high-tech medicine, this was no longer true; your cancer became the doctors' property, to stalk, to do battle with. Your body was just the battle site. The best you could do was follow the progress of the war and hope your side won.

While I hardly approve of denial as a coping mechanism, I see it not as the opposite of fighting back but, eerily, much the same thing. Both approaches are rooted in the status quo of one's life: the plans and expectations that were in place before trouble hit. And both approaches crave only trouble's nonexistence, so life can go on in the same old way.

I think we have to allow ourselves to be transformed by trouble — stopped cold by it. We have to let trouble open a door to a new world.

This is the shattering imperative I now wear on my sleeve. I came out of Barbara's eight months of struggle with pancreatic cancer in a state of permanent celebration of whatever comes along. I came out loving life with an evangelical fervor, and now preach a nonstop sermon of salvation through life's overlooked details, especially what seems wrong: the arguments, the friction, the slaps in the face. The only other choice is to be defeated by them.

"I'm scared," Barbara said. She only said it once, but the words chilled my heart. It was Saturday morning, her first day back from the hospital following an unsuccessful operation to remove her tumor; she'd just been diagnosed with advanced, terminal cancer. We were still in bed, with a whole day to face.

Mortality was suddenly part of our lives: the Grim Reaper, for God's sake. He was in bed with us. This was not supposed to be happening. Barbara's words made me feel the blade of his scythe.

The words were Barbara's moment of reckoning, and she chose to step into her fear and into the unknown. Every moment is a door either to walk through or not. To choose not to walk through that door is to stay in ordinary time, clinging to what you have and how things are supposed to be.

On that Saturday morning, we started letting go of what life was supposed to be, and it became simply itself, rich beyond measure. Suddenly it was strewn with miracles. Miracles are as easy as sunlight, as easy as kindness. "What can I do for you?" one of our neighbors asked Barbara. "I'll do anything — I'll clean your toilet bowl!"

This fleeting, luminous world is full of portals that lead beyond what we can even imagine. At a bookstore one afternoon, I flipped through a volume I had no intention of buying. It fell open to a page in which Albert Einstein was quoted as asking: Is the universe kind?

A few months earlier, such a question might have made me wince. On this day I embraced it, and I knew the answer was yes.

*December 2001*


## THE BLUE PEARL

You want to convey sympathy, but come out instead with a shudder. Someone you care about has just been diagnosed with …

Well, in this case, breast cancer.

News like this never fails to overwhelm, even at a safe distance. When I heard about Kay's condition from my sister, I felt crowded by it, pushed to the very edge of adequacy. I wanted to whimper; I rallied, after a few heartbeats, only because I knew that wouldn't be of use to anybody. I offered, of course, "whatever I can do to help," but I wanted to offer the blue pearl.

I offer it now, having rummaged for it beyond my fear and self-pity. Would that it could be issued routinely at the time of diagnosis, especially to those who are lost and don't know where they'll find their courage. It'll be there when you need it, I want to say, though Kay already has it, of that I'm sure.

The blue pearl is mortality's unit of currency. It's passed between the wounded like a secret handshake — secret only because the polite constructs of everyday life require discretion, averted eyes and an allegiance to the fiction that we're strangers. The blue pearl has no tolerance for this, because the truth is, we're "strange" to each other only on the surface.

Thus, when my wife was diagnosed with cancer, I noticed a charged change in conversations. For instance, here was my friend Herb, constructor of crossword puzzles, divulging that he'd lost his son in an accident some years earlier. I was his editor; we talked routinely on a weekly basis, but not till now had there been room for such a disclosure in our amiable chats. His telling me this was like a warm hand on my shoulder — "Yes, I too am mortal" — and gave me courage. This is the blue pearl.

I came across the term during one of my forays into Eastern religion. Swami Muktananda, the Siddha yoga master, had talked about a "blue pearl" the size of a sesame seed, which became apparent in the rarified subtlety of deep meditation. At the time, I wrote it off as one more treasure — if it really existed — that would be forever out of my reach. But after Barbara was diagnosed with terminal cancer and our lives scraped bottom, I realized that such a treasure has no intention of hiding from us.

My glimmer of its existence came on a moonlit night as I stood in the empty parking lot of my neighborhood Osco. Barbara was home from the hospital, recovering from major surgery and newly diagnosed with cancer; I had just made my first purchase of prescription morphine. I'd paid the pharmacist, at the same time, for a gallon of milk, but as I left the store with bulging breast pocket and unbagged jug, the security guard stopped me, demanding to know where I was going. His eyes told me I was stealing the milk.

Had I expected "sympathy" from the world? Certainly I hadn't expected to be accused of theft! The misunderstanding was untangled in a few minutes, but I emerged from the store trembling with disbelief, my self-possession unraveling like a dirty bandage. I looked up at the moon; its silver light streaked the lifeless lot. I felt naked, but something in me refused to give and I met the moon's glare. "We'll get through this," I heard myself vow, gripping this moment fiercely, holding on for dear life.

Most of the time, so little is asked of us.

Many years ago, when my 3-day-old daughter was hospitalized for a mysterious viral infection, the words bedecking the waiting room of the pediatric ward caught my eye. "The will of God" — read the hand-stitched sampler — "will never lead you where the grace of God cannot keep you."

I extend the blue pearl to everyone who has just been served notice of mortality, to everyone entering the cancer universe, to everyone looking around wildly for comfort and courage. Life is more than we've been told it is, more than we can imagine. All of us will have a chance to hold hands with the stars.

*February 2002*

## THE SANDMAN

Baby asleep in my arms, his soft cheek pressed into my shoulder. I hover at the crib and delicately peel him off me. How long it's been since I was a sleeping infant's bed of flesh — I'd forgotten the fragility of such a moment. Can I set him down without waking?

What a night, playing Great Uncle Bob, being part of the Saturday night baby-sitting team for 7-month-old Jackson. I was flooded with memories — of strained veal and ticklish tummies, of wondrous grins, wobbly steps, sudden spills, big tears, piggy-goes-to-market and "Miss Lucy called the doctor, Miss Lucy called the nurse."

Mostly I remembered a me I haven't known for a dozen years: the passionate parent, indefatigable at peek-a-boo, fearless with a storybook, meeting the energy of babyhood right there on the living-room floor. Kiddy books aren't for the timid. They're to be sung at the top of the lungs. "Miss Lucy called the lady with the alligator purse!"

I remembered, with a pang, when my voice — when parenting itself — needed only to be enthusiastic.

At one point Jackson stood at the coffee table, in pre-perambulatory "cruise" mode, looking around for new worlds to conquer. I scootched beneath the table on my back and lay there looking up at his baby-fat knees, wondering how long it would take him to notice me. When he figured out where I was, he dropped to the floor in glee, as though the world had never seen antics so funny. "Babies," I exclaimed, "are God's antidote for teenagers!"

It was the cry of a dad aching for the good old days, though, phew, a few hours into this adventure, the three grown-ups in the room were starting to wilt and Jackson's ego began disintegrating. We softened our voices, rounded the edges of our merriment and slowly he drifted off to sleep. My sister (the grandma) carried him upstairs. Success!

Except she seemed to be up there an awfully long time. After about 45 minutes she reappeared — carrying Jackson, who was wearing a fresh pair of pajamas and an "I'm back" grin that was a little too wide.

And thus began the second, slightly more desperate, phase of my evening of baby-sitting and remembering. Oh yeah, there's this other aspect to babies. They stay awake, even when it's clearly time for beddy-bye. The tireder they get, the more they ratchet up.

And soon enough Jackson's grin collapsed into wailing frustration. I've got to earn my great-uncle stripes right now, I decided, and hefted him up, rocked him, tried to find the precise vibration that would calm him. And then we began singing, more earnestly than before; everyone's peace was at stake.

I give the assist here to Allen Sherman, the outrageously comic songwriter of my own teenage years. Sue and I, it turns out, still know an entire album of his by heart. I'm not sure why this is what we chose to sing, but it worked. By the time we got to "Don't buy the liverwurst" (the "Down by the Riverside" parody), Jackson's head was plop against my shoulder. He was out.

And suddenly it occurred to me that among the ultimately discarded roles of parenthood — Tooth Fairy, Santa Claus, Easter Bunny — that of Sandman may be the most rewarding of all.

I held him and reflected on my "other" child, the 15-year-old, and felt stirred by life's long rhythms. With a baby, all your energy is spent on building a bond. Sleep's brief separation is a break in that bond. But in adolescence, there's only separation …

Well, no, the bond is there, I realized; it shows itself in brief flickers of need. On Sept. 11, Alison called me from school to ask, in tears, "Are we at war, Dad?" And just a few days ago, at dinner, that same checking in, that same groping for my perspective: "What exactly is Enron all about?"

I set Jackson in his crib and backed away. His sleep was sound this time, a jewel to savor. Easy, easy. Shhh …

*February 2002*

## GRIEF AND COMPOST

The blade of the hoe bites into the earth and as the soil opens up so do I. Life, oh God. My backyard aches with it.

I am a widower in my fourth spring of grief, and something in me has changed. A friend said four years, that's how long it takes before you can really start to live again. Maybe he's right. Here I am, with my feet planted in the weedy plot recognizable as a former garden, methodically breaking the surface, a square foot at a time — claiming the spring, in other words. Claiming the summer.

The hoe breaks up the viny tangle, and once again this piece of ground — eight paces by six, something over 400 square feet — will be a garden. This is rich soil, full of earthworms. I love the living feel of it that passes up the handle of the hoe into my wrists and forearms, and work with an unhurried fluency. My heart swells. Why, I wonder, did it take me so long to get back to the dirt and sun and this elemental relationship with the planet?

I tried gardening that first summer after Barbara died; a lot of what I did then was out of stoical determination to stay the course. I had a not-quite-12-year-old daughter to raise, and I thought I owed her as much continuity as possible, so I threw some tomatoes in the ground — they'd always been my friends — and some other stuff, even a scattering of petunias. But I took no pleasure in it. I knew gardening as a communal activity; working at it alone felt grim and unreal. I was a trespasser in my own yard.

To grieve is to reduce the size of your life. You have no choice. I pulled back from the edges of what I cared about. I put the garden tools away and shut down the whole operation. How odd to let go of something you value — to jettison not just joy and exercise but political convictions. When I stopped gardening, I no longer had any reason to maintain a compost pile. Doing so had been a ritual, a duty, a sacrament.

As a composter, I had valued the slop and glop of life: banana peels, coffee grounds, eggshells, apple cores and everything blue and suspicious at the back of the refrigerator. This wasn't garbage, it was organic matter. It broke down and became humus, the organic component of soil. To landfill this material — amid the plastic shrink-wrap and used Bic pens and broken furniture of American life — seemed not just illogical but fundamentally wrong, a sin against the cycle of life.

Funny, then, that I had no will to keep the compost pile going. It was as though only in the context of family could I close the circle of life. With Barbara's death, the circle had been breached, and in my grief I bled kitchen waste.

But here I am, four years later, proud owner of a new pitchfork with which to turn the resurrected heap. Grief and compost: There is a similar alchemy at work. Grief is lifelong, but it has its shifts and movement. Dark loss gives way to hope, and I feel it now, pushing up through me as I work the hoe and lay open the once-and-future garden.

I chop at the soil on a glorious Saturday morning (I love this humus-rich soil, so deep and silky) and mull the stirring in me. It hardly matters what happens next — whether I plant at all. I will, of course; and indeed envision broccoli, cabbage, lettuce, peas, melons, peppers. And more, an herb garden: savory and basil and thyme and lemon balm and chocolate mint. And while I'm at it, raspberries. How about strawberries?

But there's no hurry. What matters is that I'm out here now, on a sunny day, pushing against the edges of what I care about.

*June 2002*

## THE DRIVING LESSON

This is my daughter's foot on the accelerator, my daughter's hands on the steering wheel. I'm trying to keep my cool, but come on, she's just a kid — with 2,500 pounds of vibrating steel, and my life, and her own, under her uncertain command. She gives it a little gas and, vroom, we're off.

Oh, shaky colt, wobbling on spindly legs. Am I talking about her or me? It dawns on me that this is where parenting gets serious.

For Dad, every driving lesson begins on Memory Lane, with the wheels spinning. Alison was in diapers not all that long ago; she was just learning to walk. When I look at her I see what I used to see, baby fat and innocence and instantaneous mood change. I see her eating snow in the front yard, watching "Sesame Street," dressing up as a princess-ballerina for Halloween, bursting into sudden tears, crying "I'm tired! Carry me!" when my arms are laden with groceries.

Now she's turning left onto Sheridan Road and suddenly she's an adult, or as close as she's ever been to one — an adult on training wheels. It's her first time in real traffic. Since her completion of driver's training last month, she has only put-putted around empty parking lots, trying to master the clutch on my old Corolla, but today I've commandeered a Ford Tempo with automatic transmission from my buddy Melanie (who rides in the backseat, slumped down so she doesn't have to see the road), and we're taking on the city, which is already in progress.

This is delicate — this knowledge transfer taking place, father to teen ager. The act of driving, it turns out — I'd forgotten — is made up of countless minute skills and judgment calls, each one separately encountered, conquered and blended into a whole so seamless it's ultimately a bore. A list of the day's accomplishments seldom includes braking properly, avoiding pedestrians, making successful left turns or pulling neatly into parking spaces. All that matters to us is being there; getting there is taken for granted.

But today the getting is everything; the "there" could be anywhere. It's no more than a pretext — let's go to Aunt Debby's — for being in traffic: negotiating stoplights and parked cars ("uh, you're drifting a little close, honey") and kids on bikes and moms pushing baby carriages and SUVs emerging ominously from parking lots, the ever-shifting landscape of transition. The traffic asks us, over the course of a few miles, to make, oh, maybe a thousand little decisions, instantly and correctly.

What a giving up of power this is, to sit in the passenger seat and see each new decision loom up — intersection! yellow light! car door opening! — and be able to do no more than give advice (the calmer the better). What bracing helplessness. The only brake my foot can hit is an imaginary one.

This is my daughter behind the wheel, tentative, without confidence yet, but determined to negotiate her latest rite of passage. As I look at her, I realize I know her too well, yet I don't know her at all. I don't know the person she is becoming: decision-maker, responsibility-taker, driver. It awes me. My baby!

I have the urge to take over and do what's easy — just get us there. We're at such an early stage in the process she might even let me. Alison herself, making her inaugural run in traffic, hardly knows her new self any better than I do. In this rare moment, we're figuring it out together, and it is to this adult-in-progress that I deliver my carefully modulated advice:

"OK, at Pratt you'll be turning left. This is no big deal. Yeah, that's right, pull halfway into the intersection, wait for the traffic to clear, yeah, OK, now!"

And we're almost home, but the road we're on is a new one to me.

*June 2002*

## SALAD DAYS

Maybe it was about the time our frizzy-haired junior guide, walking backwards, pointed out the roof where they found the pumpkin last fall that I felt my composure give and just surrendered, ceded my objectivity. I could taste the future again, sweet and sharp, the way they serve it in college.

My 16-year-old daughter was at my side, complicating my sudden onrush of undergraduate memories and postgraduate regrets. We were here because of her, after all — looking at prospective schools. My gut churned with pride and helplessness. She wasn't gripping my arm or wearing a white gown, but it felt as though we were walking down a long aisle, at the end of which I would give her away.

College was certainly my own getaway vehicle — the first place, it seemed, they told you the truth and made that mental light bulb flicker. And here it all was again: tradition and dorm food, Frisbees and Socrates, words in stone and the eagerness of youth. This was College Tour 2002. Alison and I went east, looked at five campuses. The facts we gathered were varied and exhilarating, but I was undone by the questions that echoed between them. Will she prosper here? Can I pay for this? Has my life been equal to the possibilities of my own youth?

It was Dad Syndrome, updated. We relive our lives through our children, which is one thing when you're doing chalk drawings on the sidewalk or sitting through the Disney classics, but quite another when you're mulling your first encounter with antiwar politics, all-night rap sessions or the poetry of Dylan Thomas. Who I am now is still intimately linked to who I was as an undergraduate, tasting freedom, sipping the elixir of language, resolving to change the world.

"The force that through the green fuse drives the flower/Drives my green age ..." Those were my salad days.

All I knew was that everything felt green and unformed again, as I traipsed through dorm rooms and biology labs with my daughter, listening to core curriculum requirements, enrollment data, spiels and anecdotes. "Last year they showed 'Jaws' in the pool. That was pretty neat."

College is about saving the world, sure, but first you have to seize it, turn it upside down, hoist pumpkins up to the roofs of staid old ivy-covered buildings. How else do you express the glory of your encounter with the great ideas of the past? You have to make them your own. You have to shock your parents.

But how foolish, I reminded myself, to be thinking thoughts like this when I'm the parent now. To sober myself up, I thought about money.

After the tour was over at Cornell, I asked our young guide if she could say a little bit about tuition. Sure, no problem. She opened a thick publication sitting on a shelf in the administration office and pointed to a number. Oh gosh. My knees went weak. The cost of all that poetry. "The force that drives the water through the rocks/Drives my red blood ..." It felt as though she were peeling back the bandage to give me a glimpse of the wound.

OK, so sending your kid to college — the snazzy ones, anyway, up on hills — is like buying a new BMW every year for four years. Talk about your getaway vehicles. I drive a nine-year-old Corolla that needs body work.

But this is how it is. You give this opportunity to your kids, somehow. And in the giving you grow both frantic and wistful, trying to pay for it even as you long to be a part of it.

I tallied up my life. What have I learned? What difference have I made? Would I have pleased the ones who gave me a push, way back when? I've done OK, I finally decided, because here I am, standing with a beautiful 16-year-old on the verge of seizing the world. Or at least a very expensive pumpkin.

*September 2002*

## POET'S MOON

The doorbell rings and suddenly, as if bugs exist to manifest human emotions, this big black thing scuttles across my living room carpet to help me answer it. It's not a cockroach — no way, not in my house — but my quick, horrified stomp is a fair imitation of La Cucaracha.

I was already in a fret over the impression my cluttered house was about to make when the creature squirted out of nowhere (whatever it was, fat and armored, with twitching antennae). Gotta act fast. Caved in its roof with a decisive splat, but, my God, it's as ugly — and damning — dead as alive. Now what?

My top and bottom halves swing into independent action. I open the door wide and plaster a "Hello, Melanie" grin across my face, exuding welcome-to-my-palace enthusiasm; meanwhile, I'm deftly herding the crushed corpse across the carpet with the side of my foot, into the vestibule and, so the plan would have it, out into the night.

Except, of course, Melanie, the love of my life, is standing there. She'd come over because the moon was so pretty. Crescent moon, which she called a "poet's moon." She wanted to take a walk with me beneath it. Oh, my heart.

This is how smart my foot is. It thinks it can flick the dead bug past Melanie with a move so lightning-quick she won't notice. It thinks it can do so accurately.

Did I ever imagine there was dignity in middle-age, dignity in widowerhood? Maybe other aging "singles" have their nagging sources of mortification in the realm of the opposite sex. For me, it's the house I live in with my 16-year-old daughter — sad old shell, full of stains and clutter.

We try, the two of us, to make the place pleasant and homey (buying new towels at Bed, Bath and Beyond, for instance), but the truth is, ever since Barbara died four and a half years ago, a window has been open that neither of us can close.

Mostly, Dad and Daughter have retreated to their respective redoubts, she to her room, me to … the written word, you might say. Journal, work, poetry. I live here more like a house-sitter than the owner, taking in its randomness with a dazzled amazement.

This is not my preference. Even when visitors aren't expected, I have urges to reclaim full possession of the house. When we bought the place 17 years ago, Barbara, within hours of the movers' departure, had maneuvered the living room furniture into an inviting rightness that stunned me. It was so quick. How did she do that? She had staked a claim on a bare room full of boxes and made it jell. A house became a home.

This wasn't just cleverness and an eye for decorating. Maybe it wasn't even just Barbara. Maybe I had something to do with it as well, though I don't remember much about my own role, except to insulate the water heater and mess around with the bathtub drain. All I know is that this was our nest — always, perhaps, a little threadbare and neglected around the edges, but comfortable, and warm at the center.

Now the warmth is gone. The warmth left when Barbara did. And without it, nothing I do feels adequate or right. Spend $15,000 on painting and replastering? A sham, a desperate mask. The house has no center, and the objects in it fill space but cannot disguise the emptiness.

And the day-to-day neglect accumulates. I confess. I let the mail pile up. I don't dust. I don't have time but in truth I refuse to make time because the clutter and uproar have a numbing effect. But it's all a great embarrassment waiting to happen. When a visitor pops in, my loss and inadequacy are on display like an open wound.

"Hello, Melanie!"

She stands in mild, amused confusion in the doorway as I complete my dance step. This is the woman I want most to accept me as I am, but I proceed to consummate the folly of pretense. I swipe my foot toward the open door, managing to bounce the ghastly, murdered bug (maybe it was an Oriental cockroach) off her shin and out into the night.

My apology is profuse. Her forgiveness is an act of grace. Together we step outside, into the light of the poet's moon.

*October 2002*

## INVISIBLE BOUNDARIES

Nothing fills an emotional void quite like the piercing drone of bagpipes. No matter the kids were rolling their eyeballs as they shuffled two-by-two into the stifling field house — this was profound, and I was on the verge of tears.

Oh, there she is. My daughter. Gulp. Eighteen years old. A college student. I stifled the impulse to wave and embarrass her still further. We had fleeting eye contact, then she turned to the business of finding her seat, one of almost 500 reluctant stars of this event.

I sympathized with their reluctance. Ceremony is about the past, not the future; and the past, represented by a thousand graying moms and dads looking on from the bleachers, wasn't quite ready to let them go. It had them in its loving tangle. They were making the best of it.

I knew how self-conscious I would have been. All weekend I'd been reliving my own undergraduate career. The previous night, after arriving in St. Paul — a seven-hour trek from Chicago — we'd gone to dinner at a Vietnamese restaurant and I couldn't shut up about the old days, and the wonder that I had survived them.

"I totally bombed calculus that first semester. Did I ever tell you that?"

She nodded. "Yeah, Dad."

But she said this without signaling impatience. She was listening to me — maybe just to be nice, but maybe, glory be, because she was interested in my sudden spill of perspective. I found myself retracing my progress, semester by semester, into young-adulthood: the inevitable, but excruciatingly slow, budding of my self-confidence. Maybe the words had some nutrient value for her. I dearly hoped so.

How odd that, when dinner was over, we got the wrong fortune cookies. I cracked mine open first. It said, "Forget about yesterday. Tomorrow will be a golden day for you."

Then she opened hers. "All boundaries," the words informed her, "are invisible."

Next morning, we were parked in front of her dorm by 8. The time had come. She was moving in. My specialty, on important occasions, seems to be promptness — no doubt a function of being a single dad. What's to stop me?

I was happy to do the grunt work, to dolly up the boxes and suitcases while Alison put her new room together. Then suddenly, as she was hanging up clothes and affixing photographs to white cinderblock walls, my job ended. The car was empty. The heavy lifting was done. I fussed with the computer cord for a while, but she had it set up right. I had nothing to do except wander outside, where I watched other extraneous dads emerge from the various dormitories looking slightly lost.

I've been a widower for six years. That's long enough to be used to the daily grind of it, but not quite long enough to be used to the transitions — the graduations, the firsts. As I sat idly taking in the sights of my daughter's new campus, my heart began throbbing with the dull ache of my wife's absence. I wanted nothing so much as to share this with her, or maybe just lean against her.

The ache stayed with me for the rest of the morning and into the afternoon. It was with me when the convocation in the field house got under way at 4 — when the kilt-clad bagpiper rent the air with a tune that sounded like but wasn't "Amazing Grace" and the color guard, consisting of more than 50 upperclassmen bearing flags representing the country of every student and faculty member at the school, followed in his wake.

It was with me when the freshmen shuffled in rolling their eyes, and when the president told us that we were now a part of the Macalester community and when we stood up and held hands with the strangers next to us and the bagpipes started droning again and escorted us across the invisible boundary.

Later there was dinner for all of us. My daughter was animated. Then she was gone, having drifted away to the student center with new friends. That was it.

I'm not usually one for ceremony, but in that moment I was rocked with gratitude for the one we'd just had — for the bagpipes and the decorum and the seriousness and the official shattering of the heart. Forget about yesterday. Let's get on with our lives.

*September 2004*

# PART TWO

# WONDER AND GENIUS

## BEGINNER'S MIND

More and more, I'm softening to the idea of being a beginner and finding joy in doing something I've never done before, to the point where I'm on the stump for a shift in the vocabulary of beginning.

"Clumsy," "crude," "awkward" — aren't these the terms we use to characterize the efforts of beginners, including our own? The prejudice locked in such words is that the state of beginning is a tedious one, a sheer linear necessity, to be borne stoically and apologetically until others come along who are newer, and worse, than we are.

These are relative terms, measuring the neophyte against the established master, but they have the ring of absolute judgment — and discourage many old dogs from learning new tricks. Who wants to be a klutz? Who needs the humiliation? As a result, we stick to what we know, and slowly stagnate.

What a tragedy — yet one more, it seems to me, that's language-based. In point of fact, having a "beginner's mind" in at least some corner of our life has the potential to open up and rejuvenate all of life.

"I wanted to work with my hands in a very basic way that would help me connect physically with really being there — a centering kind of thing," my sister told me the other day about her new pottery class. "But what I'm finding is that I'm opening this door into a vast creative world that goes on and on and on — it's endless."

It's the magic of seeing a slab of wet clay grow into a pot, however imperfectly, as you guide it on the wheel — a breathtaking thrill when it's brand new in your life, sending electrical signals to every last outpost of your being.

"One guy had two little covered pots that he'd done the most amazing thing with," she said. "He made an indentation in the top of the knob and put a marble there, and also one inside the pot. The kiln gets so hot it melts the marbles. It was so pretty, cracked and melted. I find myself just with hungry eyes looking around at all the possibilities."

She does, however, recognize her vulnerability. Beginners are always tumbling to earth. "My skill level is infantile. I'm barely crawling. You raise the pot up on the wheel and suddenly it's gouged — I forgot to cut my fingernails. Or it breaks in half." The ways to flub up, to lose control, are seemingly endless.

But flubs don't have to translate into discouragement. A good teacher will celebrate his new students' efforts unreservedly, finding ways around their gritted teeth and frustrated self-judgment, above all keeping them in the game, assuring them that gouged pots, exploded pots and every other cruel surprise are simply part of the process, not evidence (as they will think) of their innate talentlessness.

On my first day of yoga class, my teacher, who was an expert at putting newcomers at their ease, told me to take a break whenever I needed to. "Remember," she said, "yoga is for you, not for yoga." The words had the effect of a potent charm. From the first moment I knelt on my mat, I was doing yoga, not half-doing it, or pretending to do it. I was as immersed in the reality of the discipline as a master, and able to regard my inflexibility and myriad resistance as a challenge, not a humiliation.

Living effectively means knowing how to be a continual beginner, the best role models for which are children, newborns: beginning human beings. We celebrate children's art, for instance, not as imperfect adult art, but as something perfect for what it is, full of smiling suns and splashed color, out-of-control joy and unconcealed truth.

Beginners are the lifeblood of any discipline. They enter not at its margins but at the core, at the level of its most basic questions: What is it? How do we do it? Why should we do it? These are not tiresome questions best dispensed with quickly, but the font of eternal renewal.

*April 2001*

## EVOLUTION'S PUBLICIST

You think evolution, you think survival of the fittest and prickly pears with tougher spines. You think natural street smarts, the soft and the dumb get eaten and that sort of thing. Social Darwinism. Winners and losers. Above all you think practical, right? The no-nonsense tooling of species over the millennia by reality itself — cheetahs run fast so they can chase down their food supply, etc. This is the design of things.

And if nature, hurling its creations at one another in the arena of life, winnows out the wanderers, the unpurposeful, the gum chewers, shouldn't that be our model for our own lives? I've never thought so, but I've always been on the defensive. How can I criticize practicality, or indeed, survival? I'm sure the concept "survival of the fittest" is behind the health club boom, not to mention the anorexia boom, as hardbodies from coast to coast use their leisure time to achieve evolution's ends in their own lifetimes.

At the risk of heresy, I confess that I'm for soft bellies. "In soft belly, in open belly, we make room for life, we make room for healing," writes Stephen Levine. I'm for soft bellies and open minds, not just as ornaments, the way the arts are too often taught in schools as ornaments, but as a basic way of being.

But as I say, I've been on the defensive about all this, vaguely sensing that evolution itself would contradict me if it had a publicist and issued press statements. Then I spent a weekend with Ella Blue, the elfin 10-month-old grandchild of my best friend, and suddenly realized — as I watched her cruise the house and shriek in triumph as she sent the floor lamp tottering or freed a watch from a grownup wrist and tested its aerodynamics — that she was evolution's publicist!

Sheer curiosity was the driving force of her life, curiosity beyond all heed, curiosity never more than five minutes away from being fatal without an adult's constant attention. How is it that evolution has come up with a species whose young have no street smarts whatsoever, whose approach to life is to unravel it with delight, pull its tail, provoke it, taste it and swallow it, but by no means to be wary of it?

And what's more, since they lack language skills, they're doing this beyond our instructive reach. For a remarkably long time, nature protects the human young from parental and societal instruction and simply sets them loose, to form their own impressions of Planet Earth free of any chance to be told "right" answers.

They are actively living in what writing guru Natalie Goldberg calls "wild mind," which she defines by asking us to conjure an image of a big New Mexico sky. "I'm going to climb up to that sky straight over our heads," she writes, "and put one dot on it with a Magic Marker. See that dot? That dot is what Zen calls monkey mind and what Western psychology calls part of conscious mind. We give all our attention to that one dot. ... Meanwhile, wild mind surrounds us."

Perhaps we're subject to a code that guarantees that falling hurts and true love never runs smooth — that burns our fingers every time we touch the hot stove — but this needn't be all that shapes us. Ella Blue is my evidence that wild mind and open imagination have evolution's sanction, that we have a right, maybe even an imperative, to be open to the messages and wonders that find their way to us from beyond the tight knot of our certainties.

For better or for worse, I'd say follow one of those messages today, knowing that, wherever it leads you, you were meant to go there.

*November 1999*

## KEEP PEDALING

Tired old schoolyard, huge expanse of nothing much — no wonder this was the spot chosen for the new addition, to relieve the school's terrible overcrowding. But it saddened me to see that litter-strewn stretch of asphalt vanish; it was the perfect spot for one of childhood's great learning experiences.

When I walk past it, I can still feel the wild, wobbly excitement of kids learning how to ride their two-wheelers.

And a parent will understand that the bike your kid is pedaling — all by herself! — cuts its erratic path across your own heart. You've been running alongside it, your big hand steadying the rear fender, then you let go, sending her off with a loving shove. The moment is magic, it chooses itself. You let go! And off she sails, beyond your momentum and into her own … and then she looks back and the bike sheers and tilts, and you shout, though you're nearly out of breath, "Keep pedaling, honey! KEEP PEDALING!"

And there comes that instant when she hears you and pulls herself into the task at hand; she suddenly understands that balance won't be found by retreating to her parents' embrace, but only by pushing forward, into her own effort, and she pedals and creates the future.

So exhilarating was that moment for my wife and me, we didn't stop with our daughter but brought other kids to the lot and gave them that last shove and watched them find confidence and right themselves. We wanted to quit our day jobs and become full-time consultants on mastering the two-wheeler — but we ran out of kids and had to settle for a trophy, a small, hard-earned truth: In life, you gotta keep pedaling.

I call this the learning zone, that space where you find yourself making your own decisions moment by moment, in service to a goal that's real rather than hypothetical, and that you own completely. Far more than I miss that perfect slab of endless asphalt, I regret the fact that the building that replaced it, and schools in general, too often care more about reducing our children's brains to letters and numbers than guiding the children, body and soul, into the learning zone.

This is what I tried to do when I was a writing consultant in Chicago's public school system. Every class I taught would culminate in a writing session. The kids would be primed with reading and discussion, then I'd exhort them to write as though their lives depended on it: Write without stopping, don't worry about spelling, let the words happen and keep writing, KEEP WRITING!

I gradually got them to believe I meant what I said, that I wanted their words, their voices, their truths — that was all I was interested in. The results were often dramatic, the language concise and remarkable.

Here's an image (one of many) that still haunts me: "One of my friends got stabbed with a pencil because he was in a gang, but now he isn't in one because he doesn't want his family to see his shoes dangling from the telephone wire."

This was 11-year-old Jose's eloquent witness against gang life, drawn from the streets of our city — where, he explained to me, a kid's sneakers are heaved in tribute over a phone line when he dies.

As a writing teacher, I exulted when a youngster explained a piece of the world to me, even one as somber as teen gang members remembering their own dead. Jose was drawing from himself to forge a powerful sentence, one that conveyed ritual, danger, sorrow, determination, hope.

You don't have to be a professional to write like this, just a kid — anybody — with something to say, and the courage to keep pedaling.

*December 1999*

## YEAST AND JELL-O

Nothing particularly funny about a pitchfork, unless it's skewering ... oh, a pair of bikini underwear, maybe. A bratwurst?

Indulge me here. This is a joke in progress. What do you think? What object would be most likely to pry a guffaw out of that scowling, granite-faced farmer in Grant Wood's famous (and famously parodied) painting, "American Gothic"? A roll of toilet paper? How about a pineapple upside down cake?

Well, keep working on it. Something has to make him laugh or he's done for, this poster boy of dour.

His was the face that came to mind as I began pondering the nature of humor recently, thanks to my niece, who asked me, "How'd you get to be such a funny guy, Uncle Bob?" This is not an answer to her question, but here's a fun fact: Children laugh 300 times a day, while adults cut loose a spare, grim 15. It's true; I read it somewhere. Can't remember where, but it's gospel to me now. I use it to justify my life. I'm one of those people who can't stop turning everything into a joke.

Whatever the minimum daily requirement of titters turns out to be — and I'm sure 15 isn't nearly enough — I help supply it. If laughter is the spiritual equivalent of Fleischmann's yeast, I'm one of the agents who makes the bread rise.

But all I was trying to do was find my way into the conversation. I was so out of it when I was an adolescent — so clueless about the straight-ahead certainties of that age, so unable to contribute to discussions about cool hair, stick shifts or the facts of life, much less to swagger about such matters — I spent a lot of time watching other people talk. As I prowled the periphery, free of the conversation's centrifugal logic, I'd notice stuff the participants missed.

Odd pieces would sometimes fly out of the chatter like foul balls — a word, a phrase, an implication. When I ran to retrieve it, I'd find other subject matter nearby: someone's crabby grandmother, last week's homework, a dirty joke. It would have nothing to do with the conversation, but I'd bring it along and divert the others' attention. They'd look at me with surprise, their own thoughts momentarily shattered. The shattering noise was laughter.

So that was my answer to Carmen's question: Laughter stopped the action and got a lonely kid some eye contact. Now during every discussion I'm in, part of me wanders into no man's land, looking for inappropriate, chuckle-wrenching contributions — cans of spam, political sound bites, anything to stick on the pitchfork of seriousness.

To test my thesis, I decided to follow myself around for a few days and keep track of the levity. This is live: My sister is telling me about losing her credit card, then remembering she used it at Kinko's. She calls the place; amazingly, it's there. "When you pick it up," I hear myself say, "be wary if, when you say 'Thanks,' the clerk says, 'No, thank YOU!'" She laughs. Life goes on.

I'm proofreading a column of news briefs. I read that the number 1 city in per capita Jell-O consumption is Des Moines, followed by Salt Lake City. This pitches me into a fit of giggles; I have no idea why. Maybe because Jell-O is such an earnest food, laced with shredded carrots, topped with sliced bananas. It's a staple of church socials and moms everywhere, but it also wiggles. It has no food value. I work in a hushed setting, among copy editors. It's all I can do not to disrupt their concentration with the news.

I can't help myself. Life is too full of frowning guys gripping pitchforks.

*February 2000*

## DIVINE USELESSNESS

An old Massey-Harris tractor standing on its nose, a pair of giant red work gloves clawing at the sky, a heap of crumpled copper, a merry fountain of shooting rocks: Uh oh, the artists are back on the lawn, tampering with reality. And the show doesn't really begin until you leave, until you're walking back to your office and you realize you're seeing the city itself — under construction, strewn with trash, bustling with business and disaster — as a fantasy world of no particular purpose.

The site is the acre of idyllic greensward at the approach to Chicago's Navy Pier, where every spring city workers bolt down tons of steel, aluminum, wood, brick, glass, copper, stone — soaring, preposterous, breathtaking spires of it. I'm always amazed at how much effort goes into setting up such a show; I guess I associate effort with seriousness of purpose. But these objets d'art poke you in the eye with their playfulness.

How about a brief tour? Just be careful! This stuff is not meant to be reassuring or confirm old values.

Here we have … well, an 18-foot summer squash, perhaps, or possibly a loofah sponge — neither of these, exactly, but something surely inspired by a humble vegetable. Elongated ovoid, splotchy beige in color, tall as three grown men and split open, with hundreds of three-inch steel pellets painted bright silver lining the inside, creating the feeling of an invaded seed pod.

And over here, ah yes, those red gloves, spectacular against the blue sky, reaching up from a 30-foot steel tower, which is ringed with dozens of inner tubes — fat, soft things lying atop one another in slumping nonchalance. The gloves, four feet high, shoot out of the tubes in stunning pointlessness.

Let's quickly walk over to my favorite piece, that big heap of semi-tarnished copper with rainbow streaks glinting in the sun. It's at least 50 feet around (17 paces), 12 feet high and has no shape whatsoever, except, perhaps, that of a crumpled paper bag, with a silver wedge sliced at a clean angle in the center and a few cone-shaped coils of wire affixed randomly. Otherwise it's just a big heap, a sack of artful uselessness I couldn't stop looking at. The shape appealed to me beyond reason; best I could figure, this is just what a kid would love to see appear one day on the front lawn of school.

There are about 50 pieces in total, all of them massive — an exact replica of a Radio Flyer wagon, for instance, 30 feet long, with tires nine feet in diameter (this was a great favorite of kids). And that old tractor, circa 1940, suspended vertically in a frame so that ... well, so that it looks silly. While still clearly a tractor, it's stripped of all possible functionality, all dignity as a machine. Now it's art.

Don't tell anyone, but sculpture gardens are subversive. The synergy of so much audacity in steel and aluminum — so much divine uselessness — starts working on the mind, corroding its categories of understanding.
I'm walking back to work after my lunchtime art stroll, see, and I pass a construction site — immense yellow cranes, piles of scrap metal, 80-foot rolls of steel tubing in a vast heap — but what I see are singular shapes, forms in steel I understand no more than I "understand" that imploded hunk of copper or the upended tractor. I'm seeing form broken loose from meaning, resonating as itself and not as what it does.

And my heart soars. Suddenly the world is a fun place, full of stuff untied to prior purpose but sheerly, delightfully there, waiting for me to notice it and complete the connection.

*June 2000*


## THE DANCE OF LIFE

This is like tuning a radio, I thought as I rocked my infant great-nephew, seeking the precise vibration of motion that would quiet his panicky fussing and bring a contented coo to his lips.

There! Ahhh ... magic. He's happy. Two-week-old human being in my arms. We dance around the room. Great Uncle Bob, the human transmitter, dial delicately set to station Jackson Deric. We waltz; my confidence grows. This is the dance of life.

I sing a hymn today to the joy of great-unclehood, not the same as being a grandpa (unlikely to happen for a decade or so) but close enough. It's been a long time since I've been around a newborn as more than just polite background noise — "what a lovely baby!" — and actually been invited to form a relationship. This changes everything, heightens every perception, as I search the unique terrain of his face, watch his tiny fingers move, fall into his eyes. "Who ARE you?" There's no greater mystery.

My heart expands to make room for him, so eagerly I wonder if I've been living a deprived life up to this moment. When he was only a few hours old, Carmen, the new mom, my niece, asked, "What did I ever do without him?" A baby radiates through your life in every direction.

My sister — Granny Sue — told me this. She was part of the birth team, along with Daddy Sean and Aunt Angie. Think of it — a whole team. Jackson's birth was a celebration. In contrast, during Carmen's birth — just before Lamaze consciousness caught hold and transformed virtually every hospital in the country — Sue was alone in a little cell, as though in quarantine. This was merely a generation ago, but it seems like the dark ages.

"A woman had become an unconscious object from whose pelvis a baby was extracted with no concern for her feelings or emotions," wrote Elizabeth Bing, co-founder, in 1960, of Lamaze International.

I would add that the changes in birth procedures over the last 30 years have been equally profound for men. Dads are no longer reduced to chain-smoking irrelevancies, forced to pace in the waiting room and bond only with other men. They have an indispensable role to play throughout labor and delivery: coach, partner, mainstay, friend. They're part of it from start to finish, allowed at last, thank God, into life's inner sanctum.

Compare holding your son or daughter moments after birth to ... passing out cigars. This has got to be good for the human race, to have the male gender thus humbled.

I cradle the infant in my arms and feel myself transcend the generality of his existence. Before my very eyes, he transforms from Newborn — a sample human, a representative of the species — to Jackson, an individual, softly helpless and beautiful as a deity.

As I tune my movements to his wavelength, I shed a decade or more of self-consciousness, that encrustation of habit that sets in with the stopping off of the font of spontaneity. Only the smallest of children ask us to be children, but they ask with an irresistible insistence. And soon enough I find myself with my face an inch from Jackson's, emitting noises so goofy they drive my teen-age daughter from the room. But they calm him down; he stops crying.

Men as caregivers — not an unheard-of concept, but hardly basic to the model of masculinity males my age were given. Jackson is on my lap now, asleep. How fragile a baby's peace. I bond with him in perfect contentment, savoring my luck at being alive when such a thing is expected of me.

*August 2001*


## POETRY SANDBOX

Shimmer, incubate, latex, God ...

Take these words and a couple hundred more, magnetize 'em, shake well and scatter across the surface of your refrigerator. What you have now is sheer possibility — raw, electric, pregnant, mud — a verbal play pile, a poetry sandbox. Dig in!

Thanks to one of the luckiest sneezes in the recent history of human expression, the English language has been blown out of context, its words — at least a juicy, $13.95 selection of them — freed from habit, dogma, windbaggery and cliché. What potent beauties words are all by themselves, what mysteries: fiddle, goddess, onion, sex ...

And what amazing things we can do with them. For instance:

> I suffocate;
> Strange emerald steam
> From ancient mud
> Burns my song.

"That one really pulled me out of a hole," my sister told me. Her refrigerator, like mine, is bestrewn with tiny, cryptic, anonymous communiqués such as this. She was in a rut when she "wrote" it, i.e., tinkered with the available words, pushed a few together; suddenly her creativity outlets no longer felt blocked.

Mostly we think of words in clumps, yoked together like oxen, pulling tired old units of established thought across our lives. We're stuck in this thought — "Hi, how ya doin'?" "Oh, can't complain, blah blah blah" — and life stagnates, the imagination atrophies. But throw some "ancient mud" into our day, or entice us with a "shadow kiss" from "storm boy" or the "ugly man under the garden," and we wake up with a start.

These are the images of poetry, but they weren't created by officially certified poets. They're the work of friends and relatives, including children, who have passed through my kitchen or my sister's in the past few months and left behind what seem like pieces of dreams.

Purple, fissure, angel, spoon …

Such words were liberated in 1993, when a songwriter named Dave Kapell found himself struggling for inspiration and began cutting words out of the newspaper. He hoped that the words, juxtaposed in random combinations, would ignite song ideas. It was allergy season, however, and he sneezed, scattering the tiny pieces of paper.

Eventually, so he informs us in the small book that accompanies a recent version of his product, Magnetic Poetry, he hit on an idea to make the words sneeze-proof: He began gluing them to little magnets and posting them on his fridge. But once they were up there, a funny thing happened. His friends couldn't leave them alone. It turned out he wasn't the only one looking for inspiration — everyone was.

I've been charmed by Magnetic Poetry ever since I first encountered it at a gift shop in a Washington, D.C., gallery some years ago and began playing with the display model. I concocted, as I recall, the admonition "Eat raw wind" and couldn't get it out of my mind for weeks, as though I'd loosed, genie-like, some visitation from the spirit world. Maybe I did. In any case, as I tinkered with the words at my disposal — shard, balance, empty, mad — I understood that this kit was giving me a whole new relationship to language, e.g.:

> Take life
> As like an egg in honey
> But rusting
> And still wanting winter

Or:

> Storm goddess
> Scream of beauty
> Worship the bitter moon

Former U.S. poet laureate Robert Pinsky, in a forward to Kapell's book, reminds us that the root of "poet" is the Greek word for "maker." Poet, thus, as tinkerer, shaper, joiner — of ancient sounds, whose "meanings" were, and are, playfully unstable, feinting in many directions at once. The poets of old were tradesmen, building nothing less than culture itself.

Their task hasn't ended.

*December 2001*

## MIND PRISON

"You let them use profanity in their writing?"

Steve winced and who can blame him? These were 10-year-olds I was talking about, one in particular, Amanda, who'd written about her fight with a bully on the school bus. The bully had cussed her out and in her essay she quoted him with unblinking precision, raising — certainly in my neighbor's mind (we were riding the train home together as I rattled on) — some alarming questions, e.g.: Truth is nice, but what about decency? And aren't fifth-graders a little too young for academic freedom?

I would put these questions another way: To what extent do children own their own lives? And, is there a pedagogical difference between guiding and herding?

I, for one, take less satisfaction from witnessing a young person's perfect echo of our expectations in her performance than from seeing that child surprise and even shock us — not by some calculated outrage, but by revealing who she really is. This is an acquired taste. It's a little scary at first.

Alan Paton, the great South African novelist, describes in his memoir *For You Departed* how, as a young educator assigned the principalship of Diepkloof Reformatory, he set about turning this grim, foul, unsanitary institution for African delinquents from a jail into a school. "On New Year's Day, 1936," he wrote, "we took away the front portion of the high barbed wire fence and the second great gate that was in it. At first it was like being naked."

As I read this, I thought about the barbed wire around the educational process that isn't always visible. My brother-in-law, for instance, bitterly summed up his undergraduate experience at one of the nation's most prestigious universities thus: "They took the smartest kids in the country and proceeded to tell us how dumb we were."

Ivied institution, edifice of Great Ideas, before which puny undergraduates cower — sorry, this deserves rude kazoo noises. It's bad teaching and bad attitude. No matter how great the ideas, you can't leave the soul of the student out of the learning process; it'd be like teaching art appreciation to the blindfolded. ("If the eye were a living creature, sight would be its soul." — Aristotle)

When I was an undergraduate, I was sprung out of mind prison by my Advanced Writing teacher, Ken Macrorie. The hacksaw-in-the-cake he slipped me (and all his students) was a technique called free writing, which meant — start writing RIGHT NOW and keep going. Don't stop, don't erase, don't revise. Just write for 20 minutes. See what happens.

What happened was, my words found their way from my brain to my fingers. As I typed, I pumped up whole seas of experiential grist. I could begin with what I had for breakfast, move from the egg yolk to (for example) some hurt look in my mother's eyes 10 years ago to ... well, who knows, a passage from Dostoevsky or Kurt Vonnegut or Mad Magazine. Composition was no longer the tedious task of setting down what I'd already decided to say but a breathless journey into my God, I'd forgotten all about that! And out of this living process came insight and, startlingly, truth.

I hasten to add that it wasn't just the technique that made this possible; it was the fact that Macrorie was a rare teacher, whose enthusiasm for great writing was equal to his enthusiasm for OUR writing. He found the gems in our raw verbiage, coaxed out more, helped us focus and encouraged us to be fearless. He de-intimidated us, you might say, by convincing us that the humanity in the loftiest literature — in Thoreau, in Shakespeare — was the stuff of our own honest work as well. The key word here is "honest."

Knowing this, I was willing to risk pedagogical "nakedness," as I gave a volunteer writing lesson in my daughter's classroom, before the honesty of a free 10-year-old.

*March 2002*

## SWEET DREAMS

"We are all storytellers. The pressure of it is so great it continues in the nightlife of dreams."

So said novelist Richard Stern, sounding the note that matters to me most: Something, an animating force — call it the X-factor, call it magic — presses continually against our human wiring, presses against our ordinariness, and effortlessly produces blooms of unimaginable beauty. This happens 5 billion times a night on Planet Earth, as each of us dreams.

Dreams don't get the respect they deserve! To me, the fact of them contradicts every petty, self-imposed restriction of waking life, every culling of the human race into various categories of chaff. The genius mechanism works in all of us, without fanfare, without prompting. In our extraordinary complexity, we aren't merely the products of evolution but its active agents, designed, charged, to make something out of this life we encounter on a daily basis.

"Last night," wrote Theodore Roszak in *Where the Wasteland Ends*, "as on all the nights of your life, you dreamed much and magnificently, moving in an alternative reality of your own invention whose imaginative magnitude (for all you know) may have rivaled the creations of Homer and Shakespeare."

Homer and Shakespeare? Me? You? But look at our dreams — vividly rendered productions studded with metaphor, wildly whimsical and anchored in the wisdom of the ages. Makes me wonder sometimes which is the real me. Do dreams keep waking life in psychological balance or does waking life tend to the needs of the body so that at night we may dream? More likely it's that the two sides of life collaborate with and shape each other.

I had the following dream around the anniversary of my late wife's cancer diagnosis: Barbara and I are lying on the floor in the attic of an old building, our chins cupped in our hands, peering out a small window as black clouds writhe in the sky, rumble, mutate, burst into dreadful downpour. Then, suddenly, we are falling through the storm, clinging to — a mattress. But the updraft buoys us and we float to a soft landing, at which point Barbara, glowing with electrical current, says goodbye and walks away.

Not every dream is a keeper, but this one was, if only because, in the space of the dreaming, my wife was as alive as ever. That's the first amazement about my dreaming self; he spins his phantasms in convincing detail. Barbara was her old self and I was as close to her as ever, and the storm was awesome, fully occupying our attention as though we were really experiencing it. And oh, to be pulled out of our dry, cozy, spectators' security, dropped like dandelion fuzz into the middle of it! At first we were kicking in unchecked freefall, but then I remembered that if we could just hold on, we'd be safe.

Only after I woke up did "meaning" rush into the breach, did the storm become a metaphor for Barbara's cancer and the mattress, our marriage. But at the level of meaning, I felt even more awe about the dream; it was like a hand steadying me. And what ecstasy, when the updraft caught the mattress and we floated softly to the ground. Barbara's final, glowing goodbye was like a blessing.

I'm convinced that the powers at our command are immense. Bernie Siegal writes of patients under anesthesia controlling their pulse rate and level of bleeding. Untrained artists, who "can't draw a straight line," can create stunning likenesses of people simply by moving their pencil without looking down at the paper.

We're at the dawn of human potential: everyone an artist, a creator, a healer. Sweet dreams!

*August 2000*

## DEUS EX MACHINA

Everybody needs a deus ex machina. It's literature's equivalent of a guardian angel — this "god out of a machine" — but more garish, and better.

Mine lowered himself into my life some years ago in a dream. Tight little worried grad-student life I was leading at the time. I woke up laughing. This absurd figure had introduced himself as Davis X. Mackinaw, a pun on the Latin phrase describing the phony device in ancient drama whereby a god was lowered onto stage by crane at play's end to set all things right. It's the Big

Cheat, the author fixing a story that can't resolve itself with its internal logic, a literary "miracle." Blaaaat!

Since I was a graduate student in fiction writing, Davis X. Mackinaw's appearance was exquisitely inappropriate. And it was just what I needed: a disreputable, permission-giving cartoon figure elbowing me in the psyche, breaking wind in the church of literature. Sometimes what you revere becomes your worst enemy; reverence degrades into a sort of cowed obedience. You spend your energy trying to fit in. You become sad and perfect.

It was early, but Davis X. Mackinaw had dumped me, coursing with excitement, into the waking day. I'd never get back to sleep. He had tripped a lever and released me, set me loose in the middle of my bogged-down, withering novel. ME! "Fat thighs and all," as Leo Buscaglia used to say — the person I really am, not the great writer I thought I had to impersonate. I started scrawling notes on the back of an envelope, the only paper at hand, as incidents from my life started popping like flashbulbs, a cavalcade of truth. Everything I scribbled down belonged in the novel.

When I stopped writing, I looked at my sleeping wife. My heart hummed — my life was rich beyond all reason. Suddenly she popped awake and smiled. "I felt your eyes on me," she said.

How was that possible? It defied physics. Sheer intangibles — my eyes, my gaze, my love — had intruded on her sleep, awakened her as though by physical touch. The mystery of this enveloped me, this sudden sense that a force field, not wholly physical, enmeshes us. How nice it felt to love someone.

Later, daylight. Up and at 'em. The glow of Davis X. Mackinaw's permission to be myself was still all around me. I felt outsized and preposterous. I spent the morning writing in my journal, fleshing out my night-table notes; then I took the elevated train downtown to school.

The ride was magical. A few stops into it, I gave up my seat to an elderly woman in tennis shoes, whose sigh of gratitude stirred, once again, the force field, that tingling sense of connection to others. A stop or two later, two scrawny boys broke into a rap. Their energy and chutzpah filled the car. Everyone seemed to be listening to them. A woman at the far end shouted, "Go away!" But others applauded. The boys' spirit loosened the weight of silence. When they passed the hat, I felt a surge of generosity; I wasn't the only one.

At the Wrigley Field stop, half the car evacuated for the Cubs game. Suddenly Sister Fran slid past. I hadn't seen her in two years. I often feel inconvenienced by chance encounters with acquaintances, but this time I called out her name; she turned and we carried on an animated conversation for three seconds, before the door closed. ("I'll call you!" I shouted urgently, and later I did.)

Downtown. Leaving my station, I got caught in a "pedestrian tango" with an old guy in a corduroy parka. His every move mirrored mine; we couldn't get around each other. Then we broke into simultaneous smiles, disentangled and got on with our lives.

I left marveling at the feel of his soul and walked away whistling. I couldn't help it. For no good reason, I simply loved life. I was my own deus ex machina.

*November 2000*

## WASTED WORDS
*On not correcting mistakes*

Eugene was a hard case — the kind of kid who, when he came to school, sat there in grim, frowning silence. If you asked him a question, he stared you down until you looked away. Even at a school as tough as this one, on Chicago's West Side, the fury of his silence was unnerving.

When I read education stories in the newspaper, particularly the kind I call "egg production" stories — those distressing pieces on tumbling standardized test scores, which talk about schools as though they were math-and-reading mills whose bottom lines are the stats they generate, which seem to be, in turn, a sheer function of centralized tinkering — I see Eugene's face, and remember hunting for a balled-up piece of paper he tossed under a desk one morning as the bell rang.

Here's what those stories never say: Education is a lot less about "teaching" kids than learning from them.

That is, a dynamic flow of influence is involved. Unless kids are brain-damaged, they're smart; you start with that assumption. And then, if you have something you want them to know, you grope until you find a way in — that point where their interest is piqued and they open warily to what you're saying. This part of the process can be excruciatingly difficult, but it's a lot easier if you're ready to respect and be dazzled by them. Even still, you may have to get down on all fours at the end of class and poke under a desk every now and again.

I was a writing consultant in the Chicago Public Schools for a while, which meant I worked with teachers on ways to teach writing, a skill that has nothing to do — I assure you —with what your average computerized test purports to measure. Writing is an utterly personal skill; doing it well demands learning to hear and trust yourself, then constructing sentences that do justice to your inner urgencies and truths. It means learning how to say something, a detail too many schools omit from their writing curriculum.

That morning I'd read a story written by an ex-gangbanger about leaving gang life; after some discussion, I asked the kids to start writing whatever was on their minds. I often got great, surprising results from this lesson, as the kids tapped into their reservoir of life experiences, sometimes, as writers, for the first time. Mr. Johnson, the classroom teacher, and I were both surprised when Eugene — who had not contributed to the discussion — started writing with everyone else.

"He never participates in class. Never!" Mr. Johnson kept saying afterwards, as we moved chairs around to retrieve the boy's wadded-up effort. We unfolded the paper and read:

"Whin I was linsing to the store I tholt what hapin do me last fall. I almoste got shot. He shot by thise c but he mist me and it hit this lital kid."

Three short, almost indecipherable sentences, with enough misspellings (11) to make an impatient politician wad the paper back up and look for a bureaucrat to blame. But there's another way to react.

First, you can try to untangle what he was trying to say. I think it's this: "When I was listening to the story, I thought (about) what happened to me last fall. I almost got shot. He shot by these (children) and he missed me and it hit this little kid."

I value this honest effort far more than Eugene himself did. I'm sure he flung it away in disgust because he knew it was full of "mistakes" and that objective measurement would crush his effort, along with the truth about his life it contained. He just crushed it first.

My despair is that I never saw Eugene again; he stopped coming to class, leaving me unable to celebrate the risk he took and the beginning he made. He has no idea how far ahead he is of so many people, who have mastered the formalities of grammar but, when they write, don't know how to say anything.

*July 2001*

## THE INNER FRONTIER

DANGER!!!! KEEP OUT!!!!

With what trepidation do we begin a journal, do we shatter taboo and commit secret thoughts to words, to paper. Are we allowed to do this? Giving form to those vague stirrings inside us that no one knows about — or even suspects — could ... what? Get us subpoenaed? (Think what happened to Bob Packwood.) ENTER AT YOUR OWN RISK!!!!

The thrill of "getting caught" is perhaps part of the allure; some of us, oh so covertly, want that dream of being naked in public to come true. Keeping a journal is a private dare. Even if we keep the little volume under lock and key, the very fact that we've committed our interior life to the public currency of words removes us from safety, makes us vulnerable. Someone could find out about us. Oh my God!

Let me be the first one to say do it anyway; it's OK. But then I'm beyond shame on this matter. I maintained a journal throughout my 15 years of marriage and from the very start gave my wife permission to read it. That turned out to be the best of both worlds. She had the benefit of my heartfelt existential pondering and I could feel secure in the knowledge that she loved even the cluttered basement of my soul.

What I like about keeping a journal is that it says I AM like nothing else. Here's the thing: The effort collapses quickly if you aren't honest with yourself. No, more than that — if you don't push yourself right up to the edge of your own jail cell, and then step through, finding words to express what no one has given you permission even to think about. When you do this, you're shaping your identity in a secret crucible.

What a discovery for an unhappy teen-ager. I started keeping a journal when I was 15, inspired by reading *The Diary of Anne Frank* in English class. At first I tried to lift myself out of the muck of adolescence with grandiose prose, writing preambles about Freedom and Democracy and penning the requisite "warning" to unknown future readers, but never quite getting to my core.

Then one evening, with my world teetering on the brink of disaster — I thought I had failed a test in solid geometry — I wrote: "God I'm worried. Scared to death is more like it." The words, and those that followed, had the magic power of truth, bestowing perspective and control on my sad carcass. Here was this bruised, uncertain inner animal — me — so often irrelevant, it seemed, to what was supposed to matter, suddenly staking a claim on the world. I became more than what others thought about me and decided about me.

And thus began my dialogue with myself, which I have kept up, in ever-mutating form, over four decades. A while ago, out of curiosity, I started tracking the forms I've invented or appropriated to adapt journal-keeping to the changing conditions and needs of my life; right now the list is up to 103. Here's a sampling: mental grindstone; spiritual spine; parenting shock-monitor; song lyric repository; war and violence watch; Eros containment; breakthrough engine; health watch; career goad; macro-planner; detachable soul.

How bemused I feel as it slowly dawns on me that journal-keeping is no longer an oddball activity, a secret life-addendum you happen upon on your own at a time of spiritual crisis, when the rest of life rings hollow. Now it's actually a popular, indeed, publicly promoted, activity, supported by workshops, websites and even a magazine, Personal Journaling: "Read the stories of how journaling helped one man accept retirement and one woman battle a life-threatening illness."

In our fragile, violent society, a positive trend: celebration of the inner frontier. We're figuring out how to explore it together. And as we do so, we have so much less to hide.

*April 2001*

## SELF-EXPRESSION RECESS

Go ahead, scour this column from top to bottom and just try to find a grammar mistake. (If you do find one, it's because I slipped it in intentionally, just to give diligent pedants a little reward for their persnickety perspicacity.)
My point is, I know my grammar. I know how to use it and how to abuse it. I know how to push it hard enough to make it cry "Uncle!" I find it, as a subject unto itself, modestly interesting (how many predicate nominatives can dance on the head of a pun?). I certainly don't fear grammar; if challenged, I might even acknowledge I respect it, in the same way I respect directional signs in parking lots.

But mostly I regard grammar as a pompous enemy, and I am a virtual Minute Man of watchfulness, ready to yank it off its high horse the instant I see it threatening our precious freedoms — that is to say, the moment some misguided soul begins to ascribe it the value of revealed knowledge, usually in conjunction with the peasant-bashing word "standards," as in the decline thereof.

I'm not sure why I'm so passionate on this topic. Maybe it's because I sense that the least respected freedom of all — and the first to be taken away, often permanently, from defenseless children no less — is the freedom to exercise our creative genius. And often this sacrilege is perpetrated under the banner of "grammar," foisted on the innocent as an assemblage of impersonal rules, the mastery (rote memorization) of which necessarily must precede verbal self-expression.

Kids learn to write safe, rule-obeying sentences in school when they should be encouraged to set runaway verbal horses loose on the pages of their loose-leaf notebooks, which, after the fact, they can work on corralling with the help of the appropriate rules of grammar. I'm sorry, but grammar has no life of its own, no sovereignty. Its sole function is to sharpen and focus thought; it's the writer's servant — even if the writer is only 9 years old. We acquire the logic of deep grammar at the same time we acquire language itself; what we learn in school is cosmetics.

This is the diatribe my poor colleague set loose the other day when she happened to remark that she deplored the lax standards generally rampant in e-mail correspondence. It took me half an hour to shut up, to find the off switch on my lecture engine.

E-mail is one of my favorite technological innovations of the last half-decade, as much because of its liberating informality as its instantaneousness. A friend of mine, for instance, used to labor to get off one letter to me per year, but writes regularly since e-mail entered our lives. This is because she always felt snail-mail correspondence had to be a grindingly perfect effort: a reasoned composition, a big deal. But e-mail asks nothing of the sort from her. She just writes it willy-nilly, punches send, and minutes later I'm in possession of her candid opinions on a wide range of topics.

E-mail is such a new innovation it comes to us free of the school-imposed thought traps that accompany other media. E-mail is self-expression recess, a spelling-be-damned playground of thought in progress. Zap, send: "heerz what i think ..." So what if it's messy? Process is always messy.

I'm not against "standards," but when I hear people deploring their decline, my hackles start twitching immediately because usually the standards in question are superficial and merely reflect a bias for something old and familiar.

I say leave e-mail alone as a medium of raw, messy thought, closer in spirit to speech itself than to the deadly dull compositions of our schooldays. Good writing always threatens to overflow its banks. I'd rather read rich, error-rife prose on my computer screen than sentences that preen in their correctness but say nothing.

*August 2000*

## SIGN IN, SIT DOWN AND SHUT UP

*Education*

Thank God for the math teacher. Till he spoke, you might have gotten the impression the assembled young people would be making license plates for the next four years.

The occasion, in fact, was the orientation meeting for the high school my daughter will be attending, a top-drawer school full of high achievers and serious award winners, which it never lets you forget. The place is not only full of students, it's also full of itself. And the agenda this night was intimidation, of both the incoming freshmen and their parents, as though the only way to deal with so much raw adolescence was to wave a big stick at it.

I sat mid-auditorium, sinking into a deepening funk as the speakers went at us with their single note of bad cheer: homework, discipline, responsibility, test-scores-more-important-than-life-itself, beware the permanent record, cover your midriff. This place is tough; it doesn't brook slackers or class-skippers.

The math teacher spoke for about two minutes, too briefly to affect the prevailing winds. And he was obviously out of the loop; he hadn't been prepped on the night's theme of endless sobriety and general anesthesia. He expressed surprise at what he'd been hearing, then told the kids, "I hope you'll discover a toy store in our department."

That was it. He sat down and the meeting continued as though he hadn't spoken at all. But I'll take my breaths of fresh air where I can find them. The education industry is too "results driven" these days — too committed to a business model for the classroom, too desperate to produce a bottom line — to openly flaunt its little secret: We don't learn at work, we learn at play.

Once you know this, it's hard to tolerate a two-hour meeting about the next four years of your kid's education that portrays learning as a joyless grind. I'm not opposed to hard work or parental monitoring, all the stuff they extolled, but, I'm sorry, I don't automatically trust educators. When they speak with too much glee about discipline, I worry deeply. As a college writing teacher, I've seen the effects of educational arrogance and intimidation written indelibly across students' minds — and prose.

I've seen what happened to my own daughter, who, thanks to a wonderfully nurturing second-grade teacher, bloomed magnificently as a writer, then in third grade (at a different school), plunged into a hatred of language and writing because the teacher taught "the second R" as a rote, dead formula, as mandated by the standardized test by which she was judged: All written thought had to begin with a "topic sentence" and end four paragraphs later with a "conclusion." If the content in between was stillborn, no one in authority gave any evidence of noticing.

For several years I worked as a writing consultant in the Chicago Public School System, a job that took me into some of the city's poorest, most desolate high schools. Invariably, I found the students eager to express themselves — and stunningly honest and eloquent — once I had convinced them I really wanted writing from them that came out of their own lives and hearts.

But what an uphill battle, getting that point across in the brittle, tight-security environment of a struggling urban school, where order was imposed (so it sometimes seemed) by an occupying army. One day, for instance, in one of my classes a substitute teacher stood at the door and growled as each student entered, "Sign in, sit down and shut up!"

I watched in dismay as each subdued kid took his or her seat and glowered silently. Class discussion that day was a flop. But the words remained etched on my mind, a personal slogan for the meaningless order that's left after the spirit of learning is broken.

*June 2000*

## GRAND MARSHAL OF THE DORK PARADE

Caught myself the other day in one of those bitter, life-wizened moods, chewing on the soft marrow of memory. Suddenly I confided to Melanie, my pal and sympathizer, in a burst of self-realization: "You know, that was the best role of my life."

And as soon as I said it I felt myself flood with longing for the latitude to be a fool again, with hurdy-gurdy accompaniment.

The Fool — the "0" card in the Tarot deck, the great innocent, the great beginner — is underrated these days. But the ancients knew The Fool well and appreciated him. "The Fool steps out into the unknown without fear or caution. He isn't brave, but he has no fear," said Nina Lee Braden of the Tarot archetype. Zen Buddhists speak of cultivating a beginner's mind, a state of unguarded openness to whatever comes along. I just talk about fatherhood.

That's what I was doing when I had my spasm of awareness that a chapter of my life was over, that never again would I be Grand Marshal of the Dork Parade. Bear with me, please, as I recover from my chagrin that this term, purloined from a Paula Poundstone monologue, describes with perfect aptness the role I've been best suited for in life.

OK, fatherhood itself requires somewhat more, I suppose, than being a great roughhousing lovable goof — you also have to be provider, disciplinarian, teacher, worrier, co-diaper changer, imparter of values, that sort of thing — but from awfully early on, from the moment, let us say, of my daughter's first grin as a resident of Planet Earth, at a few weeks of age, up until about fourth grade when things took a serious turn (Truth or Dare became popular, for instance), the role I seized with greatest gusto was Grand Marshal of the Dork Parade.

Sometime early in my daddy days I heard Poundstone deprecatingly label herself thus on TV and I howled at how it fit my own situation as well, because fatherhood was ridiculous, but in a good way. This little life force in my co-care, relentless energy burner, tiny scientist, consumer of all available attention, pressed, in her complete neediness, against what was selfish and brittle in me, even as she demanded ... my collusion.

"The Fool steps into the unknown without fear or caution" — that's how I entered fatherhood, but doing so seemed easier while wielding an imaginary grand marshal's baton. It was unconditional surrender to my fate: to the burning wonder in an infant's eyes and the miracle of that grin on her face.

I wrote in my journal when she was 18 days old: "She smiles especially — 'goes crazy,' as Barbara puts it — when you kiss her on the cheek or nose or forehead. Her face opens up into the brightest smile and she starts waving her little arms up and down in excitement. It's too much to believe."

It was for this that I vowed to be as ridiculous as necessary, not that doing so was so hard. I just unbuttoned my inhibitions and became a co-

conspirator in the act of growing up. But almost every parent does this. "If you're happy and you know it clap your hands!" What mommy or daddy hasn't gone almost giddy with glee, at times, over the simple fact that the wheels on the bus go round and round?

This is the dork parade. What entitles you to be grand marshal is your memory of your own dignity, which you fling aside as you bid goodnight to the moon and dance for the Gloomy Kerploppus.

Maybe I took it further than some; I'm not sure. But it was this that I remembered the other day with such a sharp pang, as I sat huddled in fresh dignity. (It grows back.) Life isn't bad now, just more sober. There are no parades left to lead, only teenagers to chauffeur to their urgent destinations. When you grow up through your child, you look around and all you are is middle-aged.

I looked at Melanie and shrugged. Wanna do something foolish tonight?

*October 2002*

## NEW EYES

My car is illegally parked at the corner of State and Lake streets, downtown Chicago — one of the busiest intersections in the city, if not the world. It's high noon.

This is a delicate maneuver. I've got to get the sandwich and get out of here ASAP. Fortunately, I have assistants. My pal Malcolm, who is visiting from Alabama, has run in to Potbelly's to get the grub — ham with mustard and lettuce — so my daughter, whom we're about to visit, won't have to eat the city's boxed-lunch fare today. This was her requirement for letting us watch her paint. She's in a city-run arts program; everything about it is great, apparently, except the food.

My job is to drum on the steering wheel and watch the traffic cop in my rearview mirror. With me is Malcolm's wife, Kim, who has never been to Chicago before. She's staring out the window. My official tour of the city hasn't even started yet, and here she is emitting little oohs and ahs — at what? Her enthusiasm takes me by surprise and, in spite of myself, I begin staring out the window with her.

At first I ache with impatience. Through my own eyes — jaded, seen-it-all-once-too-often — this is nothing, just a too-busy street corner where parking's impossible. The humanity spilling around me is a nuisance, the tide I have to fight every day to get from Point A to Point B. But as I look at the throbbing corner through Kim's eyes — new eyes, freshly beholding Chicago's spectacle of daily life — a funny thing starts to happen. Instead of my showing her the big city, she's showing it to me.

Each figure looms distinct, a detail of the daily carnival of lunch hour under the steel girders of the elevated train: A bus lumbers around the corner bearing a screaming Jackie Chan ad. A bicycle messenger flies by, dreadlocks poking from beneath his yellow helmet. The street is alive with muscle shirts and muumuus, headphones, beepers, backpacks and hairnets. Ice cream cones drip. Cameras click. Cabs screech to a stop. An ancient, orange-aproned newspaper vendor sits on a milk crate, sweat glistening on his bald head, crying out, "Sun-Times, Trih-byooooon!"

By the time Malcolm returns with the sandwich, I feel exhilarated, newly attuned to the world in front of my nose. We push on with the day, wending our way, eventually, to the Art Institute of Chicago, and suddenly I find myself standing in front of Vincent Van Gogh's spare, glorious painting called "The Bedroom."

Austere room in Arles: a bed, two chairs, table, wash basin, mirror. Pale violet walls, scarlet coverlet. The room is grim, shabby, lonely. But my heart swells when I look at it. The empty room is alive, full of color and energy, inhabited by a soul.

"Do you know what I have left today for the week," Van Gogh wrote to his brother during the period in which he painted this scene, "and that after four days of strict fasting? Just six francs. ... I ate something at noon, but already this evening I shall have to sup on a crust of bread."

The starving artist rendered the contents of his pauper's bedroom — nothing more exotic than that — with such startling newness of vision the painting would, today, fetch millions of dollars. Normally this sort of irony pinches me terribly and elicits a bitter laugh, but on this day I take satisfaction in the truth it reveals.

All artists have about them the air of being visitors to our planet, who look at its wonders with a gasp. They coax us to see through their eyes, and when we do, the commonplace becomes luminous — as luminous as the fat woman in the silver blouse and silver slacks, with enormous silver-tinted hair, carrying a black handbag, crossing against the light at State and Lake today at noon.

*August 2001*

## SECRET FIRES

Did you ever once nurture a secret truth about yourself — that you were an artist? Did this truth go away, or does it return sometimes, even now, as a stab of foolish longing ... to make something beautiful?

Did you act on it?

Chances are, if you're like me (a male), you've been awfully busy crunching away at necessity for the past, oh, two, three or four decades. The dream of being an artist is a hard one to keep alive in our society, especially, I would guess, for men, whose rite of passage cauterizes them with a sense of duty and responsibility. The indefensible characteristic of art is that it's fun. At heart, art is play, a dance with the elements.

But of course art is also survival. We know this. A few of the extraordinarily talented among us are richly celebrated and rewarded, as though they've been ordained to make art on behalf of all the rest of us — to sing our songs for us, to forge our visions, to tell us who we are. Taking nothing away from the brightest stars in the human sky, I long for a world that gushes less before great talent, accepts it and honors it, but sees it as no more than the lifeblood that courses in all of us.

Art that we participate in is infinitely more valuable, for all its flaws, than art that merely dazzles — merely entertains — us. But in our bottom-line-fixated world, which distrusts the artistic impulse and too often holds it in contempt, where do we get the chance? Who extols the art of the common person?

For something over a year now, I've been attending monthly get-togethers of an organization that does just that — uniquely, as far as I know. The Chicago-based Men's Art Forum is one of those endeavors that opens up the definition of who we are, or have a right to be. It certainly loosens the screws of masculinity.

It was founded by three men: Andy Mitran, a drummer and composer; Tony Savino, choreographer and event producer; and Dick Levon, psychotherapist, painter and musician. The three met at a men's retreat weekend, in which setting — with males sharing the raw truth about their lives — the need to address, on some ongoing basis, the right of men to be artists was painfully apparent.

Participants would talk, shyly, awkwardly, about an interest in one artistic pursuit or another. "Overwhelmingly, these guys had been threatened out of their art," Andy said — by their dads, their teachers, their peers. They were told, perhaps in the strident language of boot camp, to shape up, find a sensible career. Very often, as a boy comes to feel the power of being a man, a piece of his soul gets left behind.

The Men's Art Forum helps us reclaim that piece of our soul. We sit in a circle. We check in. The macho shells crack, as ordinary guys reveal what they do and love — their music, their poetry ... it could be anything. Digital collages, whimsical furniture. Some tell stories about their lives, or simply give us their lives. They share what they've forged in their secret fires.

"Every meeting we've ever had there's been a new face," Andy said. "That's been incredible. There's 65 guys on the list who call themselves members. It gets me excited to think about spending an evening inside their brain."

The attitude, in this circle of men, is one of respect and receptivity for each person, which, like the drumming we sometimes do, has an almost primitive — primal — feel. This can be breathtaking: Tell us who you are; we're listening!

In the Men's Art Forum, each one of us has a chance to ignite the circle.

*August 2001*


## STAR STUFF

I found the sweet spot by accident when I was 8 years old, to my immediate chagrin and ongoing puzzled humility. Man oh man, how that ball sailed!

Today I peel back the perversity of paradise, as it shows up on the playground and in our blood. There's a $20 word for it — "self-efficacy" — to go along with a host of other words and phrases, varying colorfully with each human activity, all of which come down to this moment, NOW, and whether its kiss is bestowed or withheld in regard to the task at hand.

Here's what needs to be said: It's the same NOW across the board, the same present moment, the same groove and pocket and right-ticking rhythm, whether you're sitting at the keyboard and suddenly let go with the freest music you've ever played or arguing with your teen-ager and catch yourself, concede the point and all at once see things from her point of view — only to notice, an instant later, that she sees your view, too.

"Everybody can draw equally," the world-renown glass sculptor Dale Chihuly told a group of youngsters at a workshop in Kansas City as he passed out plastic squeeze bottles of paint and other equipment and set their creativity in motion. This is the secret that's slowly escaping, tickling the edges of the collective unconscious: We are all equally powerful beings, equally creative, equally endowed with star stuff. We just need to realize it, and escape our own mental labyrinth.

Even science and medicine are getting around to recognizing the influence of attitude and spirit on life's inner workings. Neither the universe nor our bodies, it turns out, function like impersonal machines. For instance, a recent study about Type I (childhood-onset) diabetes concludes that young people who believe they can stick to a diet, give themselves insulin injections, etc., maintain better health than those who don't.

This is news?

What's news, to me, is the fact that science is turning its scrutiny on intangibles like "belief." The study, notes the Center for the Advancement of

Health on its website, "is the first to demonstrate the relationship between the belief in one's capabilities of adhering to a diet and exercise regimen — what psychologists and sociologists call self-efficacy — and blood sugar control."

Good attitude means better blood, which is great for those who have a good attitude, not so hot for those who are, let's say, cowed or terrified by their situation. This is what got me to thinking about baseball.

When I was 8, I was bewildered by this game that was suddenly all around me. Everybody was playing it, so I had to, too. But it had dropped into my life almost as senselessly as diabetes. If it had been diabetes, I would have been one of the disease's doomed underachievers — couldn't catch a ball, couldn't hit a pitch ...

Later I fell in love with the game and actually got good at it, but when I was a klutzy 8-year-old, I was the worst kid out there, an aggravation to his teammates, likely as not to be named "official catcher."

There I stood at home plate one afternoon. The outfielder heaved the ball in. I was supposed to catch it and tag out the runner, but I didn't have a glove. Instead I held, for some reason, a bat, as though for protection. I still see that ball flying toward me.

I couldn't hit a ball pitched to me from 10 feet away, but I swung at this one that lofted in from 100 feet. I just meant to stop it, I swear, but I connected effortlessly and sent it back from whence it came, over the outfielder's head, down Olmstead Street all the way to Nowlin. Everybody groaned. My "hit" was utterly useless, completely outside the game.

But sometimes that's how it works. Confidence is a condition outside the prescribed boundaries. When you're trapped in a game you know you're no good at, the star in you has to make up his own rules.

*March 2002*

## PADDED CELL

Tick, tick, tick.

Is it the clock or is it my heart? My eyes open and fix on the green numbers hovering in the darkness just above the night table: 3:47. Maybe you've been there, in that moonscape terrain of twisted sheets and unwanted consciousness known as insomnia. Once it claims you, just try wriggling free.

For about a week, I feared I had lost the knack of a full night's sleep, that something had dried out in me. Dreams that should have kept spilling merrily into eternity abruptly stopped. I'd be crawling through a tunnel and emerge — in my own bed. A padded cell. The worst nightmares are the wide-awake ones.

4:11.

How do you shush the brain? Random worries attack like birds of prey. That worn spot on the kitchen floor, so easily ignored during the day, now scrapes mercilessly against my conscience, reminding me that I'm a neglectful homeowner. My portfolio is tanking, the videos were due yesterday at Blockbuster, the tomato cages are still out in the garden and the president is threatening nuclear war.

I take to lying as still as possible, but that doesn't help. Every sound is abrasive: the traffic, the wind, a tree branch scraping against the window. And weird things happen. Once, I swear, my end-table lamp popped on of its own accord — it's one of those "sensitive" lamps, you need only touch the stem. But no one touched it. Must have been a power surge.

4:23.

I give in to the fact of insomnia — spell-weaving incantation of a word. How big sleep suddenly seems, how far off, like the sky. I writhe in my padded cell, a prisoner of my senses, wide awake but not "up." I'm caught between two worlds.

Desperately, I try to outwit my own mind. Make it go numb. I think up lists. What was the address of every place I've ever lived? Name a hundred motels I've stayed at (picture the lobby, if there was one). How many girls have I had crushes on, starting in first grade? What did I do today?

4:48.

I can't peel my eyes away from the green numbers. Each minute hangs in pregnant anticipation, giving birth to the next. It's out of control. I close my eyes, but it does no good. The numbers are too luminous. My eyelids are transparent. I pull the covers over my head. It doesn't help.

I'm stuck, I realize, in time itself, in "identification with the past and continuous compulsive projection into the future" (as Eckhart Tolle defines it in *The Power of Now*). Tick, tick, tick. I need to find the present moment — and quick. My alarm is going to go off in two hours.

5:01.

A sort of surrender. OK, I'll never sleep again, fine. Immediately the panic and urgency lose their edge. The sounds go blurry and thoughts emerge blunt-edged. Sleep is the disintegration of thought, it occurs to me. Perhaps this is the limbo that gives birth to cartoonists. How would Bugs Bunny handle those late videos? They sprout legs and dance to the fuzzy margins of awareness.

I let every unwelcome thought turn to rubber. Worries mutate and step off the edge of cliffs. Seriousness makes a fool of itself. For some reason I think of yin and yang, but they emerge from their fetal twining and become two halves of a fake, press-on mustache. I stick them under my nose and feel myself sink into oblivion.

The room turns pale yellow. Somewhere there's a faint click, followed by a voice bursting with familiar enthusiasm. It's time for the news and traffic is backed up on the Dan Ryan Expressway.

7:01.

*January 2003*


## PRETEND SCIENCE
*education*

"BOR-INGGGG!"

An 8-year-old takes no prisoners. She feels what she feels and that's all there is to it, so there! But sooner or later, if you're a loving parent, especially if you also have a stake in the matter that's repelling her, you have to pry back the steel bars of her attitude and ask, "What's wrong, sweetie?"

She was learning, as a third grader, how to hate writing.

By the tenth or dozenth time she declared her contempt for my calling — "We went to the museum today and now we have to do a composition about it. Yuck!" — I became desperately alarmed. This wasn't passing pique. Some active massacre was taking place in her classroom, of a process fundamental to being human. Why not just kick her in the soul?

A year earlier, a loving, imaginative second-grade teacher had sent her scurrying on fantastic adventures in prose. Now her face contorted at the thought of writing a single sentence. And the sentences she wrote weighed in my heart like cinderblocks, so dull were they, so devoid of her spirit. "In conclusion, I'd like to say I really learned a lot from this trip" — the grinding dishonesty we wring from our children! What contrast to the celebration of donuts and stray cats and throwing up five times on Sunday with which she'd regaled us at age 7.

I feared lasting damage. As I worked with Alison on her museum essay, coaxing her to write the truth as she experienced it, no matter what — "You saw where the black painting had orange in it? Great! That's what you should say!" — I slowly wormed my way to the core of the problem. In third grade they start testing kids. And the teacher, her job shackled to its results, taught to the test.

This was not the old-fashioned kind of test, of course, but the first of many quasi-scientific probes into the brains of schoolchildren in quest of numbers. How smart are they? How well have their schools rammed home state-mandated standards? Regardless what skill was being gauged, the answer was always a number — so nicely portable, so seemingly objective. When you come up with a number, it sure looks like science.

The writing portion of the monstrosity known as IGAP (Illinois Goals Assessment Program) measured proficiency in a five-paragraph format —

opening sentence, blah blah blah, conclusion — so this became the school's writing template, standard and god. It was what the state wanted, after all, no matter it valued formal, easily measurable trivialities (e.g., capitalization) over risky honesty; no matter it gutted writing of its point, communication, and turned it into a rote grammar drill; no matter it bored my daughter to death!

Writing, like speech, is an activity of organic complexity; those who claim they can divine and quantify someone's skill level from a prompted sample — as though writing can be "scraped" from a student's mind the way you'd take a tissue sample — are, in my humble opinion, practicing pretend science. That's putting it charitably. Speaking as a parent, I wish they'd just go away. I'm tired of doing damage control.

But who listens to me? The cachet of numbers and testing — "standards" — in education, and especially the politics of education, is on the wax. Here's the president's new education bill, grandiloquently named the Leave No Child Behind Act, calling for nationwide testing for grades three through eight (you mean we don't already have this, and then some?), to "provide parents with the information they need to know how well their child is doing," etc.

Testing is the new hickory stick, the standardized whack across the behind of anyone who believes learning occurs more readily in a climate of joy than fear. Too many of my daughter's teachers (she's in high school now) talk in terms of what she needs to know for the next Big Test. Too few talk of what they love about their subject.

*January 2002*

## THE SOUL OF LEARNING

Anyone else offended — maybe just a little bit — by the term "grade inflation"? This nakedly monetary expression is the defining metaphor for the latest debate about academic standards. What a specter it raises: dumb kids getting A's, "academic excellence" going the way of the almighty buck.

It certainly has 'em all shook up at Harvard, where 90 percent of the class of '01 graduated with honors. Now red flags are hoisting all over the place, as though mediocrity has pulled a fast one. The great institution is on the defensive against those who accuse it of harboring — not, you will note, lousy teachers, but rather, lenient graders.

This is a debate about softness and mollycoddling, not about learning or teaching. What a fat target, though. A spokesman for the National Association of Scholars recently lamented, with withering sarcasm (as quoted in the Chicago Tribune), that colleges "don't want to give students the grades they deserve; they're afraid of hurting their feelings."

So that's what grade inflation is: easy A's, cheap standards, a bloat in the currency of encouragement. How disrespectful on its face, as far as I'm concerned, this implication that grades are anything at all like money, that they're a commodity tied to a gold standard, too great an issuance of which will lead to ... in the name of Professor Flutesnoot, what? Undergraduate overconfidence? Too many whippersnappers who think they know something? A dearth of dropouts?

"What is it we want from America's schools?" asks Sara Matthews in an excellent essay on the Education Week website. "Do we really want excellence in instruction for all students? Do we want all students to be successful, or is it necessary that some must fail so that the success of others may seem real?"

I think that's exactly what the anti-mollycoddlists believe, to which I say, how disrespectful to the soul of education.

The wonder of this debate is that it's not about anything at all. Grades — there seems to be some misunderstanding about this — are nothing more than temporary markers, entirely without intrinsic value. They're part of the scaffolding of learning. What matters, when you take a class, is whether you get it.

A grade is a notch on a gauge in the teacher's mind of the extent to which you have, or haven't, mastered the material at hand. It's a reference point, which ought to fall by the wayside when the class ends and you're left with the knowledge and understanding you have gained, if any. That's the product of learning, and its only reality.

When I was an undergraduate, I saw the soul of learning chalked across the blackboard of a seminar classroom one morning. It didn't bill itself as such. It was just a quote from Ralph Waldo Emerson that my teacher found inspirational. So did I, and I copied it into my notebook. Thirty-plus years later, it looms as holy text — this half-sentence lifted out of "Self-Reliance." It's been working on me all this time, a live imperative, a goad, pushing against the edges of my complacency, upping the stakes of every conversation I have with my daughter's teachers.

"In every work of genius," wrote the premiere essayist of the 19th century, "we recognize our own rejected thoughts."

Careful, it's loaded. Take it at face value and you'll never have peace again; you'll never be content with the chasm separating ordinary humanity from greatness. You'll never again regard genius as cold perfection carved in granite, but as a living restlessness, a refusal to give up, a manifestation of the star stuff we're all made from.

Emerson throws down the gauntlet. Genius is on the inside, intrinsic to your makeup and mine — and our children's. It's the not-yet-imagined future, coiled, waiting to be born in every undergraduate.

*January 2003*

## HEMORRHAGING NIRVANA

"Oh my gosh, I'm having a stroke! I'm having a stroke! And in the next instant, the thought flashed through my mind, this is so cool!"

You want a guided tour of the human brain? My guess is that you probably can't do better than *My Stroke of Insight*, Harvard-trained neuroanatomist Jill Taylor's extraordinary account of the cranial hemorrhage that shut down her left brain when she was 37 years old. But the book's value — its preciousness — lies less in the plain-language, enthusiastic science it offers us, than in the door it courageously opens to the mystery of the brain's right hemisphere and beyond ... to the pulsing miracle of life and the vast universe that is our home.

One morning in late 1996, Taylor, a research scientist who worked at the Harvard Brain Tissue Resource Center (a.k.a., the Brain Bank), awoke with a sharp pain behind her left eye, and soon enough — as her speech and motor functions failed her, as she melted into what she called a euphoric stupor and lost all sense of where "Dr. Jill" ended and the rest of the universe began — she realized this was no ordinary headache. It was, she later learned, a blown AVM: the rupture of a congenitally deformed vein-artery connection deep inside her brain. She was in the first stage of a potentially killer stroke — and she was alone in her apartment and had lost the capacity to think or act rationally or even communicate with the outside world.

Part of the joy of this book is that nothing unfolds the way you'd expect. Taylor's story at its darkest courses with gratitude and humor and, most of all, amazement, as she recounts what happened to her with Ph.D.-level clarity and awareness of detail combined with childlike exuberance. The sudden loss of her left-brain organizational and self-defining capabilities was not, for instance, terrifying. Life-threatening though her predicament was, Taylor saw her stroke as a gift of unparalleled awareness: the shattering of the self-created box we live in that we call "life."

"When the shower droplets beat into my chest like little bullets, I was harshly startled back into . . . reality," she writes of that first morning. "As I held my hands up in front of my face and wiggled my fingers, I was simultaneously perplexed and intrigued.

"Wow, what a strange and amazing thing I am. What a bizarre living being I am. Life! I am life! I am a sea of water bound inside this membranous pouch. Here, in this form, I am a conscious mind and this body is the vehicle through which I am ALIVE! I am trillions of cells sharing a common mind. I am here, now, thriving as life. Wow! What an unfathomable concept! I am cellular life, no — I am molecular life with manual dexterity and a cognitive mind!"

Taylor's book accomplishes quite a few important things in a fairly short space. It tells a fascinating story that begins with how she orchestrated her rescue that morning even as "my earthly body dissolved and I melted into the universe," and proceeds through brain surgery and eight years of slow recovery of her left-brain functions (for instance, she had to learn to read all over again, beginning with the preschool-level "The Puppy Who Wanted a Boy"); it bursts with hope for everyone who is brain-injured (not just stroke patients but accident victims and thousands of Iraq war vets); and it gives medical practitioners clear, no-nonsense information about the shortcomings of conventional treatment and attitudes toward the brain-injured: "I needed people to come close and not be afraid of me."

But to my mind, what makes *My Stroke of Insight* not just valuable but invaluable — a gift to every spiritual seeker and peace activist — is what I would describe as Taylor's fearless mapping of the physiology of compassion, the physiology of Nirvana.

This book is about the wonder of being human and as such is a plea and a prayer that we strive to be equal to how big we really are. What a piece of work is man — 5 trillion cells functioning in purposeful harmony. The two hemispheres of our brain are yoked opposites: limit-setting rationality (time, judgment, ego) in perpetual interplay with the eternal and unbounded now. Together, and only together, do these two halves of our awareness make our human destiny.

A healthy person, and a healthy society, honor and live more or less equally out of both halves of the brain. When I asked Taylor how she'd describe our current state of societal balance, she said: 85-15. "We don't just not engage the skills of the right hemisphere, we mock them!"

That is to say, we live and we strangle each other in our left-brain ego-boxes, refusing to trust or even acknowledge that a different kind of world is possible. Here's how Taylor puts it: "I realized that the blessing I had received from this experience was the knowledge that deep internal peace is accessible to anyone at any time. ... My stroke of insight would be: Peace is only a thought away, and all we have to do to access it is silence the voice of our dominating left mind."

*March 2007*

PART THREE

# 9/11 *REVISITED*

## LOW TECH, HIGH CONCEPT

Not a soul on this planet, I would venture, imagined — before four hijacked jumbo jets punched a hole in history — that you could bring down the twin towers of the World Trade Center with knives and box cutters.

Thus were the hijackers on at least one of the planes armed, so it's possible that was the extent of the weaponry on all of them. This was even more subtle than the bomb-in-the-suitcase scenario terrorism experts have warned about for years. The hijackers, with such innocuous implements, had an easy slide through airport security, apparently: The only truly lethal weapon was their resolve, which is not detectable by X-ray.

Mix a willingness to die for your cause with 50,000 gallons of jet fuel and you have one of the deadliest and "smartest" bombs ever built.

"This was low tech, high concept," an expert on terrorism told a TV interviewer on that first day, as the smoke of the collapsed towers billowed in the background. That is, we'd just been hit by an enemy who understood the modern world and its vulnerabilities better than we did ourselves, and who had manipulated them with lethal brilliance. This expert was one of the few in the endless parade of retired generals and old Cold Warriors who actually had something insightful, and responsible, to say to a benumbed nation. Most of them just kept telling us we were at war.

War was the refrain — the metaphor — that couldn't be repeated often enough, as the horror unfolded and we sat glued to the endlessly replaying footage of fire and dust. "It's clear the U.S. is at war," one official said. "It's just not clear with whom."

Did it matter that no formal declaration was made by the other side? Did anyone go to bed on the night of Sept. 11 not believing some Arab group or other was behind it all? The networks seem to think we require certainties, "answers," as we watch the news break. Remember the 2000 election? The winner is ... Osama bin Laden!

Even if that supposition proves right, the media ill served our grief and horror by scratching the itch of an old prejudice. They blamed the Oklahoma City bombing on Arabs terrorists, too, you'll recall. How dare they do so again.

But perhaps even more disheartening was the sheer military drumbeat of the coverage. Few voices could be heard calling for healing and prayer, or even restraint, much less explaining that terrorism, despicable as it is, has causes, and doesn't just emerge, incomprehensibly, out of a clear blue late-summer sky.

In our disbelief, we groped for familiar solutions. Here, for instance, was former Secretary of State Lawrence Eagleburger, opining on CNN that "We need to be prepared to act as though we are at war. ... You strike at them militarily. You have to kill some of them even if they aren't directly involved in this thing."

Reporter: "You're not taking about a long, drawn-out investigation then (before we take action)?"

Eagleburger: "I hope not!"

A day later, the "n-word" had entered the discussion — nuclear retaliation, at least as a possibility not to be ruled out. This, before we have a known enemy. Maybe we don't need one. We know where our missiles are pointed.

War is high tech, low concept. Strip away the coded language and what you ✓ have is a justification for killing innocent people.

If we pursue such a strategy, with nukes (say it ain't possible, Lord) or without them, I know two things for sure: Those we kill will be just as innocent as those we have lost. And we're guaranteeing that the terror will happen here again. Better airport security won't keep it out.

*September 12, 2001*


## MORE HEROES

At the prayer vigil I attended, the biggest cheer went up for a fire truck that happened to go by with its sirens blaring — not ceremoniously, as far as I could tell, but because it was on a routine run.

This commonplace urban sound shattered our three minutes of silence and ripped open the collective heart of the crowd. Here were the heroes of our national tragedy, still on the job, still risking their lives for our safety, this very minute for all we knew. Bravery and sacrifice and duty were on open display — the same stuff that propelled the first rescue teams into the Twin Towers, moving against the exodus, on a mission to save lives as the buildings collapsed on top of them. It could bring you to your knees.

The cheer still resonates, louder than ever. It came from a place deeper than our anger or cries for revenge. It was a cheer for life itself, for its immeasurable value. This was the rawest "meaning" to spill from the Sept. 11 events: that human life is precious and saving it is the highest calling. This is the belief that unites us, or did at the prayer vigil.

Can we honor this spirit in our response to the tragedy?

Too many of the voices I hear dishonor it. How easy to sound patriotic by calling for abstract, risk-free vengeance against a country we know nothing about, whose people have no more humanity to us than ants or cockroaches. This is the cheapest patriotism available. It cauterizes the pain, perhaps, and fills the void left by disbelief, but it doesn't bring back the dead. It just creates more of them, this time wearing turbans and burqas.

The suffering people of Afghanistan are not our enemies. The terror the ruling regime, the Taliban, has unleashed on its own female population has been described as medieval in its fury. To read of its grotesqueries — the stonings, floggings and amputations of women for such crimes as leaving their homes unaccompanied by a male relative — is to be filled with a disbelief almost equal to that of watching the World Trade Center towers collapse.

Do we have weapons smart enough to seek out the Taliban but spare its victims? More likely, our weapons will do the opposite: score direct hits on the disabled, orphaned, starving, immobilized women and children of Afghanistan, while their oppressors scatter and regroup. In Afghanistan, a woman who is ill or injured cannot, by law, be treated by a male physician. If we rain war on a country with so inhumane a government, how many women's lives would we render unsustainable? How much further misery would we create?

The unpopular truth is that "anti-Americanism," particularly in the Middle East, is rooted in something other than envy of our prosperity and freedom. In waging the Cold War, in protecting our oil interests, we have asserted a presence around the globe that cannot be called benign. From the CIA-engineered overthrow of the nationalist, liberal-left government of Mohammad Mossadeq in Iran in 1953 (and subsequent installation of the hated shah), to our present-day, children-killing sanctions on Iraq, we have thrown our strength around to much consequence and suffering.

An honest response to the terror of Sept. 11 would be to rethink our relationship to the Third World, rather than automatically declare war on it. (Some would say we're at war with it already, housing, as we do, the School of the Americas, in Fort Benning, Ga. — that notorious training ground for torturers and death squad leaders.)

To come clean about our nasty little foreign-policy secrets, to commit ourselves to global justice — to be a country that believes in more than "justice for just us," as poet Kevin Coval put it — would be to honor the Sept. 11 dead, and the heroism of those who tried to save them.

To go to war over the tragedy would be to create more heroes, pulling more bodies from the rubble. These heroes wouldn't be Americans. They'd be our enemies.

*September 20, 2001*

## COLUMBINE GROWN UP

In our irreverent age, shhh ... Sept. 11.

It's simply The Day, bathed in national quiet. We talk about it with our heads bowed, though our eyes still flash with disbelief. In our minds' eyes the towers burst into flame, first one, then the other, again and again; and in countless conversations we relive the moment we heard the news, cherishing that last flash of innocence, that illusion of an intact world, and holding onto its memory as though someday it will come back.

We know, of course, that it won't. We also know the day has not yet ended, that its rubble still has to be turned over brick by brick, shard by shard, and every last body trace scraped from the wreckage for DNA matching. We know this, and wonder how what we learn will change us.

We also know that something has to happen — some collective action, some response to terrorism. As I write, we are still standing on the edge of it all. No war has begun, no lashing out of an aggrieved superpower, so I persist in believing this is not what we as a nation truly want.

Where I go, I don't see the evidence of a 90 percent approval rating for military action, which is what the polls report. War mobilization, I'm sure, is the only large, collective response on the pollsters' list of alternatives, so people pick it, not wanting to diminish the scope of the tragedy by choosing … nothing. What I see in public, however, is not war fever but a complexity of feeling: anguish, disbelief, compassion and fear, all tempering the anger. I see a recognition that anger is a small emotion, inadequate to the real task at hand: creating a safer world.

When guitarist Fareed Haque, at the world music concert I attended over the weekend, said, "Every note I play tonight is dedicated to peace," the audience burst into applause. It was instantaneous — a collective sense that our passion must drive us inward as well as outward, into artistry, into prayer. It must make us ask: What is the good I can do? What can I give to the human race?

What I see is that Sept. 11 is nothing like Dec. 7 — we're not the nation we were when Pearl Harbor was strafed. We've lived through the Cold War, Vietnam, and the movements for civil rights, environmental awareness and gender equality. Even those who have hated these movements, opposed them every step of the way, have been influenced by them and today acknowledge, however reluctantly, their core truths. Arab-bashing, mosque-trashing and other "retaliatory" hate crimes have been swiftly condemned by every authority. We aren't "rounding up Japs" and putting them in camps.

Indeed, we have lived, since that original Day of Infamy, through World War II. If the World Trade Center and Pentagon attacks were the equivalent of Pearl Harbor, presumably we'd have to trump them with a new Hiroshima. There's no sentiment for this, not after two generations of jokes about World War III. We know that war has no winners.

All of this adds to the quiet that surrounds our memory of Sept. 11. We possess terrible knowledge about how dangerous and complex the world is, and know the wrong move could set off a chain reaction. We've absorbed one unthinkable tragedy after another in recent years: Oklahoma City,

Columbine, the twin towers. I've heard the events of Sept. 11 called "Columbine grown up."

We're starting to get the message. Evil cannot be easily isolated, put in the crosshairs of our $330 billion arsenal and — boom! — eradicated. Its seeds are scattered across the surface of the globe.

And so we wait in sobered silence, knowing that some of those seeds are in our own hearts.

*September 26, 2001*


## SECURITY WORLD

When the towers went down and the Pentagon got hit, alarm bells rang at every level of leadership and, as a consequence, I show my photo ID to get into work now — the one where I look like John Wayne Gacy.

This is just one more small way in which the world is shifting, becoming unrecognizable.

Welcome to Security World, our friend and protector. It is also, at a moment's unpredictable notice, our tormentor, our persecutor. If it sees something it doesn't like about us — a Muslim surname, too much cash, the wrong chemistry in our urine — it can turn on us, spring shut like a trap. In an eye blink we're no longer the protected; we're the suspected.

As the "war on terrorism" gets more subtle and complex, the surveillance of the commonplace thresholds of American life will likely increase and become more invasive. My fear is that it will also become more irrational. (Remember loyalty oaths?) What seems straightforward — a person's legitimacy — is really anything but.

For all its high-tech gadgetry, security is to an extraordinary extent a guessing game. I say this extrapolating from a few bizarre encounters with Security World in recent years. Maybe things are different now — maybe the industry has suddenly revitalized its professionalism — but in the world that existed prior to Sept. 11, I felt a glazed-over complacency standing guard at the nation's checkpoints.

Once at the Buffalo airport, for instance, my wife and I made the bonehead mistake of telling the truth. In answer to the requisite question from the ticket taker — "Has your luggage been in your sight the whole time?" — we said no.

What could we have been thinking? I assume, as I try to reconstruct our naïvete, that we expected some sort of follow-up discussion. Our circumstances were perfectly plausible: We'd checked out of our Niagara Falls hotel at 11 a.m. but, because our flight wasn't till late afternoon, we left our luggage with the bell captain and got in a few more hours of unencumbered sight-seeing before taking a taxi to the airport. Hardly a big deal.

But our answer set off a series of scowls and dropped jaws up a chain of command that culminated in the confiscation and meticulous search of our luggage and a brief sequester in a little room until our belongings were certified bomb-free.

My bemusement isn't over the fact that the luggage was searched, but over the sudden disconnect a simple, truthful answer caused between us and airport security. They were immediately flustered and sprang at us in a way that felt like being under arrest — because we volunteered the truth. We could have lied and spared ourselves a great deal of inconvenience.

Not only was this irrational, it was disrespectful. Security at its worst glowers at the public that passes through its checkpoints, monitoring not so much possible dangers as sheer breaches of normalcy.

Since the attacks, the national instinct has been to tighten up, as though a slackness of character — too many people doing what they want — somehow were responsible for what happened. We almost seem to be making a new national motto out of a phrase from the letter, recently released by the FBI, that was found among the belongings of several of the suicide terrorists: "The time of fun and waste is over."

This is the terrain of Security World. A tightly secured society demands, and processes, homogeneity, in the mistaken belief that this is where safety lies.

*October 4, 2001*

## MATTHEW 5:39

I don't think I'm the only one who felt a terrible moral tearing when we let the missiles fly against Afghanistan, 27 days after the horror of Sept. 11, or who now fears more deeply for the future of the human race than ever.

No matter how smart our bombs — and they're always less "smart," less accurate, than the enthusiasts initially proclaim, it later turns out — violence still begets violence.

I seriously question that the best way to fight evil is to suspend the moral context of human conduct, but that's what war is — not unleashed rage but dispassionately altered reality, in which right and wrong downgrade to mere questions of strategy. The violence of World War II, which began, you'll recall, a mere 21 years after the end of the War To End All Wars, so eroded moral standards that taking out whole cities became an acceptable strategic calculation. The firebombing of Dresden and many other cities preceded the atomic incineration of Hiroshima and Nagasaki.

Today we ache over the loss of perhaps 3,000 lives, and two tall buildings, in New York City, but these deaths are miniscule compared to the number of innocents claimed in the Good War. Yes, we beat Hitler; the war was a strategic triumph. But it was a moral disaster for the human race nonetheless, and we don't want to replicate it. Fifty-six years of pride in that victory is perhaps sufficient. It's time to look for a different way to mobilize against evil.

George W. Bush's favorite philosopher once made a suggestion to that end.

"But I say unto you, that ye resist not evil: but whosoever shalt smite thee on thy right cheek, turn to him the other also."

Matthew 5:39: a troubling Bible verse, is it not? I feel as though I'm playing devil's advocate just by bringing it up, not as scripture, not as divine mandate or pie-in-the-sky idealism, but simply as an idea. Was Jesus a coward? Was he naïve? Or was he two millennia — and counting — ahead of his time?

The concept of "turning the other cheek" has long been the straw man of pop culture; a prescription for impotence. And war, as it is engaged on the home front, is as much pop culture as it is serious news. This is where I start to feel cast into a wilderness of misgiving — when we as a nation embark on a course of action as unreflectively as if we were picking out a movie. "Tali-BAM!" went the headline in the New York Post the day after the missiles were launched.

We sang "God Bless America" and hauled out the flags, but we have not yet debated what our responsibility might be, as a grievously injured superpower, more powerful than any nation in history, to help the human race break its chain of violence. Maybe it's not too late.

Sept. 11 changed everything; we all woke up at once, gasping in shock, reeling in grief. No one, not even corporate Hollywood, has any interest in returning to "normal," if normalcy means the pursuit of petty self-interest. Surely there's more to be done with such a moment in human history than squander it on revenge.

What if the flag summoned not the troops, not the bombers, not the missiles, but an outpouring of compassion for the entire suffering world, equal in intensity to our willingness to shower aid on our own wounded and grieving? Every open conflict on the planet could be re-evaluated, with a commitment to healing it at a level where every life is precious.

Jesus said take the blow, but he didn't say run away. The vulnerability implicit in Matthew 5:39 is not that of a victim. It's the vulnerability of the hero — the cop, the principal — advancing on the armed child with hand extended, disarming him by offering him his soul back.

*October 7, 2001*

## BACK TO NORMAL

Every door I tried was locked.

There were a dozen of them, at least — every 50 feet or so, all around the building. Big, brown, ugly school doors. Some rattled when you banged on them; others seemed nailed shut, permanently decommissioned. These didn't give back even an echo.

And the silence, as I yanked, felt deliberate, the way bureaucratic silence always does. My daughter's in this building, for God's sake. She's swimming in a meet, it's only her second one, and I'm missing it — and it's raining! A flustered anger began to burn, as old, petty grievances about school and new ones about the state of the world merged with a father's panic and deteriorating sense of dignity. (How quickly that goes.) Other people manage to get in this place. Yank, yank. Why can't I?

I was running late because the rush hour traffic had been aggravated by the rain. I could have left earlier, but I'd poked around at home, lingering over the headlines: "Could bin Laden get nukes? Experts call it a nightmare." How odd it felt to pop myself free of such matters, to drop out of the national flight pattern, so to speak: OK, somebody else can worry for a while. How small and isolated I felt battling mere traffic, being merely Dad. There's a surprising loneliness and "who cares?" in the return to normalcy.

The rain intensified. I was beginning to remember how much I hated high school. And this place was half a mile in circumference — a gothic fortress built in ... what? The Middle Ages? Yank, yank. It definitely recalled an anti-kid era, a time when adults could declare, "Children should be seen and not heard." A child could enter this place and never be heard from again.

But security concerns were minimal when the building went up. They could build schools that were accessible to the public. What a naive concept, I mulled bitterly as I tramped through the mud, vainly tugging at all this obsolete access. Even before we worried about terrorists and jumbo jets and suitcase nukes and anthrax, we worried (remember?) about high school kids with guns. The world is getting away from us, and the result is that ... a dad can't even get into his own daughter's swimming meet.

What it is, see, is that when you're the father of a teenager (in my case, the widowed father), you lose tolerance for locked doors, for reminders of your own futility. All you want is to do right by the kid — but, see, I just blew it again. She hates that word, "kid."

All you want is to let her grow up, to ease things along, to get a little love back — and to be there when you need to be. And the more shut-out I felt (yank, yank), the more necessary my presence seemed, at that moment, to her transition to adulthood. She needed her old man in the bleachers, his battered heart swelling with pride as she swam backstroke in the medley relays.

But we were back at the parking lot. The mom of another swimmer, who had joined the search, said, "I don't think we've tried that one" — a metal door next to a dumpster in a sort of loading-dock area. A small sign on it said: GIRLS LOCKER ROOM.

The door opened when she pushed it.

Dignity? What dignity? I followed her in. I did it for my country. I did it for the future.

I was hoping, I suppose, that I would find myself in a corridor, not the locker room itself, but I was immediately, and ominously, in the midst of rows of lockers. And next to one of them — surprise, surprise ...

I averted my eyes, lunged for a second door, but couldn't avoid catching the look of shock on the girl's face. She was still in her suit, at least (thank you, Lord). An instant later I was out of there, this time in an actual corridor, next to yet another door. It was marked "pool." Screams and whistles emanated from the other side of it.

The meet was still going on; I wasn't too late. I walked in, feeling a blast of heat and chlorine. Things were so back to normal I could hardly hold back my tears.

*October 12, 2001*

## WAKING INSOMNIA

In the privacy of our souls, we find ourselves getting crowded these days by the possibility of sudden death. There it was the other day on the commuter train, disguised as a discarded fast-food bag.

When I sat down next to it, I picked it up by a corner — it still reeked of ketchup and french fries — and put it on the floor, out of sight but not, however, out of mind. Is this the sort of thing I should be suspicious of, I wondered? An explosive device that looks like litter? I was amazed at my paranoia: radio signals from silly land. But they beeped the rest of the trip home, as I kept glancing down at the bag and childishly speculating whether I'd know what hit me when it went off.

"Normalcy" has been stolen from us even at the level of litter, apparently. It's a situation that's ripe for panic, overreaction and foolish lashing out — throwing Arab-Americans off airplane flights, jettisoning other people's civil liberties — as we grab for our old life, the one that fit us like a BarcaLounger. I call this predicament "waking insomnia": We can't be numbly unaware of our surroundings anymore, sleepwalking through our days, so certain we know what to expect of life we don't have to notice what's really in front of our noses.

We're suddenly in the position, it occurs to me, of the young Buddhist monk described by Jack Kornfield and Joseph Goldstein in the book *Seeking the*

*Heart of Wisdom,* who kept falling asleep while he was meditating. The master cured him of his spiritual sluggishness by having him meditate while sitting on the edge of a well.

We're all on the edge of that well — vulnerable and threatened, unable to rock backwards and disappear into the reverie of our private lives. This is not necessarily such a bad thing.

You may have heard, for instance, about the remarkable speech made by a United Airlines pilot only four days after the hijackings. (I read about it in The New Yorker.) "The doors are closed now and we have no help from the outside," the pilot noted. If this plane is hijacked, "I want you all to stand up together," he said, telling the passengers to throw whatever is available at the hijackers, rush them with blankets and pillows, get them down and keep them down.

"There are usually only a few of them and we are two-hundred-plus strong. We will not allow them to take over this plane," he said. "I find it interesting that the U.S. Constitution begins with the words 'We, the people.' That's who we are, the people, and we will not be defeated."

The stunning part of the speech, to my mind, was the end of it, when he asked the passengers to turn to their neighbors, introduce themselves and say a little something about themselves and their families — breach the anonymity, in other words, and open up little two-way passages of trust with one another. Voila, a hijack-proof plane! And the terrain of citizenship extended.

The time is ripe for unprecedented reevaluation of ourselves and our world on just that model, it seems to me — finding potential in ourselves and those to the right and left of us we had never before dreamed possible. I don't see much hope in the other direction we could go as a society: increasingly armed, isolated and paranoid, increasingly dependent on technology and the impersonal machinery of government to keep us safe.

All of this, finally, is a meditation on war, as I sit at the edge of that well. Life is fleeting and precious. We know this with a newly wakened wonder. Yet our insomnia hasn't penetrated the assurances issued about this war's necessity, or found its way into the dark and rubble of Kabul and noticed, and been shaken by, the humanity of our targets.

At the very least, I think, we as citizens should be mindful of whom we're killing. It's too easy to fall into a sleep about this, to be awakened only by retaliatory acts of terror.

*October 18, 2001*

## HOW TO SHOCK THE WORLD

With the ingenuity and sense of leverage against superpower weak points that the terrorists have already shown, they could really bring us to our knees by suddenly (oh, the horror!) ... turning nonviolent.

I mean, what if Osama bin Laden simply gave himself up? Sure, it'd be a suicide mission, but it would be one Allah was likely to bless, if he did so before winter set in. We'd have to stop bombing Afghanistan if we had our billion-dollar man, and this would allow humanitarian organizations to begin trucking food to the country's desperate poor, 7.5 million of whom are in imminent danger of starvation, according to the United Nations.

Bin Laden could then claim the credit for saving their lives and we'd be caught looking — the instant heavies, exposed as the ones who planned to continue bombing a starving country. Whoops, war over, and we have egg on our face. We were last seen ignoring U.N. Human Rights Commissioner Mary Robinson's plea for a halt to the bombing so help could reach the hungry and dying. All our global sympathy as aggrieved victims might leak away like so much jet fuel.

Think how vulnerable we are, as we prosecute this war with high-tech fury. Bin Laden could cry "Enough's enough," turn himself in for humanitarian reasons, and win the war of world opinion. I say this with bitter facetiousness, of course, certain that this is one "unthinkable" act we'll never see — an act that shocks the world by saving lives.

We could shock the world in such a way ourselves.

What if "America Strikes Back" meant such a thing? What if it meant more than killing bin Laden, for which purpose the president just allocated $1 billion to the CIA? Compare that to the paltry $50 million the federal government spent last year — a little less, actually — to improve the national public health infrastructure (which is suddenly important because of the anthrax scare).

I ask all this with patriotism unfurled, mulling that number: 7.5 million Afghanis in danger of starvation. I want my tax dollars to go toward rescuing them, not pushing them into the grave. Our missiles aren't the whole cause of their plight; drought, three years of crop failure and vicious Taliban misrule have created the crisis. But we're making a bad situation worse. And by pushing on with the war despite the crisis, we may be closing the window of opportunity for delivering aid before the onset of the cruel Afghani winter.

Just as I had feared, now that war has become our response to the Sept. 11 atrocities, now that it has fixed national, and media, attention, military strategy has become our moral lodestar, defining what matters and, indeed, what is good. Thus, the success of the Northern Alliance, a brutal bunch cut from the same cloth as the Taliban itself, has suddenly become crucial, and their fortunes fill the news. The looming starvation of millions, to the extent that it's reported at all, has a sort of footnote feel to it.

Patriotism ought to be more than just cheering from the bleachers for our side to win. How richer is the patriotism that rallies not simply to defeat an enemy but to do good. This is always a more arduous and complex undertaking.

We made a feint at doing good by dropping thousands of food rations — packed with such goodies as beans with tomato sauce, shortbread cookies, peanut butter and moist towlettes, and costing $4.25 each — into the mountains of Afghanistan; the same day, we began heaving million-dollar cruise missiles into its cities. (And the food packs look like the cluster bombs we also drop, causing Afghanis, including many children, to mistake the latter for the former and blow themselves up.)

We're tapping into bottomless billions to kill a bearded fanatic; we begrudge a few million to help the starving. The patriotism of many, many Americans cries out that such numbers be reversed.

*October 25, 2001*

*UPDATE: In December 2001, the U.N. World Food Program, with the help of private relief organizations such as Oxfam, delivered 116,000 tons of food to Afghanistan and mass starvation was quietly averted, though the possibility in this shattered country remains ever on the horizon.*

## LAMB OF GOD

The other day I thought how lucky I was to have hold of my wife's hand as she died.

Later, when a sudden memory of her laughter, say, made a direct assault on my sanity, I was unable to doubt her death. This is a blessing. If at some secret level you harbor the hope that a lost loved one will return, will fling her keys on the living-room floor again, just once, or throw a ratty sweater over her head after work and flip on "Seinfeld," you cannot grieve properly or go about the business of being a survivor.

One of the conditions of consciousness is a blind spot about not-existing. We all cherish, in our heart's vault, a child's assumption that we're the center of the universe. Only the death of a loved one can tear this assumption from us, rip it from the seat of being. Mortality has no exemptions. Healing from great loss begins with knowing this.

So the spectacle of the post-Sept. 11 search for news of missing spouses, friends, fiancés, children — for their bodies, or at least traces of their DNA — was almost too heart-breaking to bear. New York — not just New

York, the whole country, the whole world — became a land of the lost and disconnected, as numberless thousands knew the worst but, lacking the hard evidence of a corpse, were unable to stop hoping and begin mourning.

Then their plight faded from the TV screen and from my immediate awareness; I began not thinking about it, even as I vaguely understood that, as with so much else about the tragedy, I hadn't come to the end of it.

A chance glance at a death notice in a Chicago newspaper not long ago, more than a month after the hijackings, confirmed this. What caught my eye was the face: a smiling young woman in a big sweater. Her picture was surrounded by six inches of 8-point type. Vanessa, the notice said. Beneath it were the words: "A missing victim of the Sept. 11 tragedy." Those words were electrically charged. I needed to read about her. Here was a clue, perhaps, about how long it takes healing to supplant hope, and life to go on .

"There are extraordinary people in the world who touch and enhance all who come in contact with them. They are the lambs of God." This is how it began — this public goodbye.

What followed was the accounting of a life: She was a Suzuki violinist, an equestrian; she was on the debate team and golf team. She was selfless, she radiated warmth, she loved her family — how this mattered, even to a stranger. Here was a life blooming in front of me. She'd been a financial researcher, hired in mid-August, which meant she'd been on the job only a month. Slowly, such details define the enormity of a national tragedy.

There was a memorial service for her that day at a suburban funeral home. I almost felt I knew her well enough to attend. The words of the death notice pealed like bells: "God has blessed us with Vanessa."

I thought about how every fireman, every cop, who died on nine one one was given his or her own memorial service, no matter how wearying this was to the ones who knew … all of them. This is how it has to be, I thought, because each life is the center of the universe, and each death provokes an upsurge of sympathy for all humanity.

But thinking about this in the context of Sept. 11 and its fiery political aftermath made me flash on a terrible possibility: Someday we could have too many deaths to be able to mourn each one.

When I read, therefore, about the carpet-bombing of Afghanistan, I refuse to rejoice or sign off on its necessity — not without thinking about that last hour at my wife's bedside. I only know what I have learned: that life is precious. And that this is a political statement.

*November 3, 2001*

## THE LEGACY OF 9/11

Is it too late to go back to Sept. 11, to summon disbelief afresh at a level so deep it might be signaling the end of the world? Can we bear to peel off the certainties with which we have papered over the wound and endure, one more time, five minutes, let us say, of pure bewilderment?

I suggest this as a spiritual exercise simply because those first moments, before we "understood" anything at all, retain an infinite capacity to move and teach us, to warn us about how fleeting life is and maybe open us, as individuals and as a nation, to a deeper resolve to live our values.

I'm thinking the least of our values have held sway since that day. We've settled, as our response, for carpet-bombing Afghanistan, an action that is abstractly punitive and asks little of us personally. For most of us, the war on terror amounts to watching it on TV, displaying the flag (perhaps) and — GOING SHOPPING. That's the national purpose we've been called to, when those first moments seemed to suggest that so much more would be needed: our blood (a pint at a time), our heart, our spirit.

When I ask my country what I can do for it, I encounter a leadership void. I encounter transparent platitudes about good vs. evil that leave me heartsick and queasy. I believe that as we shop, the war on terror, which we're told won't be over anytime soon, is inflicting terrible pain on innocent people we could care less about.

Indeed, the number of Afghan civilian dead as a result of our furious and wanton aerial bombardment could well, by this point, exceed the number of Sept. 11 dead in New York, Washington and Pennsylvania, a ghastly little piece of war-on-terror marginalia. As of a month ago, that number, gleaned from an array of foreign Internet sources by University of New Hampshire professor Marc Herold, was approaching 4,000.

The national indifference to this is deafening. How is it that such a number exacts no emotional toll on us — because the Afghanis are dying in increments of 10, 20 and 50, rather than all at once? Or is it just because the newspapers aren't breathing a word to us about any dead at all, except our own?

If we were really pursuing a foreign policy based sheerly on doing good, rather than on raw economic self-interest and covert agendas, such as running an oil pipeline through Afghanistan, wouldn't the "collateral" death toll matter?

Before Sept. 11 hardens into history, let's reclaim our disbelief about what the world has come to. Let us reclaim our stricken conscience, personified in those early hours and days by a shamed Hollywood pulling some of its big-budget schlock action flicks out of the distribution pipeline. Let us reclaim that moment when the collapsing towers shook us free of petty self-interest, before the platitude-utterers reassured us that evil wore a turban and a beard, and lived in a cave. In this resurrected state, perhaps we can remember wanting more than an enemy.

In this state, perhaps, we can hear the sense Jim Hightower is making when he proposes a national purpose bigger than "going shopping."

"I find (and polls confirm)," the Texas populist writes in his newsletter, The Lowdown, "that Americans yearn to be part of something BIG, something that calls us together in common cause besides military destruction."

How about liberating ourselves as a nation from oil dependency? He suggests a national effort to do so that's the size of the Manhattan Project, or larger, and public rather than top-secret. Let us, he says, pull together the best scientific minds, along with the heart and goodwill of every citizen, to achieve the necessary breakthroughs in the mass use of pollution-free alternative energy sources — "fuel cells, biomass, solar, wind, geothermal" — to achieve energy independence in 10 years.

We built The Bomb, and put the future of humanity in jeopardy. What a fitting legacy it would be if Sept. 11 spurred us to take on a project that served humanity, and saved it.

*February 2002*

## FRESH DAWN

Here it comes, Sept. 11 — a permanent scar on the calendar now.

We're all feeling our pulses quicken as it approaches, wondering, perhaps, what forgotten detail, what suppressed feelings the anniversary will flush. (Oh yeah, I drove my daughter to school that morning, and then later she called in tears and said, "Are we at war, Dad?") This was the day America was ripped open with half a dozen box cutters. It was the day that changed everything. Its claim on us has yet to be plumbed.

Anger and patriotism have poured out — the easiest (and worst) kind of patriotism, in my opinion. Long before the shock of the day's crimes wore off, the media started feeding us an enemy to blame, and soon enough we were at war, bombing cities, caves, wedding parties. Somehow this was self-defense, a logical response to what had happened. It relieved us of the need to fall to our knees, to grope for understanding and transmute horror into reverence.

My hope is that we begin to understand the day in all its political and human complexity and reclaim it from the Defense Policy Board, the president, the attorney general and network television. Sept. 11 should be a day that unites us with the rest of suffering humanity, not one that severs us from it. But the year separating this Sept. 11 from the last one has done just that.

10 years

Recently, for instance, the mainstream Council on Foreign Relations issued a report lamenting that the United States has image problems abroad: We're widely perceived, it concluded, as "arrogant, self-indulgent, hypocritical and unwilling or unable to engage in cross-cultural dialogue."

The Council's recommendation? Throw a division of public-relations specialists into the fray to spruce up America's image, because, in the words of chairman Peter Peterson, "If we're going to fight (a war on terror) effectively, we'll need the cooperation of a lot of countries."

A cumbersome evasion of reality seems eerily operative here, which begs slicing with Occam's razor. Maybe the problem is that we're perceived to be what we, in fact, are; and the best way to solve our image problem is to relate less arrogantly to the rest of the world — beginning with Iraq, the country of some 23 million people currently in our crosshairs. We see an enemy (and smell oil); the rest of the world gazes on a frightful sea of collateral damage.

Sept. 11 was about the death of 2,830 people, an ethnic, racial and national panoply of souls. They died — most of them — at work, suddenly, in circumstances so ordinary they should have been immune (who didn't feel a spasm of outrage over this?) from mortal concerns. Yet some of them, likely having no idea what had happened, found themselves forced onto ledges 90 or 100 stories above the earth. Fleeing an inferno of jumbo jet fuel and burning infrastructure, they stepped into thin air.

I thought about these nameless leapers the other day because of a story my sister told me after she got back from Hawaii. On Maui, she had a chance to leap from a 30-foot cliff into a deep natural pool — a once-in-a-lifetime adventure opportunity, which she took after only a slight pause to gag on the fear reflex.

What struck her, she said, was how long it took her to reach the water.

And so I multiply this "long time" to fall 30 feet by 300 and conclude that those who jumped from the World Trade Center on Sept. 11 lived, perhaps, half their lives in that space between leap and oblivion. Whatever terror, whatever grace, accompanied them for this miniature eternity belongs to us. It's part of the legacy of this day, even if our only access to it is through our own imaginations.

If we strip ourselves, even for a moment, in memory of our fallen countrymen, of all but our innermost resources, if we imagine their long leap into the unknown, we will, I'm sure, be less likely to squander Sept. 12 when it arrives. Our only hope is in a new day, fresh dawning and free of the hatreds and encumbrances of the past.

*August 2002*

## GROUND ZERO

You take the E train to America's newest — most nondenominational — shrine: a big hole. The pieces of earthmoving equipment on its periphery look like toys.

What are they excavating here? The faith and values system of the new millennium, I think, or perhaps merely hope. We see what we want, no doubt, when we visit what's left of the World Trade Center.

I don't know that you can go to New York and not visit it. I've got a niece who lives in town, and an old college friend, and a daughter who wanted to tour some East Coast colleges, but when I thought about making this trip, I thought, first: Ground Zero. It yanked at me from a third of the way across the continent. Not a day has gone by in the past year when I haven't thought about it … when 280 million of us haven't thought about it.

Not that seeing the long-cleared site would answer any questions or reveal anything new. It's an immense city block surrounded by a chain-link fence that's covered in green mesh — as though, somehow, the site still required privacy, seclusion from the public's gaping, hungry eyes.

You emerge from the subway, it's a bright Sunday afternoon, and you're immediately part of the crowd, snaking around the sidewalk at a casual pace. At intervals the plastic mesh is torn and you peak inside, at tiny trucks, a crane, a lift basket bearing its rental phone number: (800) 654-PRIDE. Overhead, unfurled from a stark black building bordering the site, is a five-story American flag. An equally large sign beneath it says: "Thank you for never giving up." Poking above the fence, on a hill of excavated earth, is a cross welded from two snapped-off lengths of steel girder.

And you shuffle along, looking up. Mostly, people brought their own reverence. A man next to me reads the Bible as he peers through a hole in the mesh; it's open to I Corinthians. The only for-profit enterprise I saw was a guy selling bottled water.

After 20 minutes you reach the official viewing area. There are flowers stuck in the links of the fence. People take pictures — of a sprawling construction site, dominated by a three-sided hole maybe six stories deep at the far end, large enough to dwarf the semi parked there. Water puddles at the center. You see a few men in hardhats. Gate 3. No trespassing. Violators will be prosecuted.

Stay as long as you want, but you have to use your imagination to conjure what occurred here a year ago, to reconstruct two towers 110 stories high. The dominant impression is nothing much, business as usual, bleak emptiness.

Only as you move along does a chill fall across the heart. The horror of Sept. 11 is still etched in the buildings that border the site. That black building with the flag — when you get close enough, you realize, my God, it's a ghost building. Blown-out windows, crumbling façade. It's black because it's sealed, top to bottom, in protective black netting, like a shroud. The shroud is 30 stories high.

At street level, shuttered businesses still have their signs up: Stan's Pizza. Burger King. Unsuspecting people once ate their lunches here. The businesses are now dead things, arrested in the middle of life, like the ruins of Pompeii.

Does it make you angry? No, this is too big for normal emotions. The shrine engulfs it, as it does the earthmoving equipment. You do not try to control what you feel, or understand it, or give it a name. You kneel to the consequences of violence.

In the heart's silence, a groping, a nascent vow. Blessed are the peacemakers. You move on.

*September 2002*

## A GOD THAT FEARS

I put off my post-election, competitive migraine for a day by attending, with my sister the psychologist, Joan Borysenko's workshop on the mind-body link in medicine, or mind-body-spirit link, if you want to get truly controversial. This is the future: "Life force medicine," as some call it. Medicine that is unafraid to explore nonlinear paths to healing rather than cling solely to the linear mechanics of curing.

Borysenko, who is, among many other things, a Harvard-trained psychoneuroimmunologist, gave laymen like me a dazzling glimpse into some of the mysteries of this realm, e.g.: "Emotions are the interface between body and mind — where thoughts turn into molecules."

I tagged along because I have high blood pressure, a condition as common as, oh, low voter turnout in U.S. elections — and just as mysterious — and wanted to get some insight into why, for instance, my B.P. is always higher at the doctor's office. If I can control it unconsciously, at the level of fear, why can't I learn to control it consciously?

The workshop nudged open some windows for me; it also, unexpectedly (nonlinearly), gave me a perspective on the big disappointment of the 2002 midterm elections, which reflected, you might say, a lack of recognition of the mind-body-spirit link in politics. If there is such a thing as a societal immune system, we didn't vote for it. We live in a society afraid of the future — in the sense that the future of a wound is its healing.

How might the immune system work at a societal level? John Dear gives us an idea of it in an essay called "Confessions of a Sept. 11 Chaplain," published at nonviolence.org:

"During those initial weeks, an unusual spirit of compassion came over the entire city," wrote Dear, who counseled hundreds of bereaved family members after the World Trade Center towers collapsed. "We felt united. We spoke to one another on the streets. We talked on the elevators. We nodded to each other. We looked at each other wondering, 'Did you lose someone?' Everyone tried to do something to help. Everyone tried to offer a smile or a kind word.

"But as soon as the government began to call for revenge and war, that beautiful spirit of compassion started to wane. ... The city was no longer allowed to grieve."

Dear's words echo what Borysenko said when I asked her about 9/11: "We reacted in an optimistic way at first, but then it became a political thing. We got stuck in 'what can we do to keep ourselves safe?' We have a society that feeds on fear. The optimism that gets generated is overcome by fear."

A state of continual fear is surely as harmful to the body politic as it is to an individual organism. At first, we filled the wounds of 9/11 with courage, prayer, citizenship, an outpouring of voluntarism, a sudden reverence for the common good. We spontaneously organized ourselves into a healing mode. We became better than who we had been before the crisis — accessed the divine in our nature, which is always present.

Then an old frenzy claimed us, a desperate lashing out at the darkness. We became "ourselves" again: Armed America.

Think how unsafe we are: We're not just fighting the rest of the world, we're fighting ourselves. In the decade of the '90s, our prison population doubled, from 1 to 2 million people. We have the highest rate of incarceration of any country in the world, this nation that seeks to impose its will on the community of nations: 690 people per 100,000, edging out Russia (678 per 100,000), almost double Iran's rate (355) and six times China's (110). Since 1980, government spending on prisons has outpaced spending on education twelvefold.

What is man but a god that fears? So asked playwright Maurice Maeterlinck, and I wonder when we'll find the political will to respond. The God in us is unarmed.

*November 2002*

## WAR WITHOUT END

The echo of Flight 93 reverberated in a recent USA Today headline: "U.S. forces say they're 'ready to roll' to Iraq."

We can't just go to war. We have to go heroically. Thus we polish our weapons with the memory of blood nobly spilled. We rally our resolve by recalling the charge of unarmed passengers up the aisle of a Boeing 757 to thwart a band of knife-wielding hijackers and save the White House, as though that's how we'll rush Saddam.

No matter we're a superpower preparing to unleash holy high-tech hell against a broken, impoverished country in an engagement we can't possibly lose. No matter we ain't the underdog and all rhetoric to the contrary is morally dishonest. Only underdogs can be heroes, so we summon the martyred innocents of Flight 93 to bless our itchy trigger fingers. Let's roll!

This is the problem, as good minds and mediocre ones alike fixate on the brutality of Saddam Hussein and the specter of weapons of mass destruction, and call for war: Every war transcends its pretext. Even the good guys commit war crimes. Wars do not end.

You think Nam was over in '75? Think again. Maybe for you it was, but consider the fires that still burn and the landmines that explode over and over for the ones who fought there. The official death toll of U.S. servicemen in Vietnam is around 59,000, but in point of fact that toll never stopped climbing. By some estimates, nearly three times that number — more than 150,000 — have either committed suicide or died in accidents that may have been driven by a death wish. Agent Orange, of course, is still claiming victims. And the divorce rate among Vietnam vets is over 90 percent. An emotionally or physically shattered GI may never be granted a cease-fire.

The artillery shells that keep exploding are literal as well as psychological, of course. In Vietnam, an unknown amount — thousands, or maybe millions — of unexploded bombs, grenades, mortar rounds and landmines still litter the countryside, going off regularly, maiming and killing farmers as they plow and children as they play. Ditto everywhere war has raged. Some 18,000 people worldwide are victimized annually by such ghost ammo, according to the Campaign for a Landmine Free World.

And then of course there are the mystery illnesses that follow in the wake of our ever more toxic wars, from the maladies of Agent Orange to Gulf War Syndrome to the high incidence of Hodgkin's lymphoma among troops who fought in Kosovo, which has been blamed on the use of armor-piercing shells made of depleted uranium.

Today our troops may be ready to roll and we're all with them in spirit, but the day after tomorrow, after the survivors come home and dig in for the long siege — of cancer, post-traumatic stress disorder or God knows what — they'll be on their own. No headlines, no cheering, just the rest of their lives. And from on high: denial. War's over, fella. Get a job.

You think you can call for a discrete little invasion? Disarm Saddam, go home — and afterwards, peace? That was the public relations gimmick 88 years ago, when the great powers of Europe went at each other in the War To End All Wars. Since then, we've upped the carnage-output capacity of our war machines, oh, a thousandfold, maybe. This is not a force we can control.

Saddam Hussein didn't invent weapons of mass destruction. We did. The good guys.

Worst of all, I fear, we're altering human society. Every major war of the last century and a half has led to new developments in the technology of mass slaughter, and a corresponding increase in our ability to think, and do, the unthinkable. Killing one's own kind is not genetically natural. "Piranhas will turn their fangs on anything, but they fight one another with flicks of the tail. Rattlesnakes will bite anything, but they wrestle one another," writes military psychologist and violence expert David Grossman.

Most soldiers are a lot more ready to die than they are to kill, Grossman notes. But improved training techniques have changed this, turning the average Joe into a more brutally dispassionate killer. And the cult of militarism has spread like a virus through civilian society via mass entertainment.

War-making is a grubby business, a mounted skeleton, the only scourge among the Four Horseman whose agents are men. Mankind loses every war. If we're serious about peace, disarmament isn't a state we can demand only of our enemies.

*December 2002*

## TWENTY GANDHIS

As the fifth anniversary of 9/11 approaches, many of the nation's values — tolerance, forgiveness, personal freedom, perhaps even courage itself — remain trapped in the wreckage.

It may take another anniversary, another 9/11 — Sept. 11, 1906, to be precise — simply to remind us of what lies buried beneath the fear and cynicism, the ignorance and politics; and, even more importantly, to wake us up to the urgency of reclaiming those values and healing as a nation.

Led by a president incapable of protecting us but eerily adept at exploiting tragedy, we went off on a howling revenge quest against "the axis of evil" and proceeded to compound the horrors of 9/11 worldwide — turning this day into an excuse for torture and domestic spying and the indiscriminate "shock and awe" bombing of a country that had nothing to do with what had happened.

Around the country, and particularly in New York City, the wakeup call is about to be sounded, as grieving Americans — grieving as much for the future we're bequeathing our children as for the past — proclaim 9/11 a day of healing and peace, not revenge. The memory of Mahatma Gandhi will help drive the message home.

*No other
9/11*

The twist of historical fate juxtaposing the birth of "satyagraha," the world's first large-scale nonviolent resistance movement, with the terror attacks on the World Trade Center and the Pentagon, is downright chilling, like the sound of rhythmic tapping coming from beneath the rubble. Someone's still alive down there! Hope floods the heart.

Liz Graydon, a former middle-school teacher who is now education coordinator for New Yorkers for a Department of Peace, saw mention in a newsletter from Nonviolent Peace Force, which does peace work in Sri Lanka, that this Sept. 11 would be the 100th anniversary of Gandhi's movement for social justice. Not surprisingly, "The date just jumped out at me," she told me. It immediately became the focal point of plans to commemorate 9/11, and the stunning aptness of it has lit up the national peace network.

In August 1906, Mohandas K. Gandhi, a young Indian lawyer living in South Africa, was stunned almost to paralysis — "an impenetrable wall was before me," he later wrote — upon learning about the law the province of Transvaal had just passed, known as The Black Act, requiring Indian nationals to submit to a humiliating registration and fingerprinting process. Its intent was obviously racist, a first step by the white government to marginalize and eventually expel "coloreds" from South Africa.

"I clearly saw that this was a question of life and death," Gandhi wrote. ". . . the community must not sit with folded hands. Better die than submit to such a law."

Gandhi called a meeting of the Indian community on Sept. 11, which about 3,000 people — Hindus, Muslims and others — attended. One angry speaker, according to Gandhi's account, declared: "If any one came forward to demand a certificate from my wife, I would shoot him on that spot and take the consequences."

Gandhi had another idea: "It will not . . . do to be hasty, impatient or angry," he said. "That cannot save us from this onslaught. But God will come to our help, if we calmly think out and carry out in time measures of resistance, presenting a united front and bearing the hardship, which such resistance brings in its train."

Gandhi's vision, which he came to call satyagraha (a combination of Sanskrit words literally meaning "seize the truth"), held the day, indeed, kept the Indians of South Africa unified through eight years of intimidation, abuse and imprisonment. In 1914, the government agreed to end all anti-Indian discrimination. And of course, this movement continued in India itself until 1947, when British colonial rule finally ended.

Graydon, who used the 1982 movie "Gandhi" in her middle school curriculum, said her students were invariably skeptical that nonviolence could accomplish anything. She recalled one boy who conceded, halfway through the film, that it was pretty convincing, "But c'mon, Miss Graydon, there are 6 billion people on the planet. You'll never get all of them to be nonviolent."

She noted that the population of India at the time of Gandhi's movement was 300 million. "We don't need 6 billion Gandhis," she told him. "We need 20 Gandhis."

New Yorkers for a Department of Peace, in conjunction with the M.K. Gandhi Institute for Nonviolence, has organized 32 screenings of "Gandhi" around the country on Sept. 11, including, in New York, at the Regal Theater, across the street from Ground Zero. As far as I can tell, many other events are being planned that day, both in conjunction with and independent of the New York event, that will draw inspiration from this mystical confluence of anniversaries.

"Nonviolence is the greatest force at the disposal of mankind," Gandhi said. "It is mightier than the mightiest weapon of destruction devised by the ingenuity of man."

Maybe the time has come to learn how to use it.

*August 2006*

PART FOUR

# A HOLE IN GOD'S GRACE

## GUARDIAN ANGELS

On a too-ordinary day in January, a mom and her three little boys went to the store to buy laundry soap.

I know this kind of day and so do you. Errands, fast food, kids, whatever. Same old, same old. Sept. 11, you could say, was such a day. Every so often, the sky opens up on days like this and something precious beyond bearing is plucked from you, without warning, without mercy, and the universe is altered forever. And wherever you are — the Burger King, let's say, at Fairplex Drive and Holt Avenue, in Pomona, Calif. — is instantly a shrine, its plastic and vinyl furniture splashed with lamb's blood.

Yessenia Rochin, the young mom, walked her three boys over to the fast-food restaurant because her youngest, Osvaldo Martinez — only 2 years old — spotted it as they left the store and wanted to go in. It was a little after 1 p.m. Lunchtime.

What happened next was a miniature 9/11, devastating only a dozen or so lives, maybe, rather than thousands or millions, but no less horrific in its random malice, and perhaps even more disturbing in its implications for our general safety. Look, nobody talks about guardian angels anymore. There's a hole in God's grace, you might say; there must be. What happened to Osvaldo Martinez looks, dreadfully, like evidence of a breakdown in some invisible medium that allows us to live together and makes us human.

Mom and kids ordered their meals and sat down at a table to eat. At 1:17 p.m., a stranger walked up to them, put a gun to the little boy's head and pulled the trigger.

Bang, bang. You're dead.

News accounts never come with a moment of silence built into them, but something is called for here, some hush, some shutdown of consumer consciousness, at least long enough to let us hear the frantic flutter of angels' wings. A child is dead on the floor of Burger King.

Killer, age 24, was named Daniel Moreno. He was with some other guy. They ran out of the restaurant (what else are they supposed to do?) and apparently Moreno told a passerby, "I just shot my son." But that was untrue. He didn't know Osvaldo Martinez. He had no connection to the family he'd just shattered.

Police got there quick. Down the street was a strip club and in front of the strip club was a telephone booth, which is where police found the suspect. They attempted to subdue him with pepper spray. He shouted, "Shoot me, shoot me" and pulled the handgun out of his pocket. They fired and in an instant Moreno was dead in his vertical coffin, taking with him all the answers.

Fifteen minutes, two corpses. Case closed.

This story has so little rational meaning it's almost as though it didn't happen. Reporters did their best with the feeble ironies, e.g., that the family had moved from Compton to Pomona two years ago because they thought it was safer. But we're getting used to the idea that no place is really safe anymore, aren't we? Terror has found a way to reach every last one of us, if it wants. And we know this little boy's death won't be the last one that rips our hearts like a fishhook. We almost lack the curiosity to ask why. That just makes it keep hurting.

No one knows why anyway. Two people who had been with Moreno that day were arrested, but later released without charges. They offered no explanation of their friend's actions; maybe they had none.

All we're left with are the two deaths, like bookends, embracing 15 American minutes, one used handgun and a why the size of heaven. Let's kneel, now, inside those 15 minutes and grope for comprehension. What is it that used to protect us? Through what hole is it leaking away? How is that we know so much about how to kill and so little about how to heal?

*February 2003*


## ROLE MODEL IN THE DARK

The oddest thing that ever happened to me at a movie theater occurred during the credits of "Dead Man Walking." Lights pop on, I grope for my jacket and reconnect, blinking, with the reality I'd suspended for two hours, when the guy sitting next to me — a stranger — reaches over and shakes my hand.

"Thanks for being the way you were!" he says.

That's it. No further explanation before he withdraws from my life. I don't remember his face, just that hand thrust at me from across the armrest, that wakeup touch: Our lives are public even when we're in the midst of profoundly private communion, in this case, with Sean Penn and Susan Sarandon on the big screen.

But no explanation was necessary. I knew what he was referring to, though I hardly expected thanks for it. I had cried through the whole wrenching movie, about murder, capital punishment and forgiveness.

It was no big deal; I well up all the time. I guess I've lost most of my self-consciousness about such physical functions, but a stranger's sudden gratitude reminded me, oh yeah, manliness, strength, the sucked-in gut, that fiction of control — we're not supposed to have an emotional life more complex than "tough it out." So here I was, a role model in the dark, letting a fellow guy know you don't have to fight back every tear. You can sometimes just let 'em loose, and still be a man.

Crying is a noble human endeavor. It's certainly one of the most useful living skills I've picked up. Life is big and rending. You can't survive grief, for instance, if you consider every tear a failure.

But, of course, you have to rediscover, as an adult, your capacity to cry. Most males have their tear ducts cauterized by early adolescence; it's part of the passage to manhood.

I remember the squalls I had as a boy, over fights in the schoolyard, wicked twists of fate, the fortunes of the Detroit Tigers. I was such a bad sport — my team loses a close one and off I'd storm to my room, wailing and cursing and kicking things. From inside the storm, how terrible it felt, how shameful … to be crying! When you're a boy, crying is a loss of control, akin to loss of bladder control. A boy has to plug both leaks.

And the tears equal the self-pity. There's no distinction between emotional immaturity and its physical manifestation, which makes matters tricky when, as an adult, you feel life's tectonic plates shift, when people die, when loss lays bare the human condition and understanding slowly pushes against those very tear ducts.

I started learning how to cry again in the '70s, thanks to the phenomenon of encounter groups: sudden permission to hug strangers, share secrets and love the human race. I was overwhelmed the first time I went to one, but the tears came afterward, as I sat, in my emotionally rearranged state, alone in bed at a friend's house and turned on the TV.

On screen was an old "Bonanza" rerun, with Hoss and Little Joe, Ben, Adam, Hop Sing, the whole Ponderosa bunch. I have no memory of the plot that night, but whatever it was, something got to me and before I could hit the off button, my face was a streaming font of tears. I couldn't believe it. I hadn't cried when my father died, but here I was blubbering to "Bonanza," shedding tears beyond cynicism and through the theme song. I couldn't stop.

The pretext for the tears mattered less than the tears themselves, which washed me to the very edge of myself, to that opening beyond which lay the rest of the universe.

*February 2000*


## THE MUD RACES

Last summer, a hard-eyed little punk went for a drive and shot randomly at Jews, Asians and African Americans from his car window, killing two people in two states, wounding many more, and finally swallowing the barrel of his .22-caliber Ruger semiautomatic and taking his own life so he could avoid arrest.

The spree vaulted organized hate into the news, as well as the term "mud races." Ugly, squatting thing. Two little words: They punched a hole in time. Out crawled, oh, Julius Streicher, the Nazi propagandist who was hanged at Nuremberg. There he was, like bad sci fi, standing in the middle of the '90s in full parade dress, smirking, dusting himself off, releasing his ideas into the wind.

Turns out he also picked up an electric guitar.

Like rock and roll, hate, apparently, is here to stay. A Chicago area group, the Center for New Community, recently released a 10-year study on the phenomenon of "hate rock" — white supremacy with a backbeat. There are at least 26 bands and 13 U.S. record labels (with names like "Panzerfaust"), so I am informed, that specialize in making music out of the bile that motivated at least several of the mass murderers who grabbed headlines last year. The purpose of the music is to win young converts.

All of which is forcing me to meditate on the phenomenon of hate, or rather, dehumanization, a more accurate term because it conveys something colder and more systematic. It's making a comeback and becoming increasingly public, which is to say, less secretive, less ashamed of itself.

Most attempts to counter organized hate, it seems to me, are aimed at driving it back underground, refusing to let it gain a foothold in respectability, which has some value, certainly. Respectable, state-sponsored dehumanization efforts, from slavery to Nazism to contemporary ethnic cleansing, wreak the sort of havoc that nuts on the margins of society can only dream of, even if they have websites and rock bands, even if they have guns.

But I worry. Our official wedge against organized hate, as we flex our legs in the new millennium, is the smiley face of political correctness. This is a pretty thin layer of protection. I doubt it will hold if the pressure builds, if the music becomes too popular, if the economy nosedives and the need for scapegoats becomes irresistible.

In my lifetime, I have seen some astounding progress in the area of hate containment. We've eliminated segregationism from the seats of government and ethnic jokes from family reunions, but rage simmers in American society, seeking form. Hatred and the dehumanization of one group or another are simply too handy as organizing principles not to be used again on a large scale, especially to justify future wars.

I remember, for instance, how awash we were in hate-mongering during the first Gulf War. In the employee break room where I was working at the time, I noticed a poster someone had tacked on the bulletin board depicting a stereotypical, burnoose-clad Arab on a camel, a U.S. jet flying overhead, and the words, "I'd fly 10,000 miles to smoke a camel." This was flat out racism, anonymous and feel-good, masquerading as patriotism, as it so often does. Stunned, furious, I yanked it down.

But the spirit of hate was on the loose. Letters to the editor during that period were full of public-spirited cries to "pound Iraq into the sand," which in fact we did. Thus a war about oil became "personal" and popular, as a war against the mustachioed, beret-clad face of evil.

What I'm saying is that hate is not the exotic province of swastika-bedecked men with buzz cuts who think white people are in mortal danger from "the mud races." Hate is far more ordinary than that.

*January 2000*

## IN LOVING MEMORY

The plea for a better world pushed quietly out of the sand and weeds. I came upon it and didn't quite believe it — shrugged, moved on, then came back and stood for 30 seconds, beach paraphernalia in hand, at the top of the steps, reading, then reading again, the words on the brass plate:

"In loving memory of Liza Olsen (1952-1996) ..."

The plate was affixed to a bench at the end of a narrow road off Red Arrow Highway, where the bluff drops 30 feet to the blue, endlessly stretching lake. The town is Union Pier, Mich., an hour's drive (barring traffic jams) from Chicago. It's one of a string of resorts that dot the eastern shore of Lake Michigan — arty little tourist villages with great beaches and gift-shop economies: pottery, scented candles, fudge.

These are perfect, miniature worlds, self-described as "quaint" and "off the beaten path," to which people escape from the big city for long weekends. The problems you expect to encounter here can be handled with a good sunscreen. What you don't expect is mystery. Much less do you expect, tucked into the scenery, a moral honesty so uncompromising and plaintive it could break your heart.

What could be more humble, as a memorial, than a bench? Stranger, rest here. This is what we are offered by someone who loved a woman named Liza Olsen. Nothing is said about her except the span of her life: 44 years. But the words on the plaque continue, expanding the embrace of the memorial beyond her to "other victims of violence who have gone to the light."

These are the words that pull you back, that demand to be read again. Other victims of violence? Does it really say that? What happened to her?

You look around. It's Sunday afternoon. The dirt shoulder is jammed with cars and SUVs, in blithe defiance of the no-parking signs stenciled on a nearby fence. There's a steady flow of foot traffic — moms and dads in their bathing suits and flip-flops, children clutching pink plastic inner tubes — up and down the railroad-tie steps that are set into the bluff. Everyone here, it seems, is going to the light, or coming from it. This is the pursuit of happiness in high gear.

But no one is standing by to explain the meaning of the bench. No one else is paying the slightest attention to it, though occasionally someone stops to sit on it.

The world he brings with him is not the world I live in. It's a witch's brew of cold nights, endless violence, corrupt cops and expedient lies, linked by the earnest urgency of his narrative. "You hear about the kid who was shot at Howard and Ridge?" Larry will ask. "Last night." His eyes search my face. "Shot off his bike, here" — and he points to the center of his forehead, never letting his eyes leave mine. "He's dead. The Kings got him."

This is my own neighborhood he brings me news of — a neighborhood I know as tree-lined and friendly, middle-class, safe ... safe enough, anyway. My daughter walks around in it. I've lived here for 20 years. It's my home. But Larry never tires of telling me how bad it's getting — "The cops are selling guns, you know that, right?" — as though this is his end of the bargain, to warn the complacent, in the manner of Cassandra, the truth-teller.

And this is an interesting role for a man who lies so shamelessly. He lies with the conviction of a Boy Scout, hand over his heart, swearing by his God and mine, "This is it, this is the last time you'll see me. All I need is money for the bus ticket. Please, Bob, please ..."

For a while he was coming by with his 17-year-old son, who at first stood in silence as his father begged, eyes downcast, enduring the humiliation. But after a few visits Deion started looking at me, talked cheerfully about his new school. One day in the fall I gave Deion money for school supplies.

When, after a considerable absence, Larry rang my doorbell and told me the boy was dead, killed in a drive-by, I could only stare blankly, unsure whether to believe him. I listened in an emotional void. Even after I decided he was telling the truth, I was unable to let grief and sympathy flow — these were the emotions Larry sought out every time, worked loose with practiced skill, always, inevitably, as a prelude to asking for money.

I had long ago decided I'd given him too much. Now I wanted him only to go away. This was a relationship on the far edge of being human. I dreaded the need waiting patiently at the end of his stories, even this one, ready to pounce on my charitable impulses. I hated the mean calculations he forced me to make. Dead son? That's worth how many dead presidents?

But I gave him money, finally. Less than he asked for. I pushed the door shut on his entreaties; my heart hung in my chest like a lump of plaster. He grabbed my hand and squeezed it. He said goodbye.

I knew he'd be back.

*January 2000*

## THE AMATEUR

She looked tall and ordinary, in T-shirt and blue jeans. I spotted her as I turned the corner from Glenwood onto Pratt, on my way home from the train station on a recent hot afternoon — a young woman, late 20s maybe, just standing there, fidgety, tense, smiling the false smile of someone who wants something from you.

Yeah, I know that look. I see it on half the street corners downtown: a pseudo-friendliness that surges out of the gloom and desperation as I walk past. "Spare some change?" Sometimes I give in to it, reach into my pocket — even my wallet. But mostly, no. I walk past with averted eyes, letting the false smile, the real need behind it, dangle in midair. And doing so troubles me each time, feels like the violation of a code: Give eye contact. Listen to people; be generous of spirit. Judge not lest ye be judged.

But it's too much. The need — as in need a meal, need to place to stay tonight — is overwhelming. I feel cornered by one broken life after another, alone in the moment with each one, jealously protective of the silver in my pocket. "Sorry, not this time." How long has this been going on, this public outbreak of panhandling and homelessness? It exploded in the Reagan era, seems to me, when the social safety net was cut.

When I saw her, I felt a weary give in my heart, a surrender to familiar numbness. Here's one more person with urgent troubles that I want no part of. Numbness is a political statement: I abstain. C'mon, I'm just a private soul, lost in my own life. I can't be your salvation.

But she didn't say anything as I walked past. Instead, she fell into stride next to me, maintaining that little soft embarrassed aren't-we-friends smile.

We walk a few steps, then: "Where ya headed?"

Silence. But I look at her. I mean my look to convey skeptical neutrality: Yes? What is it?

This is delicate. I can no longer pretend she isn't there, not when she has attached herself to my journey. But to acknowledge her at all is to confer a legitimacy on our sudden, chummy intimacy. Her presence fills me with alarm, anger and, at the pit of my maleness, a dangerous curiosity. Is this going where I think it is? My glare is harsh, but it's a bluff. I am no longer numb.

"Do you live around here?" Her voice is upbeat and perky, as though a real conversation is in progress. She has freckles, and walks with a slight stoop as her hopeful eyes probe my face. I can't stand it. I'm unable not to respond.

"Yeah. Not far."

She's hustling me, but I play along. If I retreat from the moment, I'll have no chance to control it. We walk in silence for a few more paces. There can be no doubt what this is all about, but even so, I am surprised, finally, when she blurts it out.

"Would you like some company?"

This is the thing. The proposition wasn't, you know … coarse, lacquered in cheap endearments: hey honey, hey big guy. What you might call a past, no depth of existence. Here, boy. They came when you whistled. They had a function. And they were worth money to their owners.

We have to understand what we have done. That's the only way to make sure we're not still doing it.

Slowly, the tide starts to turn. Illinois recently became the second state, after California, to require all insurance companies doing business within its borders to search their archives and divulge details of insurance policies written on slaves. Last week the Slave Era Policies Register was posted.

It's a raw, stunning document, peeling back 150 years: This is how it was. You can comb through the names and occupations and policy numbers at your leisure, feel the back of your neck tingle. Here, boy. Daniel, Delia, Dick. Laborer, house servant, farmer. A human being dies. A piece of property is mourned.

This is our legacy, our Founding Contradiction. How long can we pretend it's over and done with when we haven't even acknowledged its impact? Slavery permeated the American economy, North and South. Northern insurance companies wrote policies for slaves in Fayette, Ky., and Natchez, Miss., and Edisto Island, S.C. Everybody benefited. Except the slaves.

Eliza, Enoch, Fanny, Ferdinand. Blacksmith, carpenter, bricklayer, washer and ironer. The estimated current value of their unpaid labor is $1.4 trillion.

As I studied the site and felt the slow rise of a nameless emotion — part rage, part grief, part dread — I thought about how we're all caught up in the callous shortcomings of our time. How can we ever see beyond it? Are we done with the owning of human beings?

Not so long ago, a number of Fortune 500 companies were outed for the practice of purchasing "dead peasant" insurance on their low-level, possibly minimum-wage employees. Wal-Mart had 350,000 of them — life-insurance policies taken out on workers they could have cared less about, without the workers' permission or knowledge. When the janitor died, the company collected. The family got nothing.

How oddly intertwined is the history of corporate America with the history of human chattel. The 14th Amendment, ratified in 1868, made citizens — persons — of newly freed slaves and prohibited states from abridging their rights. Looked good on paper, but somehow failed to stave off a century of Jim Crow laws.

Yet the 14th Amendment helped somebody. Turns out the new business concept known as the corporation had far more success, in the wake of the Civil War, becoming recognized before the law as a "person" than former slaves did.

Of the first 150 cases involving the 14th Amendment heard by the Supreme Court, 15 involved African-Americans and 135 involved business entities, notes Doug Hammerstrom on reclaimdemocracy.org. And the amendment was so narrowly interpreted that blacks won only one case. "The expansive view of the 14th Amendment that comes down to constitutional law classes today," he writes "is the result of corporations using (it) as a shield against regulation."

We've been much better at turning a profit than redressing injustice, than healing the Founding Contradiction known as slavery. The ex-slaves got nothing but more bitterness. The fight for reparations — 40 acres and a mule, and a chance to forgive — is far from over.

Isaac, Isabel, Ishmael, Jacob, Jem, Joshua. There were 4 million of them. They weren't meant to be part of history. They were meant to be worked to death and forgotten. But they're with us still, mute, single-named, yoked to their policy numbers, yet managing to shake our deepest assumptions of who we are.

*August 2004*

## TRUSTING HER ANYWAY

"Sir . . . sir."

Need has a tone of voice that's hard to ignore, as badly as I might want to. It pierced my purposeful hurry this night. I had stopped at the store after work and was carrying two plastic bags of groceries — milk, OJ, cottage cheese — which were cutting into my hands. My briefcase was slung awkwardly over my shoulder and I felt tired, stressed, put upon.

Words can hardly convey how little I wanted to turn around just then and find out who was summoning me.

I live in Chicago, a city with lots of dark corners, a city of want spilling up from the margins. The want is perpetual, as much a part of the cityscape as Lake Michigan — always there, sometimes roiled up, sometimes dangerous. I resist it with a weary heart, having no clue what my relationship to it ought to be.

I turned around. A woman was standing in front of an apartment building about half a block behind me. I walked back to her, lugging my groceries and briefcase. She was skinny, scrawny, with a scraped-raw look to her face and terror in her eyes, which instantly made me forget about the weight of my own life.

The story tumbled out. Her name was Shadima. She was HIV-positive and three months pregnant, and was starting to bleed. She needed to get to Mercy Hospital as soon as possible.

This encounter happened last fall, when Hurricane Katrina and the FEMA-bungled aftermath were in the news, when the inhumanity of our social structure lay bare on the nation's front pages, and suddenly I felt swept up in the middle of something life-or-death and Katrinalike. A sense of urgency overrode that layer of protective skepticism that normally helps me keep my spare change in my pocket and prevents other people's problems from breaching my daily agenda.

"I can't call 911," she said. "The paramedics will take me to St. Francis. That won't help. I need to get down to Mercy, where my doctor is."

This hardly seemed time to quibble. I was instantly prepared to take her — to bridge the "FEMA gap" or whatever you want to call it, that abyss of meanness and indifference that separates a life of dignity and freedom of choice from a life of poverty. We used to have a social safety net, but I've seen it rent to shreds in the last two decades. I figured a bleeding woman has a right to see her own doctor.

Come on, I said. Follow me. I was about two blocks from home. She started spilling out gratitude and fragments of her life story as we walked. When we got to my house, I told her to wait on the front porch. I stashed the groceries. When I went back to get her, she was on her knees, praying.

I wish this story had a happy ending — you know, a crisp, bright, Hollywood feel-good sendoff. Baby saved, social gap bridged, understanding all around, and maybe a nice red ribbon for Yours Truly, for being such a good neighbor. Instead, I'll likely feed the cynics with what I'm writing — the ones with the pat answers and the ready "sucker" label to slap on every would-be do-gooder. I can't write a cynic-proof column about Shadima, but I'm only writing about her at all, six months later, because . . . I'd do the same thing again.

When I came upon her praying, with a focused desperation, oblivious to my presence, I lost perhaps my last protective objectivity, which explains why my suspicion mechanism never kicked back in when, in retrospect, it should have. The twists and turns of her desperation had such a compelling logic — and the ultimate goal was so urgent — I didn't have it in me to override her requests and just say, "I'm driving you to the hospital now."

First she wanted to stop at a 24/7 pawnshop in the neighborhood so she could pawn her wedding ring so she could afford to get home. Well, OK. But the pawnshop, it turns out, was closed. I said I'd give her money for cab fare home. That settled, I was ready to drive her to the hospital, but then she said — through torrents of tears and gratitude — she couldn't let me do that. "I'm afraid I'll bleed all over your car," she said.

The upshot is that I gave her money for transportation to and from a hospital many miles from the neighborhood, a total of $80, pretty much what I had in my wallet. Compared to what was at stake, the twenties I handed her felt thin and meaningless — four yuppie food stamps, as I've heard them called, spit out earlier that day by the ATM.

She left in tearful gratitude, trying to press a gold-colored necklace into my hands as collateral, or something. I resisted, the necklace fell between the driver's seat and the gearshift console. (It's still there, unretrievable.) I saw her get into a cab.

Later that night, when I told my street-smart friend Jose about the incident, he gave me a cold glare and said, "I know this woman." After I'd gone to bed I got a call from him. "I'm out in front of the 7-Eleven," he said. "She's here in the parking lot right now. She's working."

I went to sleep in total defeat, woke up at 3 a.m. flagellating myself for being conned, yet in awe of the thoroughness of her performance . . . or maybe Jose was mistaken, and it wasn't a performance at all. What I know is that six months later, my wounded doubt, my sense of the ambiguity of giving, feels permanent. If I erred, it was on the side of trusting too much, and I plan to keep doing that.

*April 2006*

PART FIVE

# EINSTEIN'S DOOR

## BREAKFAST ON VIEQUES

Do I dare call it a vision? Maybe it was no more than a burst of naïve hope, on the patio of an old sugar cane plantation on a tiny subtropical island, amid bougainvillea and hummingbirds, in the middle of a war, while I was eating breakfast.

The island was Vieques, truly one of the world's tender spots, 52 square miles of beauty and paradox due east and an hour's ferry ride from Puerto Rico. I've been nourished by the place, and by the sudden, sharp spike of freedom I experienced — freedom from the inevitability of hate and violence in human affairs — ever since I visited there a year and a half ago.

The pang was palpable as I ate breakfast with Sue and Margaret on that April morning. A cluster of half-ideas seemed to take root in the compression of the moment, as though my mental soil were as fertile as the earth beyond the Casa del Frances, which was alive with orchids and coconut palms, mango and banana trees, ferns and fronds and all manner of nameless succulents.

Half a world away, ethnic cleansing and aerial warfare raged in Yugoslavia. The weapons of that war had had trial runs right here in paradise; for almost 60 years, Vieques has been the site of the Atlantic Fleet Weapons Training Facility: They test bombs here. Two-thirds of the island is under control of the U.S. Navy. You can be snorkeling off one of the white-sand beaches and hear the thunder of war games in the distance. It's a matter of acute controversy.

A week after I left, a civilian was killed when the pilot of an F-18 fighter jet accidentally leveled an observation tower with two 500-pound bombs during a training exercise, virtually uniting Puerto Ricans in passionate agreement that the Navy should get off Vieques. Numerous sit-ins, forced removals and arrests later, the Navy, with its barbed wire and Quonset huts, remains.

All this — the sumptuous excess of life surrounding us on the crumbling veranda, the violence in the headlines, and the eerie, discordant, unwilling role of Vieques itself as a proving ground for modern weaponry — was pressing on me as we talked over pancakes and coffee, straining against the protective shell of common knowledge. And the book I'd been reading, *Selected Poems of Robinson Jeffers*, contained a curious line: "Humanity is an atom to be split." What did that mean?

It reminded me of a famous comment Albert Einstein made at the dawn of the nuclear age: "Our world faces a crisis as yet unperceived by those possessing the power to make great decisions for good and evil. The unleashed power of the atom has changed everything save our modes of thinking, and thus we drift toward unparalleled catastrophe."

As our free-ranging breakfast conversation moved from past-life regression to education and the creativity of children, I felt something give. "Civilization" — or the life I'm despairingly used to —suddenly cracked. Possibility flooded in: a sense of human potential and the value of life. Couldn't this be what mattered above all else?

Maybe the stuff of life, so lovingly given to us and richly ours to mold, need not be squandered on the least worthy of causes. I thought about the war games being played on these coral reefs, the impunity with which we blow up brain coral and angel fish and litter paradise with depleted uranium dust. I thought about the linear bludgeon of war, and its crude contrast to what was visible to my senses, and to my heart.

I felt Einstein's door open. The new mode of thinking begins with the realization that the Garden of Eden is still right here. We only think we've been exiled from it.

*December 2000*

*UPDATE: SAN JUAN, Puerto Rico (AP) – The U.S. Navy has set aside $200 million for the removal of military waste in Vieques island, just east of Puerto Rico's main island, authorities announced Tuesday. The money will be used in the next seven years to remove explosives in the island's eastern region, the site of most previous military training exercises, said Richard Mach, with the Navy's environment office. More than 9,000 acres of the almost 23,000 acres that the Navy occupied for several decades will be scanned for contaminants, he said. The Navy previously used Vieques as its main Atlantic training site, combining air, sea and land maneuvers. It ended them in 2003 following years of local protests after an errant bomb killed a civilian guard. About 775 acres have been cleared since the cleanup began in 2005, with officials uncovering nearly 15,000 live munitions and recycling about 1,900 tons of scrap.*

*The Associated Press, March 26, 2008*

## TURN THE OTHER CHEEK

It had to be done that way, with federal agents decked out in full battle regalia, brandishing assault rifles? What paradoxes are compressed in that instantly famous photo: rescue and overkill, justice and terror.

Certainly the intransigent faction who believed 6-year-old Elian Gonzalez should not have been returned to his father got what it wanted, a readymade poster of tyranny: Soldier Waves Weapon at Screaming Child, Rips Him from Embrace of Loving Family. Small matter that's not the reality; the government action righted a wrong, seized the boy from the grasp of his politics-besotted relatives and returned him to a father who loved him. No one was hurt, but measured force was necessary.

What a shame, then, that a right action had to look so wrong — thanks to the fundamental dishonesty not of the mission itself but of its design. The planners, anticipating violent opposition, had to protect the agents (hence the battle armor, goggles, etc.); they also had to convey seriousness of intent. This was not a "request" for the boy's return to his legitimate parent, it was a demand. And something has to back up a demand.

The government decided to go with the threat of violence, a big bluff — the agents weren't going to shoot up the place or kill Elian in order to save him. Little Havana isn't Vietnam (or Kosovo). If the military action is on American soil, collateral damage isn't an option. So why the assault rifles, then? Why such a dishonest display of authority?

The disheartening answer is that nearly everyone believes in violence at some level as an effective tool, the ultimate way to get what you want. Worse, nearly everyone believes violence, so long as it's wielded by the good guys, is a tool that can be "surgically" applied. Zap, remove the obstacle, clear the path, make the world safe for democracy. So even when moral and political compunctions against the spillage of blood are operative, the only way we can imagine taking effective action is by arming ourselves to the teeth.

Haven't we had 2,000 years to come up with alternatives? For that many years, in any case, professed Christians and the nations they dominate have had no excuse not to ponder Christ's radical social imperative, "Turn the other cheek," and practice the spirit of it in their civilization-building labors.

Talk about failure of religion. What an abysmal job Christianity's adherents have done selling this notion, even to themselves. Where does it rank, in potency and ability to command respect, among such catchphrases of popular culture as "Lock and load" and "Make my day"? Forget about it! Turning the other cheek is for wimps. It's synonymous with backing down. Pacifism is the equivalent of passivity.

Remember that scene in *Witness*, where tough guy Harrison Ford, a big city cop stuck among the Amish, finally loses patience with the nonviolent mandate of his hosts and punches out a couple of hecklers? What a crowd-pleaser. His companions, meanwhile, stare down at their black boots, helpless prisoners of a tradition that has robbed them (so it would appear) of their manhood, but grateful for the respect that's just been earned for them.

Oh, Hollywood! Curse it for its inability to dramatize moral courage. To turn the other cheek does not mean to turn away, to back down from confrontation, but to stand utterly present and awake to it, uncowed by the hatred coming at you, ready to deflect it, defuse it or simply absorb it, but never to give in to it — and never to give in.

"What are you doing here?" I asked, pleased to see him, but worried something had gone wrong for him.

"I came back to bury my cousin," he said. "He was shot 13 times."

Oh.

Let us begin our national dialogue on violence. Isn't it time? Let us move beyond metal detectors and SWAT commandos, beyond anger, blame, exasperation and retribution, beyond politics, beyond shock, beyond fear, and look into one another's eyes. We are all so alike, and we know so little about each other.

*April 2001*

## LOVABLE MOBSTERS

Killjoy here, spoiling another togetherness moment with my loving family — spoiling it for myself, anyway — by souring on the moral content of the evening's video fare.

The movie we'd rented was *The Whole Nine Yards*, which came daughter-certified as "funny — you'll like it, Dad." Our entertainment tastes generally mesh these days, but I'm still sheepish and apologetic about our moviegoing past, when, on the car ride home, I'd let slip some irritation with the film we'd just seen and inadvertently crush the kid's enthusiasm. So I'm wary of my critical nature and rein it in as best I can when the point is to just have fun.

But, my gosh, I've got to ask: What's the deal with lovable mobsters?

Cuddly murderers — specifically Bruce Willis and a certain gorgeous starlet (Amanda Peet) who punctures the jugular of a decidedly uncuddly mafioso while wearing nothing but her semiautomatic — are at the heart of this amiable entertainment. To get with the laughs, unfortunately, you have to swallow a few little moral fishhooks: Cold-blooded killers can be lots of fun. They make good pals. Only wimps have consciences.

I'm not a moralist. I don't go around looking for "wrong thought" and smite it with an axe when I find it. I didn't want to get exercised over a flick as innocuous as this one, but the fact of the matter is, a movie is never just itself. Good or bad, it taps into the national collective unconscious, our great body of myth and self-understanding, where Manifest Destiny meets Main Street and good triumphs over evil. This is our story unfolding here: who we are and who we're becoming. Out of this cauldron emerge trends and fads and national policy.

The symbolism that carries a movie resonates well beyond both the big and small screen, in other words. And this is the level at which I found myself watching *The Whole Nine Yards*, and felt my heart sink.

If it had been a better movie, with a little more artistic integrity — and not such an eager-to-please, yuk-a-minute piece of fluff — I wouldn't have been so appalled at its underlying premise: that while killers may have moral problems (yada yada yada), they sure know how to cut the red tape. And if you're lucky enough to have one like you — as is the movie's pathetic, conscience-saddled everyman, Matthew Perry — you can get first-class service from banks and maybe even a better life. Lucky you!

The movie gives us our own personal hit man. It indulges our national road rage, our collective "I've had it up to here with …" (supply your own pet peeve: marital conflict, work, other people and their problems). Gangsters don't live in the world of petty annoyances. They don't whine when they're inconvenienced, they just shoot the obstruction. We can't do that because we're, you know, morally constrained. The movie shows us a way out of that tiresome state.

And it does so shamelessly. Bruce and his lethal galpal are adorable and the punks they perforate are ugly and anonymous. What's the problem? The joke about Hollywood when I was a boy was that its shoot-'em-ups were bloodless. Now its bodies generally fall to the ground spewing crimson realism — more than enough of it, thank you. But the realism stops with the blood and brain matter. Otherwise, movie mayhem remains abstract and consequence-free.

I'm sorry, I worry about this. And not just because of all the alienated loners in our midst with access to handguns. I worry about the way movies feed the national psyche. The Big Myth *The Whole Nine Yards* perpetuates is the myth of amoral force — that it can be controlled, "humanized" and used in the national interest. Think smart bombs and surgical strikes.

Having a lovable mobster on your side is like having a killer attack dog named Daisy. Or an atom bomb named Little Boy.

*September 2000*

## BANG, BANG

The doll that showed up the other day on the office freebie shelf twinkled with sheer malevolence. I'm used to seeing books stacked there, and manufacturers' promos for random products — salad dressing, T-shirts, shampoo, dried figs — but a bulked-up action figure poised to rip flesh gave me a bit of a shock.

"Gosh, an Evil Toy," I thought, grabbing it furtively and secreting it to my desk, where I studied it in its plastic case and ruminated about the roots of human violence.

Folks who worry about the effects of popular culture — rock music, video games, etc. — on impressionable young minds could well get Vega stuck prey were dying off from eating poisoned mice, which had fled outside after ingesting exterminators' pellets. I didn't want to be part of such a process, but of course neither did I want to share my humble, messy-enough-as-it-is abode with rodents.

Dilemma, dilemma — but not one I gave a whole lot of attention to. When one of these street-smart scuttlers was unlucky enough to get stuck in the stickum, I crushed it under my foot. It died with a distinct little crunch, and I threw it out with the trash. Not a pleasant job but, hey, that's homeowning.

Then I had a dream:

I'm crouched in a thicket of bushes. Mysteriously, someone proffers me a handgun, warning: "You'll need it for protection." Sure enough, a stranger comes blundering along, unaware I'm hiding a few feet away. His presence is intolerable; he's invading my space. So I open fire and down he goes; his eyes, full of shock and pain, meet mine as he falls. Now here's another one, and another. They're simply strangers going about their business, but I pop each one in a frenzy of self-protection. Each death is wrenching, and has a hideous, crunchy sound that's all too familiar. I wake up with a wildly pounding heart, thinking about mice.

This is a small matter, perhaps — a disturbance in the otherwise tranquil waters of conscience that could have been avoided so easily. If I'd just called the exterminator, as I have in years past, the little invaders would have died quietly and, for the most part, beyond my awareness. Out of sight, out of mind. (And too bad about the hawks.)

But now I'm stuck with my dream and my misgivings about the taking of the lives of animals, even small ones that scurry along the floorboard and leave droppings behind the toaster. My dreaming self, as usual, is way ahead of me, pushing the matter to a question I feel embarrassed to ask publicly. But I do so despite my embarrassment because it nudges open a corner of the heart that's too often closed like a fist: that corner where necessity brokers its compromises and violence, in its name, receives our sanction.

Do animals have souls?

Do they belong within what James Garbarino calls our "moral circle," which contains everything we value and would never harm? Garbarino, the author of *Lost Boys*, a compassionate study of violent teenagers, confesses that he found himself growing inconveniently aware, as he listened to the boys' stories, that cruelty to animals and cruelty to humans are on a moral continuum. This awareness slowly turned him into a vegetarian and made him give up a boyhood love, fishing.

My thought is that perhaps the world changes — its tenor shifts — less by massive and noisy political initiatives than by the quiet, courageous forays we make into our own hearts, pondering the awkward questions we unearth and choosing to expand our circle of caring.

I have, I hope, most of a year to think through how I'll handle next year's mouse invasion. Maybe as I do I'll meditate on Binti Jua, the lowland gorilla who, five years ago — on my birthday — saved the life of a toddler who fell into the moat surrounding the gorilla exhibit at Chicago's Brookfield Zoo. She shooed the other gorillas away and gently cradled the unconscious boy until her human keepers took him from her.

However much intelligence, or soul, we concede to her, or animals in general, and whatever place they occupy in our value system, the boy she rescued was apparently within her moral circle.

*March 2001*

## COLLATERAL DAMAGE

I can't stop thinking about "collateral damage," the term Timothy McVeigh repopularized before he died.

He secured his immortality in the annals of cold-bloodedness by referring thus to the 19 children his fertilizer-and-racing-fuel bomb blew up six years ago — and at the same time affixed the asterisk of hypocrisy to our hatred of him. His language mimicked the language of patriotism. McVeigh was our caricature.

How easy and painlessly abstract to revile him: to curse that wooden face, to call him a monster. "It's understood going in what the human toll will be," he wrote of the deed that left 168 innocent people dead and hundreds more injured. Surely this is a smug soul on its way to hell.

Yet, how hollow to exact our justice on him, to shoot him with poison and watch him die, then scrutinize his final words for signs of remorse, as though any of that ... could help. He gave away nothing, except, eerily, a hand-scrawled copy of "Invictus," that staple of high school English class. He cheated us by refusing to let us execute a being with human feeling.

McVeigh — Sgt. McVeigh — had the demeanor of a prisoner of war and spoke with military lingo. "Collateral damage" was a term of the Gulf War, the war in which he served with distinction, and learned his lessons. He repeatedly cited our actions in Iraq, an incredibly popular war in which we outkilled the enemy by a ratio of 10,000 to 1, as a justification for his own preposterous act of war.

He shocked the nation by applying the lessons of the Gulf War domestically, rubbing in our faces our lack of remorse for, let us say, the 400-plus people, mostly women and children, who were incinerated on Valentine's Day of 1991 when two of our smart bombs went through a ventilation shaft in the Amiriya bunker in western Baghdad and destroyed it.

This site is a national shrine in Iraq, just as the grounds of the Murrah Federal Building are a shrine in Oklahoma City. If you ever visit Amiriya, you will be able to see the "nuclear shadow"-like images of mothers and children on the heat-blackened walls, and the handprints of children on the ceilings as they were roasted alive on the top decks of bunk beds when the temperature in the bunker rose to 2,000 degrees Centigrade. Our bombs, and our tax dollars, did this. It was collateral damage.

I think the key to finding "closure" about McVeigh's terrible deed lies in understanding that he did not act in isolation. He just gave us some dead we could care about.

We can choose to pray for McVeigh to rot in hell, but the comfort in that is cold indeed. If we truly want peace — if we truly want to honor Oklahoma City's 168 victims of terrorism — we have to do more than vent our anger. We have to search our souls.

Never again should we bomb civilians, or downgrade matters of terrible moral import to the status of strategic questions. The environment itself is collateral damage in the wars we wage. In Yugoslavia, for instance, according to Mother Jones, our targeting of Serb oil refineries and other industrial sites wreaked ecological havoc on the country, including the Danube River — the storied Blue Danube — into which thousands of tons of industrial toxins spilled. (Vinyl Chloride Monomer Waltz, anyone?)

At the very least, let us stop lying with the bland language of Pentagon spokesmen. If war is contemplated, let us gauge its necessity with full awareness of its likely toll on children and rivers and all other innocents, and understand that not all of the collateral damage will be on enemy soil.

*July 2001*

## SUNDAY SCHOOL

These aren't men, they're boys.

That was my first, chilling thought — that they look like high school students, the ones whose faces show up in the news these days after a shooting spree. They were a little older but not necessarily any smarter; they certainly had no greater understanding of the value of a human life. But they had guns. And they were grinning.

The old photos of "Kerrey's Raiders" accompanied last month's story in the New York Times Magazine about the commando raid Bob Kerrey led on Thanh Phong 32 years ago. The raid, as we all know now, left more than a dozen women and children dead, their bodies heaped atop one another in the middle of the village, as though they'd been executed.

Regardless what really happened that night — whether it was a "war crime" or merely a tragic goof — the terrible unraveling of events, and the public soul-searching of the former Nebraska senator ("I was so ashamed I wanted to die"), have provided yet one more naked glimpse into the nature of war, the preparation for which we budget $300 billion annually.

It is also a glimpse into our collective soul: This is what we do. We put guns into the hands of young people and proceed to endanger not just their lives, but their consciences. We ask them to become killers, to enter a moral free-fire zone, where decisions of incalculable weight — should this person live or die? — hang on a thread. In the temporary context of war, life is cheap, and triggers squeeze easily; but later, for the survivors, the moral significance of their actions can turn into lifelong guilt, which, of course, they have to face alone.

This is one more fraud we commit as a society in the name of short-term, and often dubious, expediency: It's OK to do this; it's for the national good. As far as I'm concerned, the lies by which we turn civilians into soldiers are equal to the lies we told unsuspecting defense workers at the beginning of the nuclear age, when we were building up our arsenal: These materials — uranium, thorium, polonium, beryllium — are completely safe. You are in no danger.

The implicit lie of the military chain of command is the lie of responsibility, that those who merely carry out morally ambiguous orders bear no responsibility for the harm they inflict; they were just doing what they were told. If nothing else, we learn from Kerrey's now-public anguish that, on the contrary, those on the front line suffer the most grievously for having unleashed hell, because the blood on their hands is real.

"The greatest danger of war," said Kerrey, recounting a truth that came to him in a dream (the messenger was his uncle, who was missing in action in World War II), "is not losing your life but the taking of others', and … human savagery is a very slippery slope."

It is never justified to put your personal moral sensibilities on hold, but this is what your commanding officer inevitably demands, often contemptuously: "This was war. This wasn't Sunday School," said Capt. Roy Hoffman, Kerrey's CO, when he was interviewed about the Thanh Phong incident. In other words, what did you expect, bozo? Of course there were atrocities in Vietnam; we went over there to make ugly.

Well, he's right. We have no business being shocked, though every new revelation of who we are garners a response of innocence affronted. This is the national pose: We're the good guys. So we're shocked, shocked when it turns out our hands are dirty in the death of an American missionary and her infant daughter in Peru. You mean they just shot down an unarmed plane? On further examination, it turns out "fly and die" has been a tactic of the drug war throughout the '90s.

What did you expect? This is war. This isn't Sunday School.

*May 2001*

## SOLO FLIGHT

The horror is that the children are wresting themselves free not just from their parents but from their own souls.

You think about the 15-year-old's solo flight (15! the age of my daughter) into the side of a Tampa high-rise and some inner whistle of awe goes off: There he goes! Wow! He's out of the range of human empathy!

Afterwards, the media fed us ironic fodder about Charles Bishop's life, facts strewn about like pieces of wreckage, suddenly pulsating with significance: He was an A-student, ambitious, future-oriented and, most startling of all, prominently patriotic. "He was proud to be an American, let me tell you," the headmaster of his former school said.

Maybe it's relevant that he used to sing "America" with fervor, led his classmates in reciting the Pledge of Allegiance and wanted to join the Air Force, but we must not let such information define — limit — the tragedy, as though our distress is due to the fact that he "switched sides." The crucial question is why did he do it at all, not why did he do it to us?

Homicidally and suicidally lost children are our national riddle. When they shatter a school day with gunfire, they also shake the infrastructure of trust that holds society together. In the wake of every tragedy, any semblance of normalcy in the young killer's life twists in the gut, explaining nothing — but challenging everything. How come our values didn't contain him?

Why, especially, did they not contain Charles Bishop, who embraced those values with a passion?

When we look at who we are with a critical eye, it's not hard to discern that patriotism in its popular form is full of the implication of violence. Is it possible that this implication is explosive, a force we cannot fully control and direct only at the official enemy, whose humanity has been indefinitely suspended? Does what we do, in other words (especially what we budget $329 billion annually to do) come back, occasionally, to haunt us?

In the spirit of examining our values — the ones that failed Charles Bishop — I bring up Qalaye Niazi, a village about 80 miles south of Kabul, in eastern Afghanistan. The name isn't a household word, but maybe it should be. Maybe its mention should quicken the pulse and convulse the national conscience.

Our bombers hit the place hard just before year's end, on intelligence reports that senior Taliban and al-Qaida officials were holed up there. We knocked out an ammunition dump and may have killed as many as 107 villagers — innocent civilians, that is, including women and children. This is not the propaganda claim of the Taliban but a number released by the hospital at nearby Gardez.

The Pentagon has maintained that Qalaye Niazi was a legitimate target, and maybe it was, though surviving villagers claim the U.S. was given false intelligence by a local anti-Taliban warlord who wants control of the province. The Pentagon also insists there was no collateral damage, but international journalists who visited the bombed village say otherwise.

A reporter for *The Guardian*, for instance, turned an unblinking gaze at "Some of the things (the Pentagon's) follow-on reporters missed: bloodied children's shoes and skirts, bloodied school books, the scalp of a woman with braided gray hair, butter toffees in red wrappers, wedding decorations."

This is the good violence, the kind we celebrate. I don't care if the cause of this war is just. Let us acknowledge what bombs do to civilian populations and apprise ourselves of the true cost of victory. And let's look again at what we ask some of our children to do when they grow up. A few already suspect, and have their own plans.

*January 2002*

## CHILDHOOD'S END

Cute kid, 7 years old, maybe, marching in a parade. His picture even makes it into the newspaper. Hoopla and patriotism. We love our children. This boy in particular tugs at the heartstrings, bedecked as he is in camouflage outfit, warrior headband and — duct-taped around his middle — a dozen sticks of pretend dynamite.

Big boy go boom!

If the child, who is Iraqi, had simply been carrying a fake gun and pretending to kill others, i.e., playing soldier (my own favorite pastime as a youngster), there wouldn't have been much shock value in his photo, which was taken by a Western journalist during the recent festivities surrounding Saddam Hussein's 65th birthday. But here he is with paper canisters labeled "TNT" affixed to his small torso, innocently flaunting the concept of his own carnage.

The thing about suicide bombers is, they put the horror back in war. The high-tech version of war we see on TV is so surreally clean it slides effortlessly down the public gullet. Afghanistan was a neat, antiseptic operation, easy on the American conscience. The 4,000 (or whatever) dead civilians that were its toll have left no imprint on us, partly because such numbers don't make it into mainstream headlines, but partly too, I suspect, because the deaths were meted out from on high, leaving no blood on our hands.

But how the suicide bombings detonate in the imagination: the shattered glass, the torn flesh, the screams at street level, the instant panic. And at ground zero, what? A pair of bloody shoes? The killer has dispatched his own guts to kingdom come. Understandably, these dead are counted and remembered.

So to see a Middle Eastern child imitating, the way children do — and in the process "blessing" with his innocence — this gruesome form of warfare in a public ceremony chills the heart. Certainly it will enflame the passions of everyone already itching for a counter-jihad with the Islamic world.

Let us stop the madness, all of us! To me the image does nothing but send out a cry that life must be revered, beginning with the magical sheath that is childhood. The issue here is something more than a failure to protect the children of the world. God knows, they die in terrible ways and in terrible numbers, from preventable disease, starvation and violence. But the use of children, in all their developmental innocence, as fodder, or even worse, killers for the cause, poisons humanity's future and calls into question, as far as I'm concerned, our right to occupy the planet.

"I killed another child. I did this three times. I felt bad but I knew what would happen if I disobeyed. Now I see dead people and blood in my dreams and I know the spirits of the children are coming to haunt me."

This is Bosco, a Ugandan child who was abducted at age 12 by fanatics known as the Lord's Resistance Army and turned into a soldier. He was quoted in a report issued by the Coalition to Stop the Use of Child Soldiers (www.child-soldiers.org), which points out that at any given time, more than 300,000 children under 18 — girls and boys, some as young as 7 — are taking part in conflicts around the world, on the side of both rebel and government forces. They're often given horrendous tasks, such as clearing land mines. They sometimes double as sex slaves.

Make no mistake, this is a global scourge, with the First World as complicit as the Third. "Millions of children worldwide receive military training and indoctrination," notes the report. We may shudder, for instance, at a youth movement called the Saddam Lion Cubs, but here at home we have the Young Marines, where boys and girls as young as 8 get to wear uniforms, take part in rifle drills and go through "boot camp."

Furthermore, according to the report, "The widespread availability of modern lightweight weapons has also contributed to the child soldiers problem, enabling even the smallest children to become efficient killers in combat."

This is not a problem to be solved by pointing our fingers at "them" but by abating, at every level, the global arms frenzy and its lucrative trade. Let us also redefine self-defense to mean, first, disarming our own fears and passions. Violent fervor for the cause — any cause — sooner or later blows up in our faces.

*May 2002*

## THE BIRTHPLACE OF DREAD

There they were, behind ropes: two big steel buckets held together with hex bolts, about as intimidating and awe-inspiring as old water tanks. Together, the originals of which these were exact replicas — Little Boy and Fat Man — obliterated, in an eye blink, 110,000 souls (and over time, a quarter of a million more).

You could, if you wanted, rap your knuckles on them. Plonk, plonk!

I felt an urge, absurdly, to kneel — I resisted. This was a museum; we were all tourists here, not pilgrims. But the urge toward reverence was powerful as I stood before these icons of the atomic age: Fat Man, the chunky plutonium-stuffed device, named in honor of Winston Churchill, which was dropped on Nagasaki; and the far svelter and more conventionally bomb-looking Little Boy, loaded with uranium-235 on that day, 56 years ago, it blew the heart out of Hiroshima.

For better or for worse, here I was, gaping at their replicas at the Bradbury Science Museum in the surreal town of Los Alamos, which is perched on a mesa in northern New Mexico's beautiful Jemez Mountains.

Los Alamos is an actual American city, with drugstores and cafes — there was a Starbucks under construction when I was there — and public streets and schools and Boy Scout troops and private housing, but woven inextricably into the town is its sole reason for being: the Los Alamos National Laboratory, birthplace of The Bomb and today a bustling and sprawling component of our nuclear weapons industry, churning out, according to the Santa Fe-based Los Alamos Study Group, 54,000 drums' worth of nuclear waste a year.

I'd wondered if including a stop at Los Alamos in my journey this summer to the Land of Enchantment was merely an indulgence of perverse curiosity, but once I was there, feeling the history of the place wash over me, I realized I was at the center of a terrible wonder, not to be missed under any circumstance: the birthplace of M.A.D. (mutually assured destruction). The birthplace of dread.

Here, not so many years ago, thousands of the world's best scientists and engineers struggled, round the clock at times, under the cloak of secrecy, to wrest the energy of the atom, the sun's secret, from nature's grasp, and bring it under human control. In order to win a war, we made the sun "rise twice" on July 16, 1945, and in the process made the human race hostage, perhaps for the remainder of history, to its own murderous impulses.

"I am become Death," said mystical physicist and Trinity project director Robert Oppenheimer after that first blast, quoting Hindu scripture, "the destroyer of worlds."

I think we're still in a state of collective shock about the nuclear age. It may have dawned 56 years ago, but we haven't yet opened our eyes to it.

Where is the debate? Since Oppenheimer invoked the wrath of Siva, we've spent $6 trillion developing and building nuclear weapons. Hitler, the demon who goaded us into birthing the atomic age, is dead, as is the Soviet Union, the enemy against whose threat we perpetuated it. Yet our arsenal of unthinkable weapons is 10,500 warheads strong, and sites like Los Alamos are growing, not shrinking. You can drive easily around the town and ogle the frenetic construction. And the "radwaste," with its half-life that extends beyond the scope of human imagination, keeps piling up.

To make a pilgrimage to Los Alamos is to face the fact that, as a nation, we seem simultaneously to know and not-know what was wrought in this place. Our knowledge is willfully compartmentalized. We live with it, we live around it, but the reality of the destructive power we have wrung from nature has not yet begun to leak through the steel canister housing our moral sensibilities.

*August 2001*

## BIG SKY

As a pinched-horizon Midwesterner, I couldn't get over the size of the sky. Looking at it filled me up, expanded my awe capacity — deepened my breathing, it seemed, like a shot of pure oxygen. Beneath it, my expectations just naturally towered, like the cloud formations.

Bear with me as I finish wringing my heart out about New Mexico, a state enormously easy to love at first sight. Underneath that sky, everything I encountered — from the extravagance of its religious expression to the magnitude of its explosions — was outsize. Like another enchanted spot I visited recently, the island of Vieques, off the coast of Puerto Rico, this state was a startling convergence of good and evil: soaring beauty and the God of War locked in terrible embrace.

On Vieques, a tropical paradise, the U.S. Navy has been testing bombs on the silver beaches for the last almost 60 years. New Mexico, since about the same time, has been a crucial link in our nuclear weapons industry, supplying not just the site in the desert but an eerily appropriate name — Journada del Muerto (Journey of Death) — for that first atomic test blast, in 1945.

The deeper appeal of the place, to me, is that it possesses not a straightforwardness of postcard grandeur but, rather, contradictions of the soul. I could see spending a good chunk of a lifetime here just mulling these contradictions, in the hope of unearthing something worth knowing about the human race.

How is it, I wonder, that New Mexico has proved to be a magnet for, and come to have an economy steeped in, our deepest expressions of both reverence and contempt for, shall we say, God's glory?

I can understand the reverence part — why, for instance, artists flock here to live and create. All you have to do is run out to the convenience store and you get the big sky, the play of light on desert rock formations, the cloud shadows trailing across undulant blue mountains in the distance. I can understand such vistas igniting in one's breast either prayer or artistic fervor.

What's a little harder to understand is how they could also ignite indifference — not just your garden variety, despairing shrug, but an indifference as big as the sky itself, clear-eyed, passionate and willful. Only a consciousness possessed of supreme indifference could see this fragile country as a convenient proving grounds for Armageddon.

But whatever else New Mexico is, it is also that, not just historically, but to this day, with national laboratories at places like Los Alamos and Sandia playing key roles in the upgrading of our nuclear arsenal. Right now, according to the Los Alamos Study Group, these labs are engaged in, among much else, research on "mininukes," for use in the Third World. And the work isn't merely theoretical; it's down and dirty. More than 18 million cubic feet of hazardous and nuclear waste are stored at Los Alamos, according to the Study Group. There it sits under big white tents, waiting for eternity.

As I ponder what I don't understand, I think about the word the pope used recently to explain his, and the Church's, opposition to stem-cell research: his fear that a "coarsening" of the human heart toward these quasi-human cells would have dire consequences.

If we're looking for coarsening in small places, I confess I'm far more disturbed by a bit of historical marginalia contained in the booklet "Los Alamos: Beginning of an Era," published by the National Laboratory's own PR office: In the weeks preceding the Trinity blast, the men encamped at Journada del Muerto apparently hunted antelope with submachine guns to supplement their dinner menu. Antelope were also shot from the big sky, as target practice by bomber gunnery crews.

Big deal, right? Any that weren't thus slaughtered would have been nuked. This is how it was at the dawn of mankind's journey of death.

*August 2001*

## PAPER GOD

If God were really relevant in American life, the following news story might have run on the AP wire:

*The day after it became known that a U.S. mission in Afghanistan had gone horribly wrong, with one of our bombs taking out a wedding party in a village north of Kandahar, killing 40 people and injuring perhaps 100, virtually the entire Senate showed up for a morning prayer and sat with heads bowed as Senate Chaplain Lloyd Ogilvie asked God for forgiveness.*

*"We acknowledge the separation of church and state," the chaplain intoned, "but under these circumstances, oh Lord, we know of no way to express our deep remorse other than to appeal to a power larger than our great but imperfect nation."*

*Many senators wept openly as the chaplain extolled the value of human life, then, stunningly, read aloud the names of all Afghan civilians killed by U.S. forces since hostilities began last Oct. 7. This unprecedented recitation of "collateral damage" lasted most of the morning. "These men, women and children are as precious as the Americans who lost their lives on Sept. 11," he concluded. "May God have mercy on us."*

*Ashen-faced, the senators filed out of their chambers and joined their colleagues from the House, who were already gathered on the steps of the Capitol. With arms linked, the full U.S. Congress proceeded to sing "There But For Fortune," by the late Phil Ochs, which ended with the verse:*

*"Show me the country where bombs had to fall,*
*Show me the ruins of buildings once so tall,*
*And I'll show you a young land with so many reasons why*
*There but for fortune, go you or go I — you and I ..."*

*Afterward, a still-emotional Sen. Tom Daschle, D-S.D., said, "We are one nation united in a belief in fair play for all. We affirmed that today as Americans, not as Republicans or Democrats, and we did so humbly, invoking the name of the Almighty only in deepest trepidation. I think many of us came to grips for the first time with what it truly means to be a superpower, and things are going to change, believe me. We'll be slower to use deadly force after this, so help us God."*

And now, back to the real world, where the God in whose name we pay our bills asks nothing of us as a nation except rote and frequent lip service: "I pledge allegiance to the frogs of the new knighted snakes of America ..." — and every other permutation of parody and misunderstanding that schoolchildren utter daily in compulsory unison — "one nation, under God, yada yada, with liverwurst and jump ropes for all."

Ike's two-word Cold War piety gets its comeuppance in federal court after 48 years and suddenly we are a nation robbed of what we believe in, as though "God" is so flimsy a concept "his" presence depends on mindless public utterance. I'm sorry, but Congress' rush to defend God — the God of the Pledge, the God of the buck, the God of the oceans white with foam — smacks of sacrilege.

They defended a paper god, a rubber-stamp god, whose existence hardly goes beyond the word that rings him up. They defended the Known God, as toothless and familiar as an aged house pet, whose name evokes sentiment and tradition, not awe and humility. We can do anything we want in his comatose presence, which is why we like him. ("Believe in" strikes me as far too strong a phrase for such a pointless deity.)

Meanwhile, on a global level, we suffer from pandemic violence and a massive failure of religion — to address, rein in and transmute the violence. Instead, politicians on every continent wheel out God to bless their bombs and missile launchers and small arms and nuclear weapons, damn the consequences, damn the human race.

Labeling such a being "unconstitutional" seems charitably mild.

*July 2002*


## CONNECT THE DOTS

As long as we're connecting dots, let's draw a line linking militarism, pop culture, guns-and-ammo availability and the ever-mutating national pattern of "unthinkable" acts of violence on the home front.

We will never be safe in a moral climate that degrades some part of humanity to the status of expendable, which is what waging war necessarily does. This is a statement of fact, not judgment. I'm not making one of those hand-wringing pleas for the waging of nice war, where only the deserving die; that's public relations, not war. I'm merely noting that serial killers operate in the same moral vacuum, a.k.a., hell, in which war occurs, but have "inappropriately" transferred the vacuum to my neighborhood and yours.

The Washington, D.C.-area sniper who pops off innocents as they pump gas or load their trunk at Home Depot — no less than Timothy McVeigh or the high school killer children of recent years, or for that matter the Sept. 11 terrorists — can only thus play God (and if this is "playing God," what kind of role model is God?) by first cauterizing all human connection to his victims. They don't matter; they don't have souls. This is the very process of desensitization that war buildup demands.

War, of course, has a rational objective, plus accouterments of patriotism, honor and glory, not to mention automatic exoneration for all, or most, of the slaughter committed under its aegis. It is not the same as murder and perhaps even morally less reprehensible. There are compelling arguments, for instance, that the human race is better off because the right side won such conflicts as the Civil War and World War II, which justifies, according to conventional wisdom, the means used to achieve victory (including the invention of "total war" and, of course, atomic weaponry).

But war mobilization, whether for good reasons or ugly ones, makes a terrifying demand on a nation's people. It asks them to perform ritual soulectomy on a bloc of humanity, to hope and even pray (as in Mark Twain's famous "War Prayer") for their annihilation: "O Lord our God, help us to tear their soldiers to bloody shreds with our shells ..." We turn them into gooks or nips or, in today's climate of political correctness, "Muslimists," so that we need feel no jolt of human horror at their deaths.

Well, fine, if you want to do that. But the price is high. Bile has a way of backing up and permeating the system. A militarized society can get infected by its own hatred.

For instance, Ishai Sagi, an Israeli soldier who went to jail rather than serve in Occupied Palestine and is now a member of Yesh Gvul (There Is a Limit), noted, when I heard him speak recently, that domestic abuse is alarmingly high in Israel these days. He attributed the phenomenon to "the deteriorating effect on a society of designating some human beings — the Palestinians — as having no rights." Brutality, in other words, is hard to turn on and off; some soldiers bring their day jobs home.

But the indirect effect of war mobilization — the overall climate it creates — has the most far-reaching consequences. "If empathy is the enemy of violence, depersonalization is its ally," writes James Garbarino in *Lost Boys,* his excellent look at juvenile violence in America.

The problem is that the cornerstone of military culture is depersonalization. During World War II, he noted, citing the research of military psychologist David Grossman, most American GIs — 80 percent — were so imbued with fundamental empathy they couldn't point their weapon at another human being and pull the trigger. The military solved this "technical" problem by changing training procedures. Instead of learning marksmanship by shooting at bull's-eyes, recruits took aim at human figures, slowly weaning themselves of their crippling inhibition. By the Vietnam War, such training was standard.

Enter pop culture: "With the advent of interactive point and shoot arcade and video games there is a significant concern that society is aping military conditioning but without the vital safeguard of discipline," writes Grossman, quoted by Garbarino. Mass desensitization, in other words. Hollywood and other entertainment outlets join the fun and suddenly it's not safe to mow your lawn in suburbia.

*October 2002*


## SHARED SACRIFICE

Members of Congress, ten-HUT!

Rep. Charles Rangel's proposal to reinstate the draft, with the nation poised at the abyss of war, deserves a crisp salute for sheer dramatic audacity. If we're really under mortal threat, then let's all storm Baghdad — your loved ones, mine, and every last precious twentysomething among the corporate-dividend class. Why should they be denied the privilege of inhaling depleted uranium dust for their country just because they have trust funds?

"For those who say the poor fight better, I say give the rich a chance," Rangel said.

No one seems to like the idea, neither hawk nor dove, and I confess to finding it appalling myself, on the grounds that peaceniks have no business forming an alliance, however ironically, with the god of war. But I find my admiration growing for the symbolic aptness of Rangel's bill anyway; it shows a flair for targeting the sacred cows of an unjust society worthy of Gandhi.

In introducing the legislation, the New York congressman noted that people of color are disproportionately represented in the cannon-fodder ranks of the armed forces, as are — duh — the poor. We all know this, of course, but when the media informs us we're going to war, the lead paragraph never proclaims that our precious freedoms will once again be preserved mostly by people who can't get better jobs.

Rangel also pointed out, a little closer to home, that only one member of the Congress that recently gave the president its bipartisan carte blanche to invade Iraq has a kid who might be affected by this decision — that is, a GI. A few more have offspring who are officers.

Well, now this is sort of raw, isn't it? Since Sept. 11, there's been an awful lot of nostalgia for Pearl Harbor and the war that followed it, but FDR had four sons fighting in that war. From First Family to last, that was a war of "shared sacrifice." No one's even making the pretense of such a thing today.

"I believe that if those calling for war knew that their children were likely to be required to serve — and to be placed in harm's way — there would be more caution and a greater willingness to work with the international community in dealing with Iraq," Rangel explained. "A renewed draft will help bring a greater appreciation of the consequences of decisions to go to war."

This is an extraordinary assertion — that "we the people" have given ourselves a government removed from the concerns of common humanity, and thus from the sanity of common sense. Logic tells us that war is to be avoided at all costs, but only if you have a loved one who would be fed into its maw.

By proposing genuine shared sacrifice for everyone — cab drivers and congressmen, secretaries and CEOs — Rangel is seeking to restore, or perhaps create, basic governmental checks and balances out of the premise that we're all in this together.

I find the terse dismissal of this proposal by Rumsfeld and Co. its biggest selling point. The professional patriots now avoid '60s-era rhetoric about "responsibility" like the plague and cite competitive wages as the foundation of a strong military. "We've got people serving because they want to serve," the secretary of defense told Larry King.

Yeah, sure. Yet military recruiters are desperate. Granted access to student data by the No Child Left Behind Act, they're "stampeding" the schools, I'm told. An Oregon reader, whose wife is a small-town high school principal, wrote recently: "The recruiters thought that they could go anywhere at any time into any class. There were some nasty confrontations. They obviously consider the public schools now farms for raising military inductees."

This is not a society where sacrifice, either run-of-the-mill or patriotic, is shared across economic strata, but I fear things are getting worse, don't you? The latest defense budget weighs in at $396 billion, not counting the $200 billion that a war with Iraq will likely cost. Maybe soldiers' pay is better than it used to be, but I'd rather the money be spent on them when they're still in school

*January 2003*

## STARVED ROCK

As thousands of gulls wheel in a cacophonous spiral above the open water where the Illinois River rushes over the dam just beyond Starved Rock, a bald eagle sweeps magnificently from its perch on a bare cottonwood and glides across the brown water, cutting the surface with its talons.

The moment's hungry beauty makes me gasp. This is the dead of winter. The river is frozen all along its length except here, where the dam quickens the current, so it's a spot of much excitement: a place to feed. I can feel the frenzy as soon as I get to the top of this naked outcropping of rock, a local wonder infused with blood legend, and my own current quickens.

Starved Rock State Park, two hours southwest of Chicago, has secrets it keeps revealing to me: canyons, waterfalls, a massive wood-beamed lodge built in the'30s by the Civilian Conservation Corps. And now this.

My heart wants to feed on the cries of the gulls and the patience of the eagles. We count nine of them in the trees on Plum Island, far more than I've ever seen at once in my life, and I wonder at my good fortune at coming upon them — great, rare, vulnerable birds. A sense of longing opens up in me, too big for my thoughts to accommodate.

The place was named after a 200-year-old massacre of Illiniwek Indians, several hundred of whom, men, women and children, starved to death atop this rock during a siege by neighboring tribes. Ancient tragedies lose their horror, however; they turn into the fodder of poetry and local color. Now it's just a name. Starved Rock.

The eagle pulls up from its dive with its claws empty, flicks its wings a few times and lifts until it is no more than a small, black speck in the afternoon sky. Then it turns and heads back to us, finally reclaiming its perch in a high cottonwood branch. There it sits, with the others, watching.

My attempts to understand the moment and reduce it to something meaningful are just as empty; it is irreducible. Nevertheless, as I look on, at this live, noisy spot, permeated with legend and symbolism, I feel an enormous question pressing at me from the inside: Why isn't this enough?

"There are souls ... whose umbilicus has never been cut. They never got weaned from the universe."

Perhaps Ursula LeGuin was thinking of such a place and such a moment when she wrote that passage, in *The Dispossessed*. She was describing people who are not isolated from the process of life: "They do not understand death as an enemy."

If there is any wisdom to be gleaned from nature, surely this is it: impermanence, death, rebirth. Yet in our proclamation as a species that death is, indeed, the enemy, we have perfected violence to a degree almost beyond calculation. Humankind is on the brink of another war; it toys with weapons of mass destruction. And it does this out of a fear of death.

All that we have will pass, no matter what we do to try to stop it. But perhaps if we love deeply, fervently enough, this moment that we are alive — love it with the magnificence of the bald eagle — we can rise above our fear of death and re-enter the circle of life.

Though we cannot reattach the umbilical cord, we can decide to grow up.

*February 2003*

## AMERICAN RAGE

What are we going to do about American rage?

Now that we're sort of finished with Iraq — the invasion's command of the headlines is ebbing — we're forced to start looking at ourselves again, and the sad and stupid violence that is our daily bread.

Handguns, yada yada. Remember that stalled debate? Yet there they are, still as plentiful as ever, still perversely finding their way into the hands of the law-abiding aggrieved, still turning petty disputes into permanent blood stains and $3 million bond.

The scene: Dunkin' Donuts on Milwaukee Avenue, Chicago's Northwest Side, a few miles from where I live. Forty-eight-year-old Alfredo Natal, a maintenance worker for the Chicago Transit Authority, orders coffee. The counterman pours in too much sugar and Natal figures, hey man, you did that on purpose. The two had argued about something a few days earlier, so ... well, hiss, rattle. An ugly rancor coils.

Stir in one .45-caliber pistol and two weeks later Sukhdev Dave is dead, shot down behind his counter as six customers look on. Natal is arrested two days afterward. Dave, 29, an immigrant from India, had a pregnant wife who would never see him again.

The scene: New York City. Lyric Benson, a young actress whose career is just starting to happen (she was in an episode of "Law & Order: Criminal Intent"), no longer wants to live with her boyfriend. The guy, Robert Ambrosino, can't live without her. They stand arguing in the threshold of her apartment. He shoots her in the face. Then he shoots himself. Two corpses hit the floor.

These are not remarkable stories. You find them on page 3 of the metro section. Even school shootings ("Boy Kills Principal") aren't page 1 fare anymore. They're part of the background murmur, like playoff scores. The media try to keep up, giving us terse little summaries: "She was shot early Thursday in her apartment doorway in front of her mother."

The reader is left to flounder in his own reverence vacuum. A silent "my God" and then we move on. America, America. We witness 30,000 or so of these tragedies every year courtesy of the handgun. But guns don't kill people. People kill people.

Right. If someone is sufficiently aggravated — too much sugar in his coffee — he'll find a way to terminate the problem without squeezing a trigger. Tire irons work. So do broken beer bottles. Whatever. Ask the NRA.

To become a killer, all you need to do is break the human contract and seal yourself in your own simmering juices. Anger is as good as brown-brown, the mixture of cocaine and gunpowder they give kidnapped children in Sierra Leone to turn them into soldiers. When you're high on it, wow, you're a superpower unto yourself, and the scattering villagers are indistinguishable from the chickens.

Dehumanize someone today. It's fun. Peacenik bellyaching about the invasion? Here's a good response:

"I would like to recommend that you have an MRI of your head done as soon as possible. I think it possible that your leftist demented brain is entangled in a tumorous mass; hopefully inoperable."

This sentiment showed up in my e-mail inbox the other day, from a correspondent in Durham, N.C. My viewpoint in a recent column was ludicrous; he saw red. I thanked him for writing (as I always do) and he wrote back, apologizing. This time he wished me an operable brain tumor.

In the same letter, he defended the invasion of Iraq, calling it "the cleanest war that has ever been fought."

Three cheers for war. The civilian death toll is pushing 3,000 and we're still glowing with a moral rectitude that's next to godliness. We're pumped. We're armed. Watch out, world.

*May 2003*

## THE OPENING FIST

For all the hitting they do below the spiritual belt, God's charlatans are right about one aspect of the same-sex marriage controversy.

The covenant in question is sacred.

I say these words gingerly, because the language is theirs, not mine. It's the language of religious knuckle-rapping. "To vote in favor of such laws is harmful to the common good and gravely immoral" — this, from the World Capital of Sexual Hypocrisy, a.k.a., the Vatican.

"There are absolutely no grounds for considering homosexual unions to be in any way similar or even remotely analogous to God's plan for marriage and family. Marriage is holy … and homosexual acts go against the natural moral law."

The obvious expedient is to end-run these guys — by whom I mean fundamentalist fist-shakers of every persuasion — and proceed with the legal recognition of same-sex "civil unions," following the example of brave little Vermont, so that gay and lesbian couples can start getting some rights.

Those who have trouble with this notion need to ponder the definition of selfishness: It's not a matter of doing what you want; it's trying to make others do what you want.

Slowly, the redoubt of sexual intolerance is crumbling, as politicians such as Canadian Prime Minister Jean Chretien flaunt hellfire and damnation ("he's putting at risk his eternal salvation," thundered the bishop of Calgary) in order to liberalize marriage laws.

The opposition, with the extravagant overkill of its counterattack, betrays its impotence. What are religions going to do when they can't scare people anymore? They'll have to surrender to common sense, of course.

This is why our own president's moral two cents' worth the other day — "I believe a marriage is between a man and a woman, and I think we ought to codify that one way or the other" — won't slow the momentum all that much, so long as the separation of church and state holds firm and religious homophobes don't get drilling rights to the Constitution. That could set back the progress of tolerance.

But there is a paradox here, the pulse of which I feel with the tiny, continuous tug of my own wedding ring as I sit at my computer writing. Why do I still wear this ring? My wife died five years ago. I'm no longer, in any civil or secular sense, married. I don't even get a surviving spouse's tax break anymore.

But I can't part with this ring or the way it ties me to a commitment I once made to someone I loved. This is way beyond the benefits and rights bestowed by civil union (some 1,400, apparently) and even beyond parenthood — though wearing the ring makes me feel less like a single dad.

That commitment defines me, like an anchor attached umbilically to some core place I have no other way of knowing: some collective human center. To talk about it requires religious words, like "sacred." To access it requires a public blessing.

And this is where the know-it-alls and bullies of God are making their stand, staking their last gasp (one can only hope) of authority on the continued banishment of homosexual love from the common blessing.

As though the human race has too many ways of loving!

Consider the astounding fact that we're more afraid of love than hate. For instance, the ordination of the Rev. V. Gene Robinson as the first openly gay bishop of the Episcopal Church was delayed while church officials investigated the allegation that he once inappropriately touched a guy on the back and arm.

Even if there was affection in such a touch, how inappropriate could it possibly have been? And how alarmed would anyone have been if Robinson had been accused, instead, of punching a man in the nose? God blesses hate all too easily.

Let us celebrate the slow, grudging opening of that fist.

*August 2003*

## TRIAL BY FIRE HOSE

"This is America, get used to it."

A generation ago — well, two, perhaps — such a comment, surfacing with malicious anonymity at a Deep South high school, along with Confederate flags, swastikas and scrawled references to "white power," would have been meant as friendly advice to uppity integrationists and racial harmony types to shut up and wise up.

In the 1950s and '60s, civil rights activists endured their trial by fire hose — and, of course, far worse — before they altered history and made an indelible point or two about justice. They were, in the main, nonviolent, but that doesn't mean they were nice, or that they won a nation over with sincerity and loving smiles. They stood their ground and paid the price.

I reminded myself of this the other day, when I read about the grief and sheer boob-ignorance visited upon the "Peace Shirt Coalition" at Cocoa Beach (Fla.) Junior-Senior High School.

At the beginning of the school year, as reported by Orlando's Channel 6 News, a group of kids began wearing T-shirts hand-decorated with peace themes every Thursday. They also put peace posters up on their lockers. Apparently such activities were controversial — like, oh, sitting down, while black, at a Woolworth's lunch counter once was — and pretty soon people started ripping down the posters or defacing them with swastikas and those other overly familiar, bizarrely racist-edged expressions of hate. The school corridors became gauntlets of derision for the "peace kids" — some broke down in tears — and eventually a counter-group started wearing Confederate flags to school.

At first I could hardly manage a thought more articulate than: huh? But even as I felt a centrifugal spin of incredulity, anger and despair — how come people hate the idea of peace so much? — I also felt some deeper click of, oh yeah, this is how it is.

Then I thought about the young soldier I wrote about last week, Sgt. Brad Gaskins, whose severe post-traumatic stress disorder, brought on by two tours of duty in Iraq, went unacknowledged by the military on his return and drove him to go AWOL. When he was interviewed, finally, by a psychotherapist, he made a comment I continue to find haunting, and which sends an echo through the corridors of Cocoa Beach Junior-Senior High School, whether the peace hecklers know it or not.

"He wonders," wrote psychotherapist Rosemary Masters, "if God is punishing him because before he joined the Army he thought of war as something fun and exciting."

If this is true, punishment is pending for a few others as well. Our collective emotional cauldron bubbles with fear and hatred just as it did 50 years ago. And we remain a victory-smitten, warrior-wannabe society, seduced and pumped up by the thought of loosing those emotions and gloriously having it out with some baddie, no matter how inanely B-movie the notion or how ugly the reality.

The peace kids innocently tapped into that cauldron. Thus a "Wage Peace" sign was torn down and replaced with "I Love America, Because America Loves War." And ominously accompanying the outbreak of Confederate-flagwear at the school was the slogan, "This is America, get used to it."

What a failure of education. Somebody needs to talk to these kids. Not me, but people like Brad Gaskins and other vets, who have internalized the hell of war, found themselves being eaten alive with guilt and unbearable memories and, far too often, have encountered official indifference and worse on their return home.

For instance, another story that recently went off like white phosphorous concerned wounded vets' receiving bills from the Army for a portion of their $10,000 enlistment bonuses — because they hadn't served out their full terms.

The Department of Defense, which a few years ago acknowledged (as noted in a 2003 article in the San Francisco Chronicle) that "it couldn't account for more than a trillion dollars in financial transactions, not to mention dozens of tanks, missiles and planes," was threatening wounded vets with interest charges on the "unearned" portions of their bonuses, at least until media attention forced an embarrassed spokesman to call the whole thing a "snafu."

Well, this is America. Get used to it.

But at least that comment cuts two ways. There is a peace movement, and it won't go away. This is also America. And when a few kids in peace T-shirts are able to scare up the undead racism of past generations and expose the deep irrationality that constitutes much of the public's support of war, we may once again be witnessing the beginning of profound change.

*November 2007*

## DANCING WITH FEAR

I knew there was a war on against cancer and, oh yeah, drugs, illiteracy, poverty, crime and, of course, terror, and that many arenas — sports, religion, business and politics, to name a few — are often portrayed as war without the body bags. But I was still surprised to read recently in the New York Times that we've opened up a fat front:

"It is a scene being repeated across the country as schools deploy the blood-pumping video game Dance Dance Revolution as the latest weapon," the Gray Lady informed us, "in the nation's battle against the epidemic of childhood obesity."

Enough already! If I were an overweight kid, would I want Braveheart in my face? My impatience here reaches into the language center of the American brain, or at least the media brain. When chubby 9-year-olds are inspiring the language of Guadalcanal and 9/11, maybe as a nation it's time to rethink our rhetorical default settings. Maybe it's time to stop regarding every challenge, danger, obstacle, mystery and fear we encounter as a military operation, to be won or lost. We should at least be aware we have a choice in the matter.

Metaphors are the very essence of that light bulb (metaphor) we think of as understanding. When it goes off, it means — boing-g-g! — we've linked the unknown with the known, created order out of the tumult of love or the daily commute or those blood-test results. Metaphors do not equal reality, but good ones illuminate it. The wrong metaphor about what's going on, however, makes us stupid. Witness George Bush's war on terror, a flailing spasm of high-tech counterterror that seems as rational as . . . oh, calling for an air strike to take out obesity.

Ever since 9/11, I've been driven by an urgency to understand why we as a nation accepted Bush's war of revenge so enthusiastically and felt so little empathy toward the innocent, sitting-duck populations we were about to carpet bomb. A big part of the reason, I believe, is that the military response — which means defining an enemy and immediately suspending all human feelings toward it — is embedded in our language. I also believe such language has outlived its usefulness in almost every way it's applied and that a new, more complex way of thinking has begun to emerge.

Consider: A 2005 University of Florida study on doctor-patient communication, published in the Journal of Clinical Oncology, concluded that, "Well-meaning doctors seeking to explain treatment to cancer patients by comparing it to an all-out war might be wise to skip the military metaphors," according to the university's website.

"The life-is-a-journey comparison is a quieter metaphor and has the depth, richness and seriousness to apply to the cancer experience," said Dr. Gary M. Reisfield, one of the researchers. "The road may not be as long as one hoped, and important destinations may be bypassed, but there's no winning, losing or failing."

Or how about the militarization of religion? Rev. Peter Paulsen, writing at medialit.org, noted: "We no longer accept racist references in speech, much less in worship. . . . But many Western — and some Eastern — religions still describe our relationship to God in military terms. We talk of 'battling' the devil, and 'conquering' sin. We loudly sing 'Onward, Christian Soldiers' or 'Lord, God of Hosts, Mighty in Battle.'

"Despite the controversy that changing this language might provoke," he wrote, "all people of faith need to reexamine whether the 'peace that passes all understanding' can be effectively communicated — in today's nuclear age — by traditional metaphors of war."

Or the militarization of business? Dennis W. Organ, in an essay on the Business Horizons website, lamented that classical management theory is permeated with military terms — "chain of command," "rank and file," "market strategy" — that serve mainly to obscure marketplace realities.

Even though he was dubious that the alternative business-model metaphors he suggested — "the organism, the computer, the jazz ensemble" — would grab people's imaginations, I think he's on to something. Such concepts are far more complex than the "us vs. them" reductionism of the military metaphor and challenge us to embrace a larger understanding of reality.

Similarly, David C. Smith, in an essay called "De-Militarizing Language" published at peacemagazine.org, asked: "Suppose instead of thinking about argument in terms of war, we were to think of argument as a pleasing, graceful dance. How would such a metaphor cause us to conceptualize argument in a different way?"

Those who can't or won't change their thinking will eye these alternatives as further intrusions of political correctness on their happiness: the smiley-face suppression of natural aggression so that everyone gets along in false harmony. I say imagine dancing with what we fear instead of trying to kill it.

*May 2007*

# PART SIX

# COMMON
# WONDERS

## Y2K NONCOMPLIANCE REPORT

I am not a technophobe, but I am a sort of techno-fogy, crotchety about "the latest" anything and inclined to poke at it with a stick long before I let it into the house.

Not only am I not up to date on new technology and its inevitable flying wedge of jargon ("cookies?" "e-trade?"), I'm proud of my resistance. My allegiance is always to life as I know it and I ignore revolutionary change for as long as possible; if pestered, I'll ask: How's that going to help? By the time I stamp my OK on something — computers, for example, or how about those ATMs? — you can figure a thing is here to stay, or ought to be.

Well, here's a partial report on some newfangled items that do not have my OK. "Newfangled," by the way, is a term ripe with squinty-eyed suspicion, as opposed to merely "new." It ropes in developments dating back to the '70s, if necessary. Fretting over the fate of the human race can't be done overnight, you know. In any case, as long as we remain in the old millennium, we may yet have time to save ourselves from:

- *The remote control.* Here's the problem: I'll be walking past the family room and see the tube on and no one in there, just noise and flicker in the darkness. This is Waste, on both the physical and spiritual plane. Energy needlessly spending itself, information dribbling into the void. I can't stand it. Guess I grew up when there was still a distinction between on and off, when the TV wasn't used to supply background thrum, or to keep a room e-viable while you're off multi-tasking.

  What I want to do is sweep into the room with a clean, crisp righteousness and turn the thing off, a move that requires an avenging angel's grace — a quick punch, snap, click or zap. There! Done with it! (Decisive, action-figure dad.)

  Instead, the action inevitably breaks down because I can't find the remote; it's buried under a cushion or it's in a shoe, under a bra or nowhere at all. If you have to crawl around on all fours before you can wield the swift sword of justice, forget it. And since I don't know how to turn off the TV without the remote, on it stays — and I make my peace with its ever-blaring presence, just as Orwell predicted.

- *E-mail.* Actually, I love e-mail. It's been pure Viagra to my flagging correspondence life, and the spawn of spam cluttering my electronic mailbox (mostly peddling Viagra) is only a minor irritant, far more easily disposed of than real junk mail.

  But there is a troubling development on the e-mail front, which assumes various forms: the meandering moral parable, the traveling tantric truth list, the mobile wish-granting e-fairy. These entities circumnavigate our electronic globe, wasting our time in miniscule doses, spreading motes of innocuous insight and cheer. They're no big deal in themselves, but they always end with a creepy little wag of the electronic finger:

"You have two choices now: One. Delete this. Two. Forward it to the people you care about."

"The tantra must leave your hands within 96 hours."

"If you send this to 1 person, your wish will come true in 1 month ... 50 people, your wish will come true in 1 hour!!! THIS IS NOT A JOKE!!!!"

Why does this stuff want so badly to live? How did it become my responsibility? Even as I click e-liminate, I get the sense of little hands grasping at me from beyond the cybergrave.

I fear vengeance may be theirs — somewhere on the other side of Y2K, of course.

*November 1999*


## HEARING VOICES

O! Modern times! Thus would I caption my mental snapshot of this moment: Conference breaks for lunch, glass doors push open and out pour the suits. Some light up cigarettes, some breathe in the crisp air, but most of them pull out their cell phones.

I happen to be taking a walk along Chicago's usually serene riverfront, a floor below street level, when, whoops, the world shifts, its rhythms syncopate, and I'm surrounded by a dozen earnestly gesticulating marionettes, lunatics you'd almost think, people responding to voices in their heads, which of course they are. They're less here than elsewhere, a dozen elsewheres, their offices, their living rooms, in casual electronic relationship with their private lives.

The technology responsible for this scene is so small and portable it's almost invisible, leaving me, the professional people watcher, with a view of only the outward behavior, which is comically unrelated to the surroundings. To walk through this throng of jerking puppets in business suits is to step around a dozen holes punched through space.

This is one of those things you don't notice till it stops — that there's a certain rhythm to public life, a certain stride, an acknowledged commonality among strangers pursuing disparate purposes: We're all in the same place, contained by the same restraints, enduring or enjoying the same weather, alive at the same time. This indeed is what public life is, the glorious sense that sheerly because we are alive and present, we're part of it.

Now, with cell phone technology, people have the option — without to-do, a calling card or correct change — to propel themselves out of virtually any public circumstance: the sidewalk, the lobby, the mall, the commuter train, the park, the jogging path. They can stand and walk among us without being with us. Previously, only the mentally ill had this option.

I'd just never seen it happen in such a concentrated form before, with everyone on the cell phone at once, causing public life simply to suspend itself. This old social observer and techno-watchdog, ever on the alert for creeping surrealism, felt his antennae quiver. O! Modern times! Is this one more ubiquitous gadget contributing to our general dehumanization? Somebody has to ask such questions.

Forgetting about such concerns as traffic safety, pacemaker interference and brain tumors, I give cell phones a provisional pass. I'm both appalled and grudgingly delighted with their contribution to public life. They make it more complex, a game of three-dimensional chess. They create a vertical society.

That is, they give us the spectacle of strangers utterly unself-conscious in our presence, kicking back, laughing with pleasure, or perhaps furrowing their brows in urgent crisis management. What we lose in eye contact, we gain in parted curtains. Peoples' lives open fleetingly to us as we jostle past. Masks drop, shells crack; humanoid life forms resonate. This may not be good, but it's certainly interesting.

On the train to work the other day, for instance, some guy sitting across the aisle from me is putting on a masterful display of cell phone oblivion. His voice fills the car. He is so relaxed he has completely forgotten where he is. I listen in unwilling fascination as he pours out intimate details of a fight he got into at work with his boss, weaving profanity and laughter into the enthusiastic narrative. He won the fight; he's pumped.

Suddenly a woman, a mom riding with her kids, is up and shouting in his face, "Stop all that swearing. Children are present!"

Oh, sheepish plunge to earth. Burst bubble. He apologizes, returns to his conversation — but in a subdued voice, reminded that the walls dividing us are paper thin.

*May 2000*

## THE TITILLATED SOCIETY

I've just seen sights you wouldn't believe — women metamorphosing into angels and ice cream cones, men into halibut and flounder. This is a dispatch from No Man's Land.

Oh mama, love for sale, heaven in a bottle. The cables and winches of desire grind in the service of industry, pulling on your heart and mine, uniting us in sexual tension. We live in the Titillated Society. God help us when the illusion snaps.

I don't thumb through the glossy pages of women's magazines very often, but somehow the other day it was just me and a 350-page issue of Cosmopolitan. I couldn't put it down. I came away red-faced, suddenly knowing too much about the technology of beauty ("The look of the moment isn't super-shiny and high-tech. It's moist and real") and way too much about the flip side of bulimia.

As a charter male feminist, I've pretty much blamed my own gender for every stupid misunderstanding between the sexes, every crude trespass, every debasement of love into power politics. From puberty to the grave, men's instinct is to objectify women, reduce them to body parts, devalue them, possess them. This is the root of all evil. My post-Cosmo reappraisal of the matter is that women do fine without us. They objectify themselves before we even get in the door.

"Make your man drool for you like he craves a cone when he passes an ice-cream shop on a hot day. Dab yourself with an ice-cream-cone smell-alike fragrance. Spiked with vanilla extract and with notes of praline and butter ... contains a no-cal sweetener, so it's also yummy to taste. Spritz it on and offer him a lick." Sugar Cone, from Flagrance. Only $15.

What's driving this ad, ironically, is a faux-'60s sexual "frankness." Cosmo abounds with it. The magazine's fever-pitch erotic content would have been scandalous a generation ago. All that decolletage and saucy innuendo is on a continuum with XXX-porn, but in the new millennium it's perfectly hip. My consternation isn't because Eros is bad for you, but because the Cosmo world view — that celebrities lead fabulous lives, that beauty is more a matter of the right lipstick than inner peace, that supermodels don't binge and purge — is just as unreal as the "Sex? What's that?" know-nothingism of the uptight '50s.

And, of course, there's that objectification problem. For instance, Cosmo's "Figure Fixers" feature tells women how to compensate for various physical defects —small chest, thick waist, short legs, etc. — which get unfortunate exposure in a swimsuit. And lest you forget that looking great in a two-piece is how you find love, a feature called "Reel Him In" shows you "four daring-but-doable poolside beauty moves to make him your catch of the day."

Meanwhile, the Flagrance ad wasn't the only one that reduced females to a runny dessert. The pitchman for Skintimate, a shaving gel, also happened to be a sugar cone, this one life-size and sprouting gorgeous, stubble-free legs.

Why should body hair be the enemy of love? My own daughter, at age 8, was suddenly so concerned by the hair on her forearms she wanted her mother to ask the doctor about it. Turns out the wrath of God may be to blame.

Author Susie Bright, an antidote to Cosmo if ever there was one, writes in *The Sexual State of the Union* of some fundamentalist religious instruction she got as a child: "'As you grow older, and become a woman, you are going to grow hair' — (the teacher) paused — 'under your arms, and also in other places. Hair under the arms is a sign of woman's original sin, and we do not let this shame be seen.'"

Shame and titillation — strange bedfellows, indeed. In a country where 5 million people suffer from eating disorders, and God only knows how many just hate themselves, how they feed our discontent.

*October 2000*

## SPENT SHELLS

Next time you read some breathless report on the disease-free future medical technology is on the brink of handing us, as researchers continue "unlocking hidden genetic secrets" that will allow yuppies to live to 150, remember that the media, even when it reports on science, isn't all that good at putting two and two together.

Sure, on the one hand, amazing, headline-making stuff is happening in certain places — a University of Chicago research team, for instance, recently isolated a possible genetic cause of adult-onset diabetes — but on the other hand, the Bulletin of the Atomic Scientists still has its Doomsday Clock set at nine minutes to midnight.

I remain skeptical about our technology-shaped future, and feel the need, when I read about it, to see what's dark and out-of-control factored into the optimism. Technology giveth; technology taketh away. Sometimes I want to shout: Stop! A moratorium, please, on all the research, on the Biblical imperative to dominate the earth, on the rending of nature from its context, until the human race sorts out its politics and priorities and learns some impulse control.

On the same day, for instance, that the breakthrough in diabetes research was page-one news, another medical technology story — although it wasn't labeled as such — quietly informed us of a congressional debate over how much money to spend on ailing nuclear workers "who have contracted cancer or other illnesses from exposure to radiation or toxic chemicals used in nuclear weapons development and production."

The Clinton administration figures the compensation package will cost $1 billion, but Republicans in the House don't like the legislation because, if we let the federal heart bleed for the 4,000 to 6,000 people who actually are sick now, well, uh … big problem, folks. The number of toilers in our multi-tentacled nuclear weapons industry is more than 600,000. GOP realists fret over a possible price tag of $50 billion over the next decade — just to prolong the lives of workers who contract federally financed radiation sickness. Sputter, sputter!

Interestingly enough, these same Republican realists, with their pit-bull vigilance over our tax dollars, want to spend $60 billion to deploy a national missile defense system that has so far failed every test designed to demonstrate its workability. Last summer they voted down a bill that would have required more stringent testing for the system; they want it built whether it works or not.

I'm bothered about all this at a level that goes deeper than the obvious irony. I'm bothered that our optimism about technology only faces forward. I'm bothered that powerful people and their (our) money manage to find their way behind all manner of sexy new technologies, but are shy about glancing backward, about acknowledging, let alone paying for, any problems or suffering left in their wake. Where's the profit in that? Sick weapons makers are just so many spent shells.

It's as though an honest accounting would grind everything to a halt. I'm bothered that this is a risk we're not willing to take. Most of all, perhaps, I am bothered that the paradox of technology and scientific breakthrough — that there is always a cost — is never a core part of the story.

"Modern safety practices have eliminated the dangerous kinds of exposure that caused the illness in those victims," an Energy Department official is quoted as saying.

I hear a ring of self-interested falseness here, the kind the media never strenuously challenges. I grew up in the Fabulous '50s, when nuclear power was clean and safe, when spring had not yet been silenced by DDT and smoking didn't cause cancer. The future was wonderful then; we weren't churning up new problems, only solving old ones.

And I hear the same old voices touting every new technology.

*November 2000*

## GLOW COIL

At first the awareness — something's wrong — was filament-thin, a tiny disturbance in my busy, wrapping paper-strewn evening. Wasn't it getting a little cold?

I'd been in a state of pleasant productivity, wrapping holiday presents and watching "Dial M for Murder." It was two days before Christmas. This had to get done; my identity as a cheery, gift-bearing agent of Santa was riding on it. But darn ... that chill. I wanted to pull a blanket over my legs. Instead, I checked the thermostat in the next room. It was set at 68, but the temperature was, uh oh, 65. Vital sign alert!

And my life went into immediate freeze frame. This was one of those moments when you realize that whatever you're doing has no bearing on what actually matters. What matters in late December in Chicago, when it's zero degrees outside, is heat — ah, heat, softly floating out of the grates in the floor, filling up the house and making it livable. Without it, plans, goals — urgencies — seem shockingly unimportant.

Only later did I come to realize that structural breakdown was to be a sort of holiday subtheme this year, forcing on me a pained awareness of how much I take for granted as I skim along the surface of my life. The next day, for instance, as I was approaching an intersection on a busy highway, a woman stepped into traffic from in front of a bus stopped in the right lane and was hit by the car in front of me; the driver, who had the right of way, hit his brakes and skidded valiantly, but still struck her a glancing blow in the thigh.

She appeared not to be seriously hurt, just massively disoriented, as she limped to the curb. There were plenty of people around, the situation looked dealt with, so I continued on my way — feeling, once again, that chill, that tremor. The driver ahead of me had had no chance to avoid the confused pedestrian, and could have, with an instant's slower response time (say he'd been yakking on a cell phone), hit her full on, at high speed. Both lives would have changed forever; one might have ended, the other, become haunted with moral despair ("If only I'd seen her sooner ...") and maybe legal and even criminal liability.

We walk this edge, always, between the chatter of daily life and the turning of the great unknown. I remember a weekend I spent with my dad when I was a boy and a baseball game we never went to. My mom and sister were off at an Indian Princesses retreat and Dad and I had spent the Saturday bumming around; we'd gone bowling, then bought cotton candy at a riverside park. Dad was going to take me and a friend to the game that night, but when we got home from the park he told me he didn't feel well. His words were stoically minimal; I was crushed, and hated having to call my pal and say the game was off. It wasn't fair.

Dad had had a stroke, it turns out.

I try to measure the moment's small necessities against the great unknown — the profoundly unknowable — and maintain a sense of gratitude that most of the time it stays hidden and silent. But I get busy and gratitude slips away. It takes a rumble from below, a structural shiver, to waken me.

The furnace, that night, was indeed dead. And this was only its third winter; two years ago, I thought I had purchased security. Hallelujah, in any case, for technicians on call. The furnace guy came out at 1 a.m. — the temperature in the house was down to 58 by then — and said I had a bad glow coil. This is the thing that heats up to a glowing red and ignites the gas; it costs $196 (plus labor).

I later hung the spent glow coil on the Christmas tree: an artifact from the great unknown, which has its own timetable and suffers me the way the eagle, as Shakespeare said, "suffers little birds to sing/And is not careful what they mean thereby."

I think of it as an eagle feather.

*January 2001*

## CLOUD TOPS

An undulating white terrain opened brightly out the window to my left, as we climbed to 35,000 feet — cloud tops! What a lurch I felt, what an odd thrill, to look — as though flight were still a wonder — on a sight unavailable to the earthbound. You'd think I'd never been in an airplane before, for heaven's sake.

Maybe it's a function of aging, this tendency to go whoopsy-daisy when something yanks me out of my settled sensibilities. If so, it's getting worse. I had an urge to summon the flight attendant and ask, "Are we meant to see this?" The sight seemed illicit, purloined from God.

What gives? Am I a guest in my own century? I pride myself on my worldliness, so this sudden reticence — it felt almost like shyness — to look easily out on, of all things, the tops of clouds, was more than a little puzzling. I thought about all those heavenward gazers of millennia past, planted on terra firma but dreaming of being where I am right now, puncturing the clouds, soaring over the planet, and heard a tiny voice inside me go "no way."

I possess a wary soul, it occurred to me as I pondered the matter and the cabin filled suddenly with the odor of airline cuisine (the unleashed scent of packaged omelets). I lack a sense of entitlement, an imperative to go, boldly or otherwise, where no man has gone before. When it comes to technology, I am not a pioneer on behalf of the human race.

It's connected to my deepest feelings of moral recoil — at the conquering spirit of those who do claim such entitlement, from the conquistadors of the Age of Exploration to today's lab-smocked scientists, pushing the envelope in biology and physics. I wonder at the claims we stake on behalf of humanity, or the Crown, in pristine and perhaps already occupied worlds. It feels reckless to me.

I know, I know — "one small step for a man, one giant leap for mankind," and all that. This is what humanity's heroes say, and their words are carved in stone. The human race is all about "advancement." We're taught this early on. In fourteen hundred and ninety-two, Columbus sailed the ocean blue — hail, bold adventurer, seeker of wealth and glory. His boldness and entitlement knew no restraint. The indigenous population of the New World was just one more obstacle to subdue, enslave and turn into a source of wealth.

Half a millennium and a whole new frontier later: We're about to become masters of the universe. On the day the atom bomb was to be tested at Los Alamos, no one knew what to expect, and at least some of the physicists feared that maybe the sky itself would catch on fire. What if they'd been right?

Yet they took the risk, on behalf of all humanity, on behalf of life itself. The conquering spirit first of all defeats all doubt — pierces it with the aplomb with which my soaring 727 pierced the low-lying clouds over O'Hare Airport. You can't put this sort of thing to a vote; it would never come off, and mankind would never progress at all. Or so, I'm sure, the reasoning must go.

Yet here I am on this golden morning, traversing the continent, born aloft by a spirit that is not my own. The clouds vanish and a surreal vista opens up below: gray-green checkerboard of farm land, layered with snow, gouged by some great, snaggle-edged, twisting river. Words simply cannot do justice to the oddness of what you see from an airplane window.

I look in ever-fresh disbelief, my heart pounding. I can't drink in enough of it. And now, suddenly, here are the Rockies, popping out of the Great Plains in massive, coal-black heaps. I relish the view all the more for my lack of entitlement to it. I remain a wary guest in the 21st century.

*February 2001*

## THE BARBIE EFFECT

As a guy, I was scornfully immune to Barbie, but as a father, I was stuck with her in my life for about six years — tiny shoes, pink convertible, gold lamé toreador pants, the whole perky nine yards — and thus experienced second-hand the spell she cast on little-girlhood. Breaking it was a rite of passage (or at least the parody of one).

Since I had always assumed Barbie was the concoction of some unscrupulous committee of middle-aged men, I was surprised to learn she had a "mother," Ruth Handler, who died last month at age 85.

Handler's passing tugs loose a small flood of memories about her creation. It also stirs thoughts about childhood and its relationship to the $2.5 billion-a-year global industry that is Barbie and her friends (a.k.a. Mattel, which, I once heard, is the largest clothing manufacturer in the world, all of it, of course, doll clothes). Whatever might be wrong with Barbie, from anatomical and sociological standpoints, there's sure something right about her from a commercial one. For a cash cow, she's awfully cute.

I have a theory about her appeal, extrapolated from the generally favorable press she's gotten in recent retrospectives. Turns out (I hadn't realized this) Barbie is a feminist. No mere adjunct to a man, she was an independent career gal from the start, giving little girls the idea they could be anything they wanted to be, even in the early '60s, when they couldn't. Astronaut Barbie! Race-car driver Barbie! President Barbie!

Of course, she pulled all this off as a smiling empty-head in darling little outfits, fully accessorized, preposterously thin, anatomically ludicrous. If she were 5-foot-6 instead of 1-foot-zero, her measurements would be 39-21-33. (And in the real world, breast implant operations are up 275 percent this decade.)

For more than 40 years, in other words, Barbie has ridden the crest of, and purveyed, both feminist and anti-feminist values — appealing to everybody. She's the plastic-and-vinyl mini-messiah of You Can Have It All, a brilliant fusion of fantasy and product licensing. I've never known a little girl who wasn't nuts about her. (When she showed up in Moscow in 1992, crowds of little Russian girls reportedly stood outside the toy store ogling her, no matter she may have cost their parents a month's wages.)

In my house, Barbie dolls and their accoutrements multiplied almost supernaturally, or so it sometimes seemed. A major source was my daughter's older cousins, who were just growing out of the Barbie phase as Alison entered it. Perfect timing! She inherited the Barbie dream house, swimming pool and bedroom set, and eventually possessed enough tiny skirts and blouses to fill a grocery bag, and miniature shoes in limitless numbers, no matter how many got vacuumed off the living-room carpet.

As a hands-on dad, I played with Barbie the best I could, but never managed to do so in an irony-free manner. Once, for instance, in some sort of convulsive reaction to the Barbie Effect, I organized the Naked Ken Parade: a somber procession of the half-dozen or so Kens 5-year-old Alison owned, each in his G-rated buff, his removable head stuck on the tip of his arm in approximation of being carried. Alison was delighted. The parade snaked through the house all the way to Mom in the TV room. Ah, those were the days!

Those days ended abruptly with the Anti-Barbie Fashion Show, which, I swear, I had nothing to do with. One evening, Alison and some friends, then 9 or 10, told the adults to assemble in the living room and proceeded downstairs one after the other in a stiff-kneed, Barbie-style walk, wearing wigs, a ton of makeup and, the coup de grace, pillows stuffed down their shirts, all of them giggling at the outrage they were perpetrating.

Praise the Lord, the spell was broken. Barbie, once the embodiment of glamour and grown-upness, had fallen to the playroom floor. Afterwards, every last Skipper and Ken and all their plastic artifacts were shoved in shoeboxes, to be stored with the rest of used-up childhood.

*May 2002*

## THE WOMEN OF ENRON

Except for the chains and sashes, the high-heels and exotic lingerie and, oh yeah, the "nether Mohawks" (to put it delicately), the women of Enron, it turns out, are much like the rest of us. Underneath their business suits, they're naked.

Well, 10 of them are, anyway. Thanks, Playboy, for removing all doubt.

Let me confess: I'm a big fan of nakedness. The type, that is, that is synonymous with honesty. I ache for truth, seek it, at times, almost recklessly — amid the weeds and neglect, behind the façades, beyond taboo and the assurances of authority. My instinct is that our survival depends on knowing what we're not supposed to know and saying what we're not supposed to say. And what is Enron but the new millennium's most arrogant symbol of the falseness of appearances?

So when I heard what Playboy was up to, doing a spread on the "Women of Enron" in its August issue — boom to bust, no hidden assets (groan) — politics met prurience and the jackrabbit of overenthusiasm leaped up in me. This was simply too delicious a cultural phenomenon to ignore: one last noisemaker's blaaat at Ken Lay and the boys, who hid behind their boardroom dignity to scam the state of California, their own employees and the country. Let Playboy, slick and venerable purveyor of adolescent male fantasies, undo that dignity button by button. How fun. It's the genius of capitalism in action. And what a great excuse to buy the magazine.

I guess I imagined that Playboy's layout would depict brave women stepping off the edge of propriety, turning the business world upside down by exposing their humanity. Repressed sexuality transforms into greed. This would help right the balance.

Once upon a time, there was an outbreak of sexual frankness in American society; openness was healthy. Remember the nude scene in *Hair*? We're all human beings in this room, no more and no less. This era seems not to have lasted long. Big Culture got ahold of it, and bared breasts, once they were airbrushed, were no longer akin to bared souls.

Something over a century ago, Friedrich Nietzsche observed: "Christianity gave Eros poison to drink; he did not die of it but degenerated — into a vice."

Eros, I fear, is as deformed as ever. Religious fundamentalism, with all its judgment and condemnation of human sexuality, may be an increasingly marginalized cultural force, but it still has a grip on the national conscience. Thus there was an undercurrent of catty wonder in the media coverage of Playboy's stunt that these women weren't ashamed of themselves for posing nude — they would have been 40 years ago, by God. And at the very least, hadn't they destroyed their credibility as businesswomen?

But that whiff of sin is just enough to keep Playboy's game plan viable. Eros is still a vice, which the soft-core porn industry debases even further — into titillation. That's all you need to know about the Women of Enron.

Yes, I did my duty in the name of journalism and scrutinized Playboy's August issue ... and came away thinking, damn, men are suckers. This was slick techo-glamour masking sheer adolescent stupidity. I don't begrudge Courtnie, Lori, Carey, Shari or any of the others their Playboy paychecks, or even question their career moves — if you've got it, flaunt it — but something in me bleeds for the common man and the common woman, who still want to be heard and valued.

Isn't that the premise Playboy was exploiting? These were "ordinary" women — What's-her-name, over in Accounting — vaulted, by grace of their company's sudden notoriety, onto the national stage. But it wasn't really about them at all. It was about how makeup and good lighting could turn them into eye candy.

Here, darling, put on this corset ...

*August 2002*

## FORECOURT OF THE STARS

"The world," whined George Costanza, Jerry Seinfeld's buddy, "is full of no-talent celebrities. Why can't I be one of them?"

I hear ya, George. They're everywhere, oozing sex appeal, dispensing diet advice, entertaining us with their scandals — simply being fabulous. How can you not envy them? Surely, with all our eyes on them, they live lives of sustained uplift, lives that never intersect with moldy bread or bathroom fungus, or come down to such a banal moment as this one here, this second, this heartbeat.

I hate to admit it, but my inner Costanza gets as agitated as the next guy's. Celebrity status is all illusion — I know that. Take Monica. She's still cruising on sheer notoriety and world-class chutzpah. (Didn't she get a job with British TV a while ago?) But I ache, in my "George" moments, to wield such attention, to be famous, as though that would relieve me of life's grind.

My ambivalence hit me like a ton of wet cement the other day, when my daughter and I, who were visiting friends in L.A., found ourselves in the Forecourt of the Stars, a.k.a. the courtyard of Grauman's Chinese Theatre, where Hollywood celebs have been leaving body part indentations on big slabs of concrete since 1927.

I went there because I'm a student of culture, of course, not an ogling fan. Funny, though. After five minutes, my 14-year-old daughter was off to check out the gift shop while I ogled on, drifting from square to square. The stars were ripped from their eras, their slabs dealt indiscriminately across the courtyard in a veritable kaleidoscope of immortality: "Wow, there's Whoopi Goldberg!" "M'gosh, it's Joan Crawford!" I couldn't get my fill.

Here's the startling thing. The Forecourt of the Stars, this "walk of fame" so ingrained in the national identity, Hollywood's garish pantheon, far from elevating the distance between celebrity and fan, between god and worshipper, fells the luminaries like so much lumber. It reduces them to the most modest of dimensions — to, m'gawd, the size of ordinary human beings. I don't think it's supposed to, but it does. These slabs are surprisingly, even embarrassingly, personal.

What you have here are unguarded, unadorned footprints and handprints, free of gloss or PR shtick (with only a few exceptions: Trigger's hoofprints next to Roy Rogers' handprints, old cowboy William S. Hart's six-gun indentations). In short, the Forecourt is the somewhat silly aftermath of a bunch of people standing in cement.

Here's Doris Day, for instance: Like almost all the female stars, she suffered her immortalization in high-heel shoes; thus, the mark she left is almost incomprehensible: a sort of rounded flatiron-shape and a deep, rainwater-collecting circle. It took me a moment simply to figure out what it was. Oh, her footprint. And when I did, I couldn't erase the image of Doris dressed to the nines as flashbulbs popped around her, slowly sinking into the glop.

On the whole, the feet and hands of the stars seemed, well, small. Cary Grant had very average-size dogs; so did Clint Eastwood. That's it — that's what you get at the Forecourt of the Stars. The size of their feet. How stripped of glamour it all is.

And how inadvertently wonderful. As far as I'm concerned, there's no bigger fraud than the fraud of royalty — whether it's royalty of blood or talent, looks or money. I take nothing away from the Forecourt honorees; most were (or are) engaging entertainers. But why spin any of them in a cocoon of hype? Why pretend they lived in something other than the human condition?

Their talent, and all talent — as distinct from ego — is steeped in work ethic and, I would venture, deep reverence for the truth about that condition. Artistry that's worth our notice doesn't ask for flattery; it asks for the chance to serve.

*February 2001*

## LOVE ASTERISK

Maybe for starters we should change the spelling of one of our most ubiquitous four-letter words. I propose a permanently attached asterisk, to wit: LOVE*.

The asterisk would stand for "and whatever happens next." Because something always does — usually something Newtonian, like an equal and opposite reaction. Without the asterisk, "love" is only half a concept — the coil without the recoil, the spring without the sprong-g-g, the dive without the splash. Have you noticed, for instance, how many scenic spots around the world are named Lover's Leap? None of them are called "Lover's Pleasant View of the Future." These jutting rocks know something. Oh, if only we could learn it before we find ourselves standing on the edge!

I'm sensitive to the issue, I guess, because I've recently become something more than just a widower. Now (shudder) I'm a dating widower. I feel as though I've dropped my heart into a particle accelerator.

And now hearts everywhere seem open wounds — the hearts of my friends, the hearts of strangers. Open the paper, here's a murdered spouse or girlfriend. More women are killed in this country every year by someone they know intimately than die in automobile accidents. One in 12 women (and one in 45 men) will be stalked sometime in their lives. It's love* that's doing this — love* that won't let go of its initial delirium, love* stuck in the doorway, mourning its disappointments with a bludgeon.

Isn't it time for some basic safety instruction? Love* safety. Condoms are the least of it. Kids (and grown-ups, too), pay attention.

The human race has only been at this for several million years, so we're just beginning to disentangle ourselves from the fraud our mating instincts spawn. Love* stories may end with the protagonists basking in a state of exponentially rising expectations — love without the asterisk — but don't be fooled. This is a fleeting condition, an announcement that your life has just gotten harder. Heaven is no match for earth; in the natural order of the universe, hope yields to reality.

In other words, one of two things happens next: You break up or you settle in for the long haul. Neither eventuality bears any resemblance to the state that birthed it; to be handled successfully, both require exquisite skill. Breaking up is the simpler outcome, but the more common and dangerously confusing (see stalker stats above). Handling it is an art of the soul. Here are some tips:

1. A brokenhearted lover makes a mistake when he/she asks the other person why it didn't work out; that answer is likely to be defensive and abbreviated. Slowly, as you heal, formulate your own answer, which fits the facts as you know them.

2.  Chief among those facts: The beauty you experienced was real, and it touched both lives.
3.  Only something bigger than both of you could have turned sympathetic intimacy into the cold, dry stalk that has just snapped in the middle. The other person may had too many secrets, a buried trauma that choked the flow of loving. There is mercy in impersonal forces, like gravity. They give you permission to let go.
4.  When it's over, it's over. Your worst enemy is hope. It's a rupture in the container of self. You do get to have your life back, but not until you stop hoping "something still might work out."
5.  Extend sympathy to your ex. This is tough — kind of like willing life after death. But anger will eat you alive; bitterness, harden you into what you hate. Loving unselfishly means saying goodbye unselfishly. The landing is a lot softer if you come down on a bed of forgiveness.
6.  As you harness the harm, you turn it into wisdom.
7.  Time, as you know, is your friend. And love* is unavoidable; it will come again.

*September 2000*

## THE SUM OF OUR PARTS

Here's the problem: We're of value to others for reasons other than our souls. Someone wants our pocket change, for instance, or our sexuality. Or our vote.

Our world isn't organized in such a way that we can easily stand in continual, prayerful awe of one another, or of nature. Mostly, people reduce the world beyond themselves to what they can handle, control and benefit from. This isn't a moral judgment, just an observation about how society functions — in a state of dynamic compromise between enterprise and worship. Unfortunately, this tension breaks down all the time and hustlers forget they're accountable for the long-term consequences of their decisions.

The least we can do is to keep life's moral dilemmas in sharp focus, so our need to grub for advantage in the short term — to satisfy our hungers, make our profits, win our wars — is held in reasonable check and the decisions we make are tested against the touchstone of our ideals. When we fail to do so, "necessary evil" settles over the land and ends justify means. In short, the cynics win.

A while ago, I came across a useful concept for maintaining this focus, for measuring the gap between what we allow ourselves to see and what's really there. Benjamin Kunkel, reviewing J.M. Coetzee's book *The Lives of Animals* in the Nation, made this statement: "Plutarch finds that cruelty to animals fosters cruelty to humans; Carol Adams' feminist version of this argument is to suggest that we abstract meat from animals analogous to our abstraction of sex from women."

I've been haunted by this concept for a year now: our power to abstract and "harvest" something incidental from a whole being, human or otherwise, to the (possibly fatal) detriment of that whole. Doing so strikes me as the ultimate in short-term blindness, especially when, even in the short term, connecting with the whole being — connecting soul to soul — produces far more benefit to all concerned, even the exploiter.

A lifelong vague uneasiness suddenly crystallized in this concept and I now see its manifestation everywhere. For instance, do we not abstract:

- *Intelligence from the child?* This is the "business" of schools — to produce high scores on standardized tests. A back-to-school photo in a local paper showed a line of students filing through a metal detector gate while their book bags were thoroughly searched; they looked like convicts. In the same paper, Chicago's Mayor Richard Daley was quoted as saying he would no longer "tolerate" below-grade-level reading scores in city schools, sounding like the manager of a chicken farm complaining about egg production.

- *The working stiff from the creator?* Labor Day is a worthy holiday and an honest day's work fills the soul, but a recent survey found that one in four of us hated our jobs and workplace aggression was on the rise. Too often what is asked of us engages a mere fraction of what we're capable of. "What does it take to be a good plumber? You gotta own it, just like you have to own being a dad." So said my friend Jim as he showed me around a job site. When he peels open a wall and looks at the plumbing behind it, "I see a work of art." Work that denies us such satisfaction is a mockery.

- *The vote from the voter?* "Winning is the name of the game," as the apologists put it, justifying the fact that the campaign process in presidential elections isn't real political engagement. The special interests and their money are going through the bare minimum of democratic charade to abstract our single, quadrennial act of approval, a vote; then it's back to whatever government is really about (profit for someone).

Sometimes we have to suspend our awe at the immensity of life in order to get on with the little matters, like getting the needle threaded and getting the bills paid, but our larger selves atrophy without daily exercise. And our future shrinks when we devalue the present.

*October 2000*

## DISGUISED AS NOWHERE

"Wherever you are is called Here."

Feel the hush and reverence of that word. Just for one moment, don't judge it or try to escape it. Look around and touch the corners and edges of "here" with your eyes, with all your senses. Drink it in as though you had only a short time left to live. It's the best you're ever going to get.

The problem is that the place David Whyte is referring to, "Here" with a big H, often — maybe most of the time — wears the disguise of "nowhere." That's why we're always speeding past it in our minds. So I offer a homily today in praise of traffic jams, flight delays and slow checkout lines, all the commonplace terrors that force us to stew in a moment we'd intended not to notice.

Superstore checkout lines seem especially intent on teaching me life lessons. They defy technological improvement, indeed, seem to grow less efficient — or maybe just less human — the more high-tech beeps they emit. When I'm stuck in a line that inscrutably stops moving for a while, my brain's reptilian core goes into "fight or flight" mode and it's all I can do to keep a billion years of evolution from making a spectacle of itself on the spot.

I stopped off at my neighborhood chain drugstore after work the other day to buy a tube of toothpaste. This was not a complicated project; I hadn't expected to wind up with indelibly etched memories of the experience, but I did.

The guy in line ahead of me had a full shopping cart, a cosmic joke on the single-item purchaser, but the cashier processed the merchandise — mop, cleaning solvent, bar soap, yada, yada — with methodical efficiency ... until, oops, the last item. The rubber mat's on sale, the customer insisted, but it didn't ring up that way. My heart always pauses when the cashier picks up the phone and calls for a price check, because now everything's in free fall.

The runner couldn't find the mats the first time out, so had to come back for more specific directions, then returned a second time having found no evidence they were on sale, at which point ... well, I forget precisely what all happened, except the line stopped dead, and it was the only one open in the whole store, so it grew clogged with increasingly agitated customers, one of whom, three people behind me, started cursing out the cashier, whose face grew blanker and blanker and blanker.

Even when the mat matter was resolved (the customer was right), the delays weren't over. The guy wanted $60 back on his debit card and the limit is $50, so the numbers he punched in didn't work. This took a few more minutes to untangle, while I stood waiting in silent, seething endurance, feeling sheer hatred for life.

When it was my turn at last, I slid the toothpaste at the cashier. She rang me up, then handed me a receipt mixed with my change — between the coins and the folding money, as cashiers always do, as though they don't know getting it that way is a nuisance. Here was my excuse to let her have it. "I don't want the receipt," I snarled.

She withdrew the offending strip of paper as though stricken. "Sorry," she said. She was ready to cry.

And in that moment I was no longer nowhere. A sense of Here with a capital H flooded over me, as I realized how high the stakes were. Her humanity and mine, nothing less, were riding on this transaction. "That's OK," I said, pulling back my anger as best I could. But her face was a mask again. The scanner went beep as she started ringing up the next customer.

*May 2001*

## THE TRUTH ABOUT BIRTHDAYS

Every year the incredulity is fresh. I'm how old? No! You don't say!

The thing is, this is not affectation, though you'd think a guy with my advanced state of hair loss would be used to birthdays by now, and used to arithmetic: 53 follows 52 in lockstep, and so on. One's age is not a surprise waiting to be opened with the rest of the presents.

Yet as middle age moves out of its crisis stage for me and simply settles in as fact, and as the shirts and sweaters and obscene birthday cards from friends strain increasingly to appear novel, the sheer numerical value of my age intensifies in strangeness. Indeed, each successive number I rack up invokes a greater sense of wonder than the last, in inverse proportion to its likelihood to be celebrated in song and popular culture.

I have a theory why this is so. Our identity forms and solidifies in youth, which is eternal. If I ever stopped being young, I'd be a different person, I assumed. Life would have to issue me a new identity card — "Old Dog" — which would have my profession, lot in life and a few words of tired wisdom stamped on it in indelible ink.

Back when I was green and growing and busy sorting myself out from the rest of the world, old people — people my age now, that is, or even 10 or 15 years younger — seemed closer in nature to the furniture than they did to us children. They were set pieces, carved out of life. You could climb on them.

But now from the soft inside of my middle age, I gape at the truth. You don't get a new ID card! Old people are just as pulpy at the core, just as volatile and uncertain about the future, as young ones are. They still believe in the Fountain of Youth.

The very fact that I have exceeded youth, broken loose from it, fooled the authorities, stumbled and fallen into my 50s the way Alice fell into the rabbit hole, guarantees that my birthdays these days will come wrapped in disbelief and wry amazement.

Apparently no matter what happens to us on the outside — to the eyes, the knees, the bladder, the back muscles or even the bank account — the core of our childhood identity stays intact, yielding as little to arithmetic as possible. The "me" I am today is essentially the me I was when I fell off my bike at age 8 or fell in love with Lorraine, my Sunday School teacher's daughter, at 10. These events aren't simply memories — fading old photos in the mind — but rather the soft tissue of my being, the passionate slush I still swim in.

But I keep these embarrassing thoughts to myself, here at the Japanese restaurant I've picked to celebrate "my" day. The new number I've been assigned this day has a crust even tougher than the last one. The psyche has to chew on it for a while, with small, wary bites. Chopsticks help.

Fortunately, the staff doesn't do loud birthdays here, but at one point our waiter pushes a cupcake in front of me, with a single, glowing candle stuck in the center. Blowing it out will not be a big challenge, yet everyone crowds around to watch. My inner circle, I think. I am at the protected center.

I make a wish and think about my inner age. How slowly it changes. And it's not the change of a ticking clock, winding down toward zero. If anything, the change — a.k.a., the aging process — makes me feel more alive, not less. That's the real surprise.

*October 1999*

## THE IDEALISM GAP

As I traverse the Yellow Brick Road of self-improvement — re-energizing my life with good diet, exercise, regular flossing — I find myself coming ever closer to the wizard himself. Whoops, the curtain drops, there's the little faker … oh, the shock of self-recognition!

If you try to change your life, sooner or later you must confront the idealism gap, the phenomenon of being unable to do what's best for you. It's not enough, turns out, to have your courage certificate and brand new, factory-wrapped heart in hand. You need to get inside yourself in all your manipulative ordinariness; you need to get your ideals in there with all the bad habits.

I'm figuring out what this means in my present circumstances. Consider, for example, the following good idea: I pack myself a nutritious lunch that includes fruit, veggies and a sandwich on whole grain bread, but then I eat at my desk and work or read straight through, barely noticing what I'm eating beyond the slow, distant "full" sensation registering in the stomach. Two hours later I'm famished again, as though I hadn't eaten at all.

The good idea is to do nothing but eat when I eat, visualizing my improving health and strengthening immune system. Doing so has virtually eliminated my desperate 3 p.m. craving for junk food (what a colleague once called "arsenic hour").

But in my second week of mealtime virtue, my resolve has flagged and the lure of the printed word has again become irresistible; my eyes spring to any and all printed matter, on page, screen or, if necessary, my Rolodex. Indeed, I try to fill every stray moment of my life with words, in my insatiable quest not for knowledge but distraction.

Brain and stomach, those poor, dumb organs, have formed an alliance against my best intentions. But change demands that I stand firm against distraction. So what happens when I jerk the emergency chain and grind my life — this fidgeting, ingesting, perusing, grasping, cogitating perpetual motion machine — to a halt? The startled face that spins around ... it's YOU, I cry. Who'd have thought?

It's the one I've been fleeing since childhood, sniveler, nose picker. He fills the cracks and crevices of my life, he's the mortar of stress and petty suffering who links together my memorable moments, he's the skulking continuity between theories.

I am slowly coming to understand that this is who I am. I am not the me of my triumphs, applauded and magnanimous. If I were, change would be no problem. Rather, I am the me who hides in the shadows and sucks on cherry lifesavers. I am the me of bad hair days, the me who cannot look anyone in the eye, the me who ruins parties just by showing up, the me at my worst, the frantic faker in the wizard outfit, the weakest link.

I am the me who will be, finally, the last one to abandon ship. I am the me who suffers, the me who is mortal, the me who will die.

"Only that day dawns to which we are awake," Thoreau says. So wake up, creature of the interstices! My plan for spanning the idealism gap is to celebrate every aspect of life, including lapse and failure and the sunlight-deprived soul who produces them.

I celebrate back pain, that dead mouse upstairs, my sheer awkwardness around strangers, the clot of dammed anger over a reprimand, the way I have to squint on a bright day, ironic loss, disappointment, the appalling ingredients in the ersatz M&Ms I just pigged out on (titanium oxide, carnauba wax), carpet stains, gum on the new couch ...

We'll get back to Kansas yet!

*April 2000*

## THE BIG EMPTY

I report the following not to relish a bleak moment in a friend's life, but to put a stake in the ground at one of the far boundaries of being human, and being 50. Anything is endurable as long as you know it will pass.

If I ever thought aging was no more than the slow accumulation of power, prestige, money and, above all, emotional invulnerability — and I did, I confess, in that casually thoughtless way of the young — I'm learning the hard way it ain't so. If anything, the disappointments get bigger as we age; the ice floes that break off from the heart are the size of small countries.

Tragedies accrue in every life, physical entropy traps us, circumstances change, our children grow up and leave home, the world leaves us behind. You think you have faced these things. Then an incidental setback, something you ought to be able to shrug off, or some benign event — a sunset, say, an organ chord, a graduation ceremony — slams you with the full emotional force of what you thought you had philosophically accepted.

"For all the history of grief," wrote Archibald MacLeish, "an empty doorway and a maple leaf ..."

My friend Malcolm just calls it the Big Empty. It can swallow your life whole. Several years ago, he said, shortly after his son Silas had moved to California with his new wife, Malcolm drove up to his piece of land in northern Alabama, near Bankhead National Forest. He needed to lick his wounds. He had no idea when he'd see his son again.

But the trip flung him into a thicket of memories: The land is remote and undeveloped except for a tiny cabin, which Silas and Malcolm had built together. He and his wife had bought the property in the mid-'70s, when their dreams were different. The marriage fell apart some years later. On this day, thoughts of his son, his ex-wife, of loss and divorce, assailed him. He built a campfire and sat staring into the sunset; the sun was setting in the west, and his son had moved West. His spirits plunged.

At one point, in a deep hour of the night, he awoke and looked up at the sky. He could see the full moon through the leafless trees — unbelievably beautiful, but so cold and remote it cut his heart out. "I tried to stay with the feeling, but I couldn't," he said. His sadness was uncontainable. At 2 or 3 a.m. he packed up and left. That was the Big Empty.

But that, of course, isn't all there is to life. Indeed, as soon as Malcolm was in his car and heading home, he started feeling better.

He had another story to tell me that night, of what he calls the Big Full. It was a simple moment, amounting to no more than walking out to his mailbox in a rainstorm not long ago. There was no wind, the pine trees were still, but a warm rain was pouring down and for no particular reason he was filled with a sense of infinite possibility. He had remarried at that point; things were going well, but the moment was more than simple contentment. It was as though a door had opened: Life was beautiful beyond all measure.

And these are the two images I hold against my heart as I wade into my own unknown. The Big Empty and the Big Full. This is life ... sheerly, life. And sometimes the Big Empty is enormous, but it passes, oh Lord, it passes.

*July 2000*

## FLAWED HOSPITALITY

It took a cold shower to wake me up to what I'd been missing — for so long now, I'd nearly forgotten it existed. Flawed hospitality, you might call it, though the hospitality itself wasn't flawed, it was warm as could be. The edges were just a little rough.

But that's the whole point.

When the lukewarm spray fell off to a trickle, then a drip — a cold drip — my God, I realized, I'm someplace real! I knew that already, of course. The Walleye Lodge, a mile west of Bergland in Michigan's Upper Peninsula, with its hodgepodge furnishings, battered, rec-room wall paneling and ubiquitous Chesapeake Bay retriever "co-host" Drake, was no Best Western or Courtyard Marriott.

To my knowledge, none of those places are run by a couple named Smitty and D. who, every evening, ask you how your day went, or recommend driving up a stretch of Old Highway 28 at dusk ("turn left just past the Tail Feathers Lounge") if you want to see dozens of deer, or let you use their gas grill to make dinner, or light a campfire with a blowtorch in the pit by the picnic tables overlooking Lake Gogebic, if you happen to be sitting out there on a nice night, and provide you with the makings of s'mores.

As we settled into this place for a three-day stay in the Porcupine Mountains region, we all kept remarking how "relaxed' we were feeling, but it wasn't until the hot water heater gave up the ghost one mid-afternoon, after a bunch of us (including several shower-hogging teen-agers) got back from a swim off the dock, that I realized why. "Convenience" is overrated — it isn't the end-all and be-all of a traveler's needs. I didn't care that I had to wash the lake sand off my body beneath a cold trickle, because the Walleye Lodge had something more important going for it: It was a good fit for human beings.

But the cold shower alerted me to the extent of my own passive acceptance of, and ultimate seduction by, a trend I once spent a large part of my life deploring: the homogenization of America.

For a while it disturbed me deeply to see that some town had picked up and moved, lock, stock and Wal-Mart, out to the Interstate, and that I was witnessing the slow erosion of character and distinctness from the American landscape. But I've gotten used to it, it seems. Now when I travel, I expect a superhighway to get me practically door to door, because I need to get there fast, and I accept the fact that the same convenience stores and fast-food joints sprout at every cloverleaf — and that "the open road" inspires yawns and anomie these days, rather than excitement.

Indeed, how else explain the preposterous popularity of SUVs? Corporate America, now that it has managed to franchise and homogenize the on-road driving experience, has begun selling us $30,000 antidotes for our neutered sense of adventure. Today you have to go OFF THE ROAD to find experiences that don't feel precast and ersatz, as though you're not really living unless you're gunning your gas-guzzler through the Painted Desert or the back woods of Maine.

Recently, for instance, I've noticed a flurry of billboards for Dodge Ram pickup trucks that come at you not just with idealized photography — a sleek, powerful, spotless vehicle tearing up the helpless landscape — but also the smirking catchphrase "Battitude."

I'll wager the "Battitude" being sanctioned here is the type that goes crunch, crunch over tiny life forms in the outback, not the type that, say, tries to disrupt World Trade Organization conferences.

I recommend a cold shower before you plunk down your cash.

*September 2000*

## SPIDER SNIFFING

I'm not always a happy camper; sometimes I'm a petulant one. I was the one who didn't want to go to the sundown lecture at the amphitheater. "Bring your flashlights," the ranger had said, her Missouri drawl lit up with too much pep. The topic: "Spider sniffing"

Spider what? And who cares?

Sensitivity to nature has been a slow process for me, wrested, creature by creature, from the self-centered distractions of my life. In theory, I'm pro-nature all the way, but in practice I connect far more easily with words and ideas than flora and fauna. "I believe a leaf of grass is no less than the journey-work of the stars," writes Walt Whitman, and my heart stirs — yes! yes! But without a poet's intervention, I feel hopelessly dull; when it's just me and the grass, all I see is something to walk across, mow or ignore.

We were camping at Missouri's Johnson's Shut-ins State Park — breathtaking slice of the eastern Ozarks, where the Black River is suddenly compressed by converging granite walls into a series of miniature cascades. "Best swimming hole in North America," it's been called, and I don't dispute this. It's one of my favorite places on the planet.

I was there for the swimming, however, not the spiders. Left to my own devices, I would have bypassed the program, but the rest of my family wanted to go. I tagged along, and ever after have been thanking the gods of serendipity that I did. Ranger Jep drew us into the secret lives of spiders, quickly convincing us we could hardly do better on a hot summer night than to behold one or two or a dozen of them waiting silently in webs strung delicately across flimsy twigs.

Try actually seeking out something you regard as commonplace — all of a sudden it's a precious wonder. This was the principle Jep invoked as she got us, kids and grown-ups alike, out in the brush, pointing our flashlights into the darkness, looking for spider webs. "Their eyes blink back at you," she explained. "You can spot 'em 50 feet away."

Suddenly I came upon a perfect round web, maybe four inches in diameter, with the tiniest of white specks in the center. "That's an orb weaver," Jep said when I excitedly called her over.

All of us went gaga for the next half hour, shining our lights into the bushes and branches behind the rustic amphitheater, turning up round webs, webs in progress, tube-shaped webs, occupied by wolf spiders and little green crab spiders — magnificent multi-eyed creatures, bejeweled pieces of the night, blinking unperturbedly back at us.

(And spiders have no scent; the term "spider sniffing" was just a bit of naturalist humor to lure us to the lecture.)

The next day, still softened by my arachnid awakening to the subtle totality of what lay around me, I noticed a sign posted at the edge of our campsite: "Beyond this point is a sensitive wetland known as a fen. Walking through the fen to collect firewood or plants will destroy it. The wood in the fen is usually wet or green and burns poorly; firewood is available at the woodlot during posted hours. It is up to you to protect this fragile area."

I thought about the vulnerability of spider webs, and how thoughtlessly and peevishly I will swat them out of my way, and felt my impatience rupture. In rushed the journey-work of the stars, the sheer unadorned thereness of nature. Beyond the flash-pop of "oh, how lovely" lies a state called empathy, a connection with the interior existence of another being, or an ecosystem or with nature itself.

"It is up to you to protect this fragile area" — the imperative seemed to apply, all of a sudden, to so many things in my life.

*February 2001*

## ALL THE TIME IN THE WORLD

Six months into my wife's cancer diagnosis, when our psychological and spiritual realignment was well underway, I watched a dumb thriller on the tube called *Outbreak*.

So much became clear to me.

My operative attitude about death, I realized in a flash of blinding insight, is more a product of the movies than any wisdom of religion or philosophy. I've watched thousands of movie deaths in my life, and most of them — as was the case with the movie I was presently staring at — were the dramatic equivalent of switching on the garbage disposal. Slurrrp! Hasta la vista, baby!

No wonder we're so scared of death. No wonder we gawk at it on the silver screen like voyeurs, expelling it from our own lives as we watch it happen, grotesquely and painfully, to others. The sort of death we're fed in huge servings of pop culture has a clear, simple meaning: You lose.

I've met few people who don't harbor this attitude: death as unthinkable, the ultimate Suckers' Walk. Sometimes it seems to me the point of everything we do is to avoid reminding ourselves we're going to die. I'd like to suggest that this is not the most sensible way to be. I'm not speaking theoretically, or even profoundly. I'm talking about how you can change your life on a Saturday morning as you pick up a tube of cocoa butter for your daughter at Walgreen's.

Writer and scholar Stephen Batchelor offers a meditation in his book *Buddhism Without Beliefs* that put my trek to the drugstore in perspective: "Since death alone is certain," he writes, "and the time of death is uncertain ... what should I do?"

If you really let these words penetrate, they have the power to leverage your life out of its inertia. As I set off on my errand on a gorgeous spring morning, I may have thought, oh, taking a walk is a perfectly sufficient way to affirm life. But as the words sunk in, a deeper awareness worked its way loose. I had an unsettled account at this very store, I realized.

This was not what I wanted to think about; it was a fly in the ointment. I did not want to be remembering that a month ago I had unleashed a temper tantrum at a pharmacist there when my insurance card mysteriously refused to cover a prescription. He was just the guy caught in the middle, apologetically explaining, uh, there seems to be a problem. But in my petulance and confusion, I saw only a single bureaucratic conspiracy against me, and I let him have it.

Later I got the matter straightened out — the insurer had dished drug coverage to a separate carrier, so I needed another piece of plastic. It was no big deal. I was able to pick up my prescription at reduced rate the next day and, yeah, I felt a passing wave of sheepishness about the outburst. But I managed to get on with my life (resolving to be nicer to strangers in functionary positions).

Now, suddenly, a moment I thought was behind me opened afresh. I felt acutely ashamed of myself and, worse, aware the wrong could be righted. The last four words of Batchelor's meditation — "what should I do?" — reverberated like a drum. I had to apologize to the pharmacist directly.

I almost convinced myself it would be better to wait until next week, or any time that wasn't now, but the urgency was too compelling. I sought him out and said my say. He didn't remember the incident, or me, but he nodded as I talked — this kind of thing happens all the time. He thanked me; he was smiling as I left. It took two minutes.

And I felt as though I had walked across a reality bridge. This is how we'll survive, by stepping across that bridge and connecting with fellow souls. I wouldn't have done so if life had mattered less, or if I'd had all the time in the world. Once you've wrested death from popular culture, its inevitability can nourish you.

*July 2001*

## 20,000 DAYS

End of the workday — the day itself is tired, a lost cause. Just go home and have a drink. Make it a double.

I don't drink, but that's how I felt. Actually, what I use to numb my brain is computer solitaire, and I foresaw an evening given over to it. Filler time in the great gray same old, same old. Joie de vivre? What's that? I was as locked into my routine as my commuter train was locked onto its tracks. Metal on metal: the grind.

Then I read: "In life, you're reborn every moment."

The book on my lap was *Awakening the Buddha Within,* by Lama Surya Das — part of my regular spiritual transfusion therapy, my ongoing quest for interesting ideas to yank out of context, to steal and reapply to the circumstances of my own life. This statement, however, seemed as outrageous as a shaft of sunlight in a shut-in's shade-drawn room. As the train pulled into my station, I couldn't have felt less capable of — give me a break — rebirth.

Nevertheless, the words pierced me; they had the urgency of an alarm clock. Here was Surya Das, proffering this very day to me — what was left of it — as a blank slate, to be lived or not. It was my choice alone. A cynical impatience gave me a surge of adrenaline. OK, wise guy, you're on. I'll walk home by a different route. Let's see what good that does.

I stepped outside, reluctantly conceding, well, it is a nice day, one of Chicago's bursts of premature spring. I turned east, toward the lake, bemused at my irrationality; I live in the opposite direction.

But one step in the wrong direction was all it took.

I looked around at grubby Morse Avenue. Nothing about it was different, except that I was awake to it. The day's grip was broken. I was released from my routine and my blinders were off: Everything my eyes took in had an illicit allure. This is not what I was supposed to be seeing today.

Oh, here's that ugly little strip mall and the Yang-Tze River Restaurant, next door to the laundromat. Son of a gun, the place is still open; I haven't been there in 18 years. I peered through the gap in the curtains — what an odd thrill. This is where I told Barbara I loved her so much I'd get rid of my cats to be with her — a desperate communiqué. She had a terrible cat allergy; I was on the brink of losing her after a single date.

I moved on, my heart aglow with the unexpected memory of making a lifelong commitment to my future wife. It really is a nice day, y'know? I decided to stop at Panini-Panini, a storefront coffeehouse, and buy a sweet roll for my daughter, the teen-ager. This'll surprise her. Then I turned west on Pratt, a street of lovely graystones. A man emerged from one of them, trailed by a shaggy creature the size of a pony.

"I've never seen such a big dog," I gushed, breaking the code of neighborhood anonymity. "He's an Irish wolfhound," the man said. "Go ahead, pet him. He's gentle. His name's Clancy." I stood eyeball to eyeball with this Dr. Seuss cartoon and patted its head. Who was I, Sam I Am?

By the time I got home, I felt I had absorbed spring itself; it was in my step. I bounced up to my daughter's room and handed her the almond roll. "Gee, Dad, thanks!" she bubbled, delight overmastering her sullen veneer.

Later that night I indulged an odd curiosity and calculated I've been alive for almost 20,000 days. Pondering the awe that number inspired, I realized each one has been splashed with the same vivid colors, filled with the same possibility, the same magic, I drank in as a newborn. Let me not let another one go to waste!

*March 2001*

## STRANGER ON A PLANE

Witness the phenomenon of two middle-aged men warily emerging from their protective crusts to look at, listen to and wonder about each other — as they rubbed elbows, literally and awkwardly, on a long flight in coach class. At seven miles up, the ground beneath our feet is shifting.

I'm still glowing from the conversation we had, and puzzling over how easy it turned out to be to move my life from the realm of the perfunctory to the realm of the serendipitous. All it took was a word, and a total inner transformation.

When we travel, the skin of anonymity that separates us from all those strangers sharing our space is surprisingly thin. It used to make me nervous; I've always been a great one for pulling up the drawbridge, as though I had something to lose by being "found out."

Shyness is an implosion of intelligence I'm finally beginning to understand. Those of us who are beset by it have more people-perception than we know what to do with — we can grasp the insecurity behind most chatter — but we have no context for it. Human beings are so much more than their pressed shirts and public faces; they're emotionally ragged and uncertain; they ache with love and disappointment, and are as interesting as uncharted continents. This is what we shy sorts understand. But it simply makes us embarrassed.

I no longer think this is a personal failing. Our only hope is to transform society itself, to open up the niggling context in which we put one another. I don't think there's any other way.

A Sanskrit word, "namaste" — say it with me: NA-mas-TAY — has helped me put the matter in perspective. It means: The god in me bows to the god in you. It's traditionally said with the palms pressed together at the chest, accompanied by a prayerful bow toward the other person, but what matters here is the internalization of the concept. The only context that's going to do justice to that random stranger next to you, impenetrably occupying space, a humanoid life form, is full-barrel "I-thou" respect.

I am psychologically incapable of entering into small talk with a stranger — initiating the possibility that we might get to know each other — with less at stake. That is, if my sense of awe about the god in either of us is wobbly, I'd rather stay anonymous.

But on a recent flight to Connecticut, I decided to give a figurative bow to my seatmate. "Finally," I said as I squeezed past him, acknowledging the two hours of fog delay before boarding began. That turned out to be sufficient to break the crust, and slowly, over the next hour or so, we nudged forward, amid ironic commentary on the airline industry, a few small personal revelations: occupation, place of residence, reason for being on this flight.

Turned out he was an aircraft engineer, not the sort of profession well-represented in my circle of acquaintances. And I had the impression "writer" was an exotic breed in his world. Still, we fell into a slow, wry camaraderie, occasionally exchanging commentary on some aspect of the flight. The conversation was, by mutual consent, intermittent.

However, when I pulled a book from my briefcase and began reading, he asked, "Have you written any books?" And suddenly I couldn't stop talking, as though his question undid the knot that held all the threads of my life together. In a gush of honesty, I moved from my unfinished novel to my wife's cancer to the ache of being a single father. He listened in attentive silence, then gave me a nod of understanding.

Then he talked about his own family, expressing bemusement that his kids were grown and leading lives of their own: His younger boy is a Marine rifle instructor, an acknowledged top marksman, he said. Although I'm a pacifist, I couldn't have felt a stronger solidarity with his fatherly pride.

Namaste.

*May 2001*


## ENLIGHTENED HARM REDUCTION

Ever wonder what sex, drugs and pigeons have in common?

They're all capable, I've noticed, of inspiring intense aversion, although, in the case of pigeons, national policy is seldom the result. But surgeon general David Satcher's recent call for a "thoughtful and respectful" national dialogue about sexuality got a response that reminded me of the look people get when they say, "They're just rats with wings."

Pigeons are a nuisance, so what we do is curse them. It's the American way, just as it's the American way to want to punish, criminalize and squeeze the daylights out of everything we disapprove of. I may have howled when my allegiance was with the activity under society's assault, but I don't think I fundamentally questioned the response itself — hold what you dislike forever in the crosshairs of your disdain — until I took a horse-and-buggy ride around Quebec City a few years ago, and saw how Canadians treated pigeons. It was a lot like how the Dutch handle Ecstasy users.

The term is "enlightened harm reduction," a concept not completely foreign to these shores, but controversial, grudgingly permitted at best, and only under dire circumstances. We have needle exchange programs and free condom distribution because the alternative is the unchecked spread of AIDS, but you get the feeling such efforts sorely test the limits of our national patience. We'd much rather solve a problem by blowing it to smithereens. Our triggers are set at birth. Aren't everyone's?

But as my family and I clopped through a Quebec City park, our coachman pointed to a whole different attitude toward problem-solving. That huge cement birdhouse over there, he explained, was put up specially for our least-loved feathered friends: pigeons. With it, the city could influence their roosting habits, even turn them into a sort of scenic resource (and keep the population under wraps with birth-control-laced birdseed). A "Shoo! Scat!"

mentality would have left the "pigeon problem" untouched. What elegant sanity.

When the problem is slightly bigger than pigeon droppings under viaducts — recreational drug use, let's say — our instinct is to organize an armed response. In Holland, however, authorities have responded to the rise in popularity of the dangerous party drug Ecstasy not with counter-hostility and "zero tolerance," but humane concern.

Rather than trying to put rave clubs out of business, for instance, the government has begun working with them to ensure safe conditions — good ventilation, plenty of drinking water — for Ecstasy users, according to the Drug Reform Coordination Network newsletter, quoting an article in the Washington Post. Users can even have their pills analyzed at drug treatment centers, eliminating the possibility of lethal overdose.

By refusing to make its own youth the enemy, the Dutch have a far better handle on Ecstasy use than we do. We prefer to allow the problem to fester in the shadows, where we are powerless to deal with it. We even, no doubt, fuel it by giving it the lure of the forbidden.

And this, of course, is our traditional stand on S-E-X. The thought of young people doing it so unnerves us, the best we can do is forbid it — about as effective a prophylactic as none at all. Abstinence is a good idea, but "abstinence only" is a rigid moral position that ignores the utterly human impulse to experiment and test limits. It betokens averted eyes and a squeamishness about our own nature.

We couldn't even tolerate an earlier surgeon general, Jocelyn Elders, using the M-word: masturbation. Bill Clinton panicked at the outrage that surged over her recommendation of this alternative to sexual intercourse and fired her. This is how close we are to a national dialogue on sexuality.

*August 2001*

## FACE IN THE MIRROR

The weirdest thing I've been doing lately is smiling at myself in the mirror. At first, hello? Who are YOU? It was unsettling, seeing that all-too-familiar mug break into a tentative grin in the bathroom, gold crowns twinkling at the corners. I felt as though some basic condition of my life had altered.

Kind of like if one day your dog starts talking to you. "Hello, Bob. I hope you're having a good day!"

Huh? Except, of course, it was me initiating that mirror-smile, rippling the subjective waters, forcing me to notice myself. A smile? Come on! Who you tryin' to kid?

If this isn't part of your daily routine, I suggest you try it just to see how strange it is — to flash, as best you can, a sloppy old "I like you" grin at yourself. And do it without irony, even though the person you're aiming at is the one who knows every last, petty secret about you and isn't going to be fooled by an insincere gesture. Self-love is as brave and illusion-free as love gets.

My sense is that it's in shorter supply than every other variety, but it's the font of all hope. I'm thinking now about cancer and other personal disasters. A friend recently divulged to me, in distress, on the eve of an operation, that she'd never been a positive thinker, but now she needed to be. Maybe it all begins with how you look at yourself in the mirror.

Somewhere along the line, I settled on a basic relationship with my face. I scrutinize teeth and gums when I'm wielding a toothbrush and carefully assess the expanse of stubbled flesh from cheeks to Adam's apple each morning when I shave. The rest of the time, what does it matter, beyond the occasional quick glance during the day to make sure nothing's amiss (cowlick, nostril hair) and I'm presentable to the human race?

In other words, I look at my surface features without much latitude or wonder, indeed, look not at but through myself, to my aches and fears and ultimate mortality. I look critically and darkly, not at who I am but whether I'm adequate.

We look at our mates and our children this way, too, after so many years, but at least they have the advantage of independent volition; they're capable of surprising us. But myself? How can I surprise ol' No. 1? (I can always disappoint myself, but that's different.)

What happened was, I took personal meditation training from the mother of one of my daughter's friends, a Vietnamese-American M.D. whose lifework is planted in the traditions of both East and West. She was the one who took it upon herself to throw my little habit-universe out of balance, assigning me after my first session with her not just what I was expecting — sit still with legs crossed, empty the mind, feel the "qi" — but this: "Before you go to bed at night, look in the mirror and give yourself a smile."

When I heard her say "smile" I thought "grimace" — as though life were so difficult and pain-fraught that intentional, pre-emptive smiling was the equivalent of ripping a bandage off my face. But it's just a darn smile: lift the lips, coax the laugh lines up the cheeks, let the eyes twinkle. Why should that be so hard?

So that's what I've been doing, smiling through the grimace: cracking its crust, pumping up light and letting it illuminate, for a second or two, that familiar yet aging mug. Who are YOU? Funny, when I don't quite recognize the face in the mirror, I see it so much more clearly.

At stake is a lifelong allegiance to pessimism. I'm starting to make it nervous.

*July 2002*

## ARMIES OF COMPASSION

Oh Lord, the "armies of compassion" are coming. Where do we hide?

It's George W.'s metaphor for the good that faith-based funding is going to unleash — bankrolling the soul-savers to administer God along with the methadone. I suck in my breath. This issue cuts no matter which way you turn. Faith-based funding is naïve and maybe just plain wrong, but for all that, intriguing, tempting. The idea illuminates a social contradiction that has to be faced sooner or later. Maybe the time is now.

Simply put, religion brings out the best and worst in us. It's an essential part of being human and a slippery slope to intolerance; it inspires compassion and it inspires zealotry; it saves some lives and destroys others. We separate church and state for a good reason: Too many gods claim omnipotence; this is the only way to make them behave.

Some years ago a woman named Julia Brown Wolf, a Lakota Sioux, succinctly captured the contradiction for me, as she talked about the core problem faced by Native Americans. "My grandparents were wrenched away from their parents," she said. They were sent off to boarding schools and "assimilated" — which meant they were culturally and spiritually bleached, separated from their heritage. "They became boarding school Indians," suffering the consequences of loss of identity, such as high rates of alcoholism and suicide.

As a young adult, after her own traumatic experiences at a Catholic boarding school, Julia worked as a paramedic on her reservation. There she felt herself open up to the influence of her father's wisdom — though he had died when she was 12 — and came to understand disease as something that "happens to the mind, body and spirit." True healing, she realized, could not take place outside the context of traditional spirituality.

Native Americans aren't the only ones who might be culturally and spiritually severed from themselves. Many, many of us are. The result of this is addiction, violence, despair, emotional breakdown — self-hatred, a lost soul. The cure for such a profound malady will likely not be found within federal social-service guidelines. It may well require surrender to religious belief.

If Faith X can transform an alcoholic's life, stay a wife-beater's hand or open a gang-banger's eyes to human connectedness — good results that society has an interest in promoting — why not give this worthy organization federal money so it doesn't have to operate out of a tacky storefront? Imagine how many more lives could be transformed with high-speed Internet access and new carpeting.

But the moment this seems like an incorruptibly good idea, think about the generations of boarding school Indians Julia spoke of, who weren't "saved" by religion but traumatized by it, probably with the assistance of faith-based funding.

How many religions know how to respect limits and refrain from trespassing where they aren't wanted? The metaphor alone — "armies of compassion" — is reason to be wary of the president's initiative. Armies conquer territory and impose their will on public life, usually reducing it to a single dimension.

In a free society, public life is the fragile confluence of competing forces. It's the antechamber of possibility. I cherish it and put more faith in it than I do in religions generally, but I would not want a world without religion. Every private world opens onto the public one, and some of its light spills out, enriching and contributing to that world that belongs to all of us.

In spite of my objections, I welcome the questions that faith-based funding raises. Without a spiritual chord vibrating in our lives, culture goes no deeper than sitcoms and shopping malls. Public initiatives that are spiritually sterile come in one color: institutional green. We need more than this when we're whole and healthy; God knows it's not enough when we're lost.

*March 2001*

## CITY OF GOD

When you pass through Harvey, Ill., a faded blue-collar suburb of 30,000 souls wedged anonymously into the vast rust-belt sprawl south of Chicago, the first words that come to mind probably are not: city of God.

More's the pity, according to the town's new mayor, who recently trespassed on what can only be called the sacred ground of constitutional secularity — the separation of church and state — by appointing chaplains to each of Harvey's six wards.

Big problem here, for sure. The human race only succeeded in wresting these entities apart two and a quarter centuries ago, to its limitless benefit. How much sanctimonious horror was visited in the name of the one true God, backed by the king's army, before America's Founding Fathers declared, "Congress shall make no law respecting an establishment of religion"?

What is it, then, that draws my sympathy to Mayor Eric J. Kellogg's idea for revitalizing his town of ghost factories and creeping urban blight?

It's hardly that I want, as a card-carrying secular humanist, to see a political leader "start appointing Christian ministers to his constituents" and telling them what to believe. Such was the objection raised by the director of Americans United for the Separation of Church and State, and others, to Chicago Tribune reporter Ron Grossman. They conjure up the yammer of tiresome, government-sanctioned proselytizing in the streets of Harvey.

Religion has its noxious side, no doubt about it. Holy certainty is a terrifying force, never more so than in today's world.

But even so, I see value in the mayor's daring trespass. "The major problem with contemporary society is that we've lost the spiritual dimension," he told Grossman, and it's true.

Or rather, the spiritual dimension — whatever that is — is forever inadequately a part of our lives, too little infusing our actions and intentions. We can live without it, but only, at best, in shallow, consumer-oriented prosperity, endlessly distracting and arming ourselves to stay ahead of the human condition.

And in towns like Harvey, abandoned by the industries that built it, shunned by corporate America (the only businesses you see there are fast-food joints and bars, except on the big, blow-through thoroughfares), there's not enough prosperity to mask the decay.

What good is separation of church and state if all it reaps is 11 murders, 42 rapes and 800-some car thefts? Those were Harvey's bleak crime stats for 2002.

Clearly the state, or public, side of American life is in desperate need of help. We have the freedom to worship as we want in private, but that's not enough, because worship — celebration of being — has a public aspect as well.

The thing is, we do worship in public, but in the wrong ways. We worship power and celebrity and creature comfort. We worship oil and fast food and sex appeal. We worship winning.

But if tragedy strikes, if the cash simply runs low, these values leave us nowhere.

I'm not interested in the propagation of religion for the sake of religion, for the sake of the betterment of New Shining Light Ministries or New Mount Olive Baptist Church or Outreach Church (which are among the 50 churches in Harvey). I'm not interested in religion per se, as it exists in its comfort zone, dispensing rules and ritual and collecting money.

But I am interested in the idea of men and women of courage humbly standing at the edge of their faith, using their faith as a force to help others and heal wounds. The civil rights movement, for instance, was faith-driven, and in primarily African-American Harvey, the mayor wants to awaken this great force and enlist its aid against the spiritual malignancies of crime and hopelessness. I say let it shine.

*June 2003*

## HOORAY FOR JUNK

Serious little 7-year-old with her hand full of change. I pick out two damp quarters amid the dimes and pennies, nod — "50 cents, thanks" — and watch her back away, holding her wondrous purchase.

Only when her mother, who has been hovering nearby, rummaging through a pile of blouses and blue jeans, also nods and confirms the legitimacy of the transaction is the girl certain the thing is really hers: a conch shell as big as her head, cream-white, slightly flaking but still harboring in its depths the roar of the ocean.

And then she smiles. Not at me, not at anybody. She just smiles. It's instantaneous, gosh, wow, filling her face, filling the whole front yard, and then she and Mom are on their way to wherever they were going and I think, well, that was sort of nice.

Yeah, the way alchemy is sort of nice. Base metal turns to gold. A piece of junk — a tchochke I had hated for years without even knowing it, as part of the dust-gathering malignancy of clutter that had slowly taken over my house — turns to an object of joy.

And there went my cynicism about yard sales.

Suddenly, as I sat on a folding chair behind the plastic picnic table, amid old board games and dress-up shoes and half-worn backpacks and tangles of naked Barbie dolls, I felt myself surge with enthusiasm for this humble enterprise beneath the hot July sun. I was just filling in for my teenage daughter, who had organized the event, while she and her friends went down the street for bubble tea. Now I wouldn't leave.

Every passerby, every car that slowed as it went past, reignited my enthusiasm. A lot of them stopped, way more than I'd expected (yeah, sure, who's gonna buy this garbage?). They stopped, they looked, they pulled out their billfolds.

They bought that heart-shaped serving platter and the sturdy old Hi-Flyer wagon that had served us well and miscellaneous plastic Berts, Ernies and Elmos and even the orphaned knights and bishops from an old Samoan chess set. A blind woman bought a toy badminton racket.

A woman from down the street bought my daughter's one-time diaper-changing table, a piece of varnished maple with six-inch curlicue railing on three sides and two shelves for supplies. For two years it had been the center of our lives, then it had disappeared into the corner of a once-functional back porch (our realtor had referred to it as "the Florida room"), buried under Hefty bags of old clothes.

Now, for $2, it belonged to my neighbor, a young woman who spoke almost no English — and who until that moment I had no idea was my neighbor. I carried it the half block to her apartment building (my daughter having returned by that point).

This is the thing. My own neighborhood is mostly hidden from me. I know it as half a dozen homeowners who wave to me as they mow their lawns. It's infinitely more than that, of course. It's "diverse." That's why I love it, I tell myself.

I live in it, walk through it, but usually the 'hood and I keep our respectful distance from one another — this teeming, socially complex, far-from-chic Chicago community known as Rogers Park, which I have called home for 25 years.

Now here it was, the whole neighborhood, a cornucopia of ethnicities — Mexicans and Pakistanis, Haitians, Russians and Laotians — milling in my front yard, examining the minutiae of what used to be my life, which was for sale in pieces, from 10 cents to 10 dollars.

Hooray for the humble yard sale, which cuts across all cultural and social strata. It's the bargain basement of democracy.

Hooray for junk, hooray for clutter, hooray for Little Mermaid backpacks and tacky end-table lamps. Somebody out there has a use for them. In a little girl's hands, the ocean roars again.

*July 2003*

## DANCE UPON THIS EARTH

Welcome to the village, J.D.

You saw it was slightly strange for him — 2-year-old Jackson Deric, my great nephew, this boy who is ripe as a peach with the spirit of discovery — to witness the edge of the known world open up suddenly. I watched him take Roger's hand and allow himself to be led up and down the aisles of smiling semi-strangers. Who are all these people? The PA system pumped out a song by the Grace family, "I'm gonna dance upon this earth, I'm gonna find joy in all this madness."

The room, or maybe it was just my heart, filled with purpose. I don't have much ceremony in my life, but now here I was, standing in the center of a profound ceremony indeed, a daisy pinned to my breast pocket, registering the fact that I had just taken on the role of Jackson's godfather — that is, lifelong guide, mainstay, spiritual mentor.

I would have wanted to do that anyway, I suppose, but something felt wondrously right about stating my intention publicly — and about being asked in the first place, by Carmen and Sean, the parents. Now I stood next to Aunt Angie, the new godmother, as the rest of the community, about a hundred members of the Fox Valley (Wisconsin) Unitarian Universalist Fellowship, opened their arms to the boy and pledged their protective benevolence to him, and the Grace family sang, "In a world so cold and full of sorrow, I'm going to find a way, I'm going to break the chain."

And for a few minutes this cynic believed anything was possible.

Yeah, it takes a village to raise a child, and all that. Of course it does, but I've spent so much of my life being disappointed by "the village," if not railing in fury and consternation at its far boundaries. I've positioned myself as critic and skeptic, patterning my life after, oh, poet Robinson Jeffers' muse, Cassandra, the truth-teller. The job keeps me hopping.

Just today, for instance, I found myself reading an account in the Chicago Tribune about how the food packets we dropped in Afghanistan, for the purpose of winning hearts and minds as we waged war, were the same color — bright yellow — as the cluster bombs we also dropped there. The result: a terrible number of child amputees. The kids set off high explosives when they thought they'd be filling their bellies.

They're our amputees, courtesy of American tax dollars. What do you get when you mix public relations with high-tech security and a little bit of revenge? Children who will no longer "dance upon this earth." This complicates things for me, as J.D.'s godfather.

My great nephew is a dancer; it's why his parents chose to play that song at his dedication. Put on the Wallace and Grommet video and watch him go. It's a miracle of unadulterated joy; his smile, a shaft of light that pokes you in the heart. To protect and nurture him is as natural as breathing, and in so doing you want to widen his protective circle to the far horizon.

But somewhere in this widening the concept passes beyond, it seems, human relevance. It turns into national defense. Homeland security, as we call it now, pledging allegiance to the illusion that a nation is just a big village. And the impulse to protect those we hold dear gets twisted beyond recognition. For American children to dance, a certain number of Afghani children must hobble on one leg.

No one puts it that way, of course, but the vast majority of Americans cheered the destruction of Afghanistan, and later, Iraq, in the name of national security, and that was one of the predictable consequences.

"In a world so cold and full of sorrow, I'm going to find a way, I'm going to break the chain." The chain is violence, and it guarantees our insecurity.

And so as the music plays and Jackson holds the minister's hand and the village opens up to him, as I swell with love and a certainty about what's right, I imagine for an instant a world worth creating. I imagine a world in which our values won't disappear on the way to becoming government.

*September 2003*

## THE HELPLESS GOD

I'm long out of the active diaper-changing business, which may account for the sheer reverence, unsullied by worry or responsibility, with which I found myself cradling my week-old great nephew this past Mother's Day and contemplating, well, God.

This is the privilege of great unclehood, perhaps. The ache of joy is an end in itself. Little more is asked of me than to love the baby, to bond with him, so maybe that's why my lap time with him, my walking-around-the-room-time, my shhhh time, my stick-out-my-tongue-and-scrunch-up-my-nose time, felt like prayer. I know of no altar that can focus the soul quite like a helpless newborn, especially when his eyes pop open.

I've held babies before, but there's no growing used to this. The tiny, curling fingers, the lively toes, the comically ancient face — life light as a feather. Shhhh. I invite you to join me at the altar of Joey — Joseph, son of Carmen and Sean, brother of 4-year-old Jackson — for a moment or two, while I figure out what it was that seemed so important to say as I held him.

It was definitely connected to the helplessness. Indeed, my awe at beholding him increased in direct proportion to my sense of that quality in all its ramifications. Joey lay swaddled in my forearms as pure potential. This was not an abstraction. I could tell that my every curious touch of his elbow, of the sole of his foot, of his tummy, my every brush of finger across cheek, was openly received and fully absorbed, as though he needed my touch as much as he needed breast milk. There were no defenses. There was only hunger, sustenance and growth.

This was our dynamic. I was actively nurturing him as I held him — feeding him love. This is the secret of moms. I had never understood motherhood before, not at that level. And this was plenty of realization for one Mother's Day, but seems to be no more than the starting point of what I want to say.

As I held Joey, I was still under the influence of an earlier conversation I'd had with my sister the psychologist (Joey's grandma). Sue and I have wide-ranging talks when we get together, which often enough begin with the current political situation and end up groping in the unexplored depths of the human condition.

At one point she told a story from her professional experience about a teenager who committed suicide. The girl had been psychotic (saw eyes in the walls) and had endured a long period of sexual abuse, which wrecked her life. It is a common horror story worse than any invention of art and to hear it told even in cursory detail is to feel the flooring of one's heart collapse beneath a great weight of outrage. Too many such stories and you'll be mainlining hopelessness. Why do these things happen?

So there I was with newborn Joey in my arms, delicately supporting his head, watching him breathe and stir lightly in his sleep. I was trembling at the altar of his helplessness, extraordinarily alert, making small, silent vows to myself to be careful, to be loving, to be good. The pure potential of his helplessness was in perfect equilibrium with my awe.

But as I held him I couldn't stop thinking about the abused, psychotic girl who began life as pure potential just as Joey has and all of us have: as malleable beings almost unlimited in what we can become but existentially naked, requiring everything of those who care for us. Only if they are selfless will we grow. This is what an infant demands, but we must give it freely. The choice is ours.

As I held this tiny boy, I wondered why I had that choice, to be careless or selfish instead of nurturing, able to do a harm whose consequences would be born by him, not by me. And this is when I thought about the nature of God — a term I do not use glibly. Indeed, I generally avoid all God language; this is the language that blesses the bomb and the buck. It's the cheapest language of all.

But still, this is what I thought, that there was a quality to Joey's helplessness that seemed more godlike than anything else I had ever encountered. What if, I thought, the nature of God were openness and helplessness? What if destructive power were a human quality, not God's? This changed everything, from the creation myths (man expelled God from the Garden of Eden) to the day's news and our relationship with our planet.

I understood this in a brief flash, as I held the planet's future in my arms.

*May 2005*

PART SEVEN

# COURAGE GROWS STRONG AT THE WOUND

## A WORLD ON BROWN-BROWN *Peace hero*

Here's one way to stop a war. Just stand in front of it. Make it move around you. Or over you. Don't budge.

It's called being a human shield and some of the most courageous people on the planet are leaving their lives to do this — bear witness to and interfere with the business of war, that many-headed hydra. They stand in front of it unarmed, of course.

And sometimes they die and their deaths, ironically, matter, or catch our attention, in a way that the many, many innocent, inevitable and mostly Third World deaths of our planet's various wars and occupations and "cleansings" can never quite begin to. Those corpses simply pile up, and the bigger the pile, the more wearisome the anonymity.

But when a young American lies dead in the dirt in Gaza, we are hungry to learn what her college major was, and that she played the flute.

This is what it means to be a human shield and to die as a human shield. You pull the TV cameras along with you; journalists interview your friends. Your smiling face graces newspapers. There's a fuss. A spokesman for the killer even calls your death "regrettable."

And for a moment the darkness lifts.

Rachel Corrie, who was 23 and hailed from Olympia, Wash., whom friends described as "soft as a petal" and who worried about world hunger when she was in elementary school, came to Palestine in February as a member of the International Solidarity Movement, a multinational coalition of witnesses to war. Five weeks later, on March 16, she was crushed beneath the blade of an armored Israeli bulldozer in the town of Rafah. She was trying to prevent it from razing the house of a Palestinian doctor, Samir Masri.

"She waved for the bulldozer to stop. She fell down and the bulldozer kept going. It had completely run over her and then it reversed and ran back over her," an eyewitness said. And the world got a glimpse of a small, ugly moment in the ongoing occupation of Palestine that would otherwise have passed unnoticed.

Meanwhile, "elsewhere in the Gaza Strip," accounts noted, "Israeli soldiers killed a Palestinian youth in Khan Yunis and a 43-year-old Palestinian in Rafah." Some dead, you see, have names and others don't.

This is the irony the human shield movement is exploiting: If you are an American or a European or a Canadian, your presence, by choice, in the middle of a war zone has cachet. And your death, so far from the good life, is virtually guaranteed to provoke spasms of media curiosity.

I can hardly add my paean to Corrie's brave humanity without becoming entangled in the sort of irony and hypocrisy — oh, now you notice — that Corrie herself would likely have found unbearable.

Back in the '60s, you may remember, there was an undercurrent of seething anguish in the civil rights movement about the phenomenon that white deaths provoked national outrage over conditions in places like Mississippi when ongoing black murders drew yawns of apathy.

With that in mind, I turn my thoughts beyond the young woman and her life to the world she looked at with a heart too unstintingly honest to remain complacent. She could just as well have been standing beneath the B-52s pummeling Baghdad (Iraqi death toll after days of aerial bombardment is not yet newsworthy) or before the machetes of Sierra Leone, or anywhere else the world's innocents are being chewed up by war. She chose to stand at the intersection of civilization and barbarism.

In Sierra Leone, that civil war-torn West African nation where both sides have specialized in employing child soldiers to do the dirty work, war frenzy is often drug-induced. A potent mixture of cocaine and gunpowder, known as "brown-brown," is administered to the children through a slash across their temples.

Brown-brown "ensures that children will be out of their minds" when they commit murder and torture, according to the website freethechildren.org. "Ingestion ... not only compels children to act impulsively, but in addition, dulls them from the reality of their actions."

Corrie, in her fluorescent orange jacket, stands before a world on brown-brown.

*March 2003*

## CLUSTER BOMB GIRL          *Courage/heroism for Peace*

How do you change the world?

On one side of the debate, we have B-52 bombers, Abrams tanks, Hellfire missiles, daisy cutters, cluster bombs, F-16 Fighting Falcons, A-10 Warthogs, Apache helicopters, depleted uranium, 130,000 troops, an indifference to civilian casualties and a budget of, oh, $6 billion a month. On the other side, we have — we had — Marla Ruzicka.

The fight goes out of me when I think of the death of this passionate young woman, founder of the Campaign for Innocent Victims in Conflict, who took it on herself — with stunning effectiveness — to humanize the "collateral damage" of war to the U.S. Congress and the general public, and to cushion the impact of our brutal occupation of Iraq with her own body.

Sen. Patrick Leahy called her a "whistleblower in foreign policy," someone who said, "Wait, everybody. Here is what is really happening. You'd better know about this." She was the driving force, he said after her death, behind the appropriation of some $20 million in aid to Afghanistan and Iraq that he secured.

No small accomplishment for a plucky 28-year-old from Northern California who was "so pretty, blond and lively she could be mistaken for a cheerleader," as Tai Moses of AlterNet wrote.

She and her associate, Faiz Ali Salim — CIVIC's director in Iraq and the father of a 2-month-old daughter — were killed on April 16 as they drove the dangerous highway from Baghdad to the airport. A suicide bomber, apparently attempting to strike at a U.S. convoy of security contractors on the highway, pulled alongside them and detonated his explosives, engulfing their car in flames. They were on their way to visit a child who had been injured by a bomb. This is what they did. It was their raison d'etre. It was what CIVIC was all about.

Oh Lord. Words come close to failing me. Here was someone with a sense of purpose so gutsy and selfless it makes the heart clutch. She personified a worldwide sense of horror at high-tech war, at "we don't do body counts," but she didn't shrink from it in despair; she put her body in the war zone, she cradled its victims.

"Thursday was a day of splendor and bliss." These are Marla's own words, from an online journal entry (see www.civicworldwide.org) posted on Oct. 28, 2003. "The magic of Hussein's smile and the dazzle in Bador's eyes allowed me to forget the problems of expenses, budgets, and the challenging difficulties that often present themselves when operating in post-war Iraq. . . .

"Bador's dream is to become a computer technician, but her burns are so severe that she has developed a skin cancer and is now incapable of moving her fingers. Her hand is shrinking and her condition deteriorates every day. Hussein has orthopedic complications and has great difficulty walking."

This was Marla's life, shining rays of hope into the lives of children like Hussein and Bador and countless others who had been shattered by a war they had nothing to do with. She was a loving and practical humanitarian. She was also a geopolitical visionary: "My long-term goal," she told an interviewer (quoted in a eulogy by her friend Peter Bergen), "is to get a desk at the State Department that looks at civilian casualties."

But you can't do that, Marla! You're missing the point. If we look at civilian casualties — if we count them, if we acknowledge them at all — the game is up. She was the national conscience the Bush administration, in its criminal cynicism, has bludgeoned quiet with fear-inducing lies.

My favorite story about her — and the story I find most compelling and personally challenging — is one mentioned by Tai Moses, citing an article the San Francisco Chronicle published about Marla a year and a half ago. In it, she explained that she was known affectionately by the Marines in Baghdad — she made friends with everyone — as "Cluster Bomb Girl," because she was always on their case to clear up mined areas the Iraqis told her about.

This was a serious woman. Friends and acquaintances described her as vivacious, fun-loving, life of the party, "angelic and sort of goofy," but at the core she was an utterly purposeful woman, who stood in the fray, who softened bullets, who protected the innocent, who demanded accountability.

London's The Independent wrote of the aftermath of the suicide bombing: "A U.S. Army medic who tried to help her said she was briefly conscious and was able to speak. 'I'm alive,' she had told him. She died along with an unnamed French national and an Iraqi."

Those were her last words: "I'm alive."

*April 2005*

## STALE GLORY

"I thought about what death is, what a loss is. A sharp pain that lessens with time, but can never quite heal over. A scar." — Maya Lin, speaking of her initial vision of the Vietnam Veterans Memorial Wall

The most frequently visited and heart-tearing monument in Washington D.C. is nearing its 25th birthday, its place at the core of American life growing stronger with each passing year. This fact belies the early critics, who called it communist- (or Jane Fonda)-inspired, a black gash of shame, a public urinal, and howled in outrage that it was designed by . . . well, an Asian-American woman (but of course the term many people used was left over from the war, and much uglier).

More importantly, however, the Wall, which was meant to heal a national wound, not glorify a military adventure, signaled — as the critics instinctively understood — a new public attitude toward war, or perhaps more accurately, a public manifestation, at long last, of an ancient yearning for peace.

What the critics (living in a two-dimensional, us-versus-them world) failed utterly to grasp, however — and which has special bearing today as Democrats and Republicans alike grope for policy coherence that extricates us from the Bush administration's disastrous war to promote terror — is that the Wall is non-ideological, or rather transcends ideology. It's simply two sunken triangular wedges of black granite and 58,195 names.

These names are not symbols. They're not abstractions. As Robert Frost famously observed, "Anything more than the truth would have seemed too weak." Accordingly, the names are not cheapened with any sentiment, any "glorification," whatsoever. The result is something extraordinary.

"But it is the wall (rather than a nearby sculpture of three soldiers) that vets approach as if it were a force field," Kurt Andersen wrote in Time magazine more than 20 years ago. "It is at the wall that families of the dead cry and leave flowers and mementos and messages, much as Jews leave notes for God in the cracks of Jerusalem's Western Wall. ... The visitors' processionals do seem to have a ritual, even liturgical quality. Going slowly down toward the vertex, looking at the names, they chat less and less, then fall silent where the names of the first men killed (July 1959) and the last (May 1975) appear. The talk begins again, softly, as they follow the path up out of the little valley of the shadow of death."

You can't stroll casually along these 500 feet of names, nor, it seems to me, can you even hold onto your prior thoughts. The chiseled names, line after line, column after column, panel after panel, seem to whisper themselves until, at the 10-foot-high juncture of the two wedges, the whispers are as deafening as thunder. This is sheer phenomenon, as non-ideological an experience as standing under a waterfall.

"It was while I was at the site that I designed it. I just sort of visualized it. It just popped into my head. Some people were playing Frisbee. It was a beautiful park. I didn't want to destroy a living park," Lin, who at the time was a 21-year-old architecture student at Yale, said in a Washington Post interview. ". . . I just imagined opening up the earth."

Her design was one of 1,421 submitted in the spring of 1981, in a blind competition, to a panel of architects and sculptors. She later said she's certain she wouldn't have won if her name had been attached to the design.

I guess not everything government-associated is a done deal. If it had been, the future could never have opened out of the earth behind the Capitol, and we'd be stuck with one more hollow monument to war, to be commandeered as needed to justify the next one.

George Bush, for instance, had no trouble hitting that tin note on the recent celebration of the first George W's birthday: "George Washington's long struggle for freedom has also inspired generations of Americans to stand for freedom in their own time," he informed us. "Today, we're fighting a new war to defend our liberty and our people and our way of life."

Yeah, sure. The voice drones on, the listener's soul deadens, the engines of war rev again. Stale glory requires fresh blood. But I'd be surprised if the next war were announced in the shadow of the Wall.

*February 2007*


## BIRTH OF AWARENESS

One of the heroes of My Lai died a few days ago, dislodging the old horrors and a fleeting national debate the world is begging us to reopen.

Are we the good guys? Is God on our side?

"We kept flying back and forth, reconning in front and in the rear, and it didn't take very long until we started noticing the large number of bodies everywhere. Everywhere we'd look, we'd see bodies. These were infants, 2-, 3-, 4-, 5-year-olds, women, very old men, no draft-age people whatsoever."

This story only gets worse. It took almost two years before a full-scale investigation got underway and the American public slowly became aware of what helicopter pilot Hugh Thompson happened upon on March 16, 1968: a wanton slaughter of Vietnamese civilians, being carried out by American troops.

"I think a count has been anywhere from two to four hundred, five hundred bodies. . . . I think that's a small count," Thompson, who died of cancer on Jan. 6, related during a My Lai symposium at Tulane University in 1994. He and his two-man crew stood in for the American conscience on that day.

"We saw another lady that was wounded. We got on the radio and called for some help and marked her with smoke. A few minutes later up walks a captain, steps up to her, nudges her with his foot, steps back and blows her away.

"We came across a ditch that had, I don't know, a lot of bodies in it, a lot of movement in it. I landed, asked a sergeant there if he could help them out, these wounded people down there. He said he'd help them out, help them out of their misery. . . . I thought he was joking. . . . We took off and broke away from them and my gunner said, 'My God, he's firing into the ditch.'"

Thompson landed his helicopter between the ground troops and nine Vietnamese civilians — four elderly adults and five children — who were fleeing to a shelter, preventing the officer in charge, Lt. William Calley, from "taking them out with a hand grenade." Thompson radioed a gunship, which eventually removed the civilians. Until it arrived, Thompson and his men kept the American troops at bay at gunpoint.

"A short while later we went back to the ditch. There was still some movement in there. We got out of the aircraft and (Glenn) Andreotta, my crew chief, walked down into the ditch. A few minutes later he came back up carrying a little kid. . . . He was covered with blood, and the thought was going through my mind and my crew's mind, 'How did these people get in that ditch?'

". . . Then something just sunk into me that these people were marched into that ditch and murdered. That was the only explanation that I could come up with."

Thompson's realization was, you might say, the birth of "Vietnam Syndrome" — the widespread public revulsion at U.S. militarism. My Lai was not some horrifying aberration from the basic myth of America's innocence and good intentions — the berserk actions of serial killers — but rather the logical consequence of the war itself, in which civilians were the enemy, or sort of the enemy.

"I was ordered to go in there and destroy the enemy," Calley later testified at his trial. "That was my job on that day. . . . I did not sit down and think in terms of men, women and children. They were all classified the same, and that was the classification that we dealt with, just as enemy soldiers."

Calley, the most prominent My Lai participant, was convicted and sentenced to life in prison, but he was freed by Richard Nixon after three years of house arrest.

The dirty little secret that came out in the congressional investigation — which would not have happened but for the persistence of another low-ranking hero, Ron Ridenhour, who learned of the massacre from some of the participants and eventually wrote a letter to 30 congressmen detailing what happened — is that apple-cheeked American boys are capable of unspeakable barbarism. As the desperate official denial and cover-up of My Lai attested, this was sometimes what was expected of them.

The news sparked a temporary breakthrough in public awareness about the real nature of modern warfare — a big problem for the military-industrial-media complex, which is calibrated to a war economy. Vietnam Syndrome has been in its crosshairs for three decades. The result is the war on terror, a public-relations success but a strategic and moral disaster that has increased worldwide terrorism and turned Uncle Sam into the world's most high-profile torturer.

The only way to salute Hugh Thompson's memory is to stand in his example of conscience and courage and to look with unblinking eyes at what we're doing right now, in Iraq, and say no, not again.

*January 2006*

## FLICKERING DREAMS OF PEACE

*[handwritten: update for this campaign season?]*

Ever try to shift a paradigm? I salute the brave souls scattered around the continent — some of them are in Congress — who are doing just that, who are daring, right now, to challenge the conventional wisdom of war and peace at the highest levels at which the game of geopolitics is played, and are calling for the establishment of a Cabinet-level Department of Peace.

When long-time correspondent Bill Bhaneja, a senior research fellow at the University of Ottawa and retired Canadian diplomat, recently e-mailed me the proposal he co-authored with Saul Arbess for such an addition to Canada's government — inspired by U.S. Rep. Dennis Kucinich's H.R. 808 — I confess to a queasy skepticism that such a project was just too darn idealistic.

Then I thought about bird flu — and George Bush's wild musings two months ago about combating it with National Guard troops, that is, by implementing martial law to enforce quarantines. This from the man who has "degraded" (in the words of one high-level health official) the nation's public health system and underfunded and politicized every branch of government created to deal with national emergencies.

And it hit me with a jolt: The level of public awareness is deteriorating. We're now whelping leaders who haven't got a clue how to deal with complex social issues except to start shooting at them. And there's no adequate challenge to this in the media or from the opposition party, and apparently no public context big enough even to allow for debate.

For instance, there was Hillary Clinton the other day telling potential supporters of her run for the presidency, who I'd wager are against the war by a large margin, that the United States must "finish what it started" in Iraq, as though there's a consensus what, exactly, we started and what "finishing" it would mean, and how many more dead Iraqis and U.S. servicemen we might expect before we attain our unarticulated goal.

It was sheer politician-speak, in other words, betraying no courageous intelligence, no insight that our brutal occupation might be fueling the insurgency and creating the terrorists we're obliged to keeping fighting. But the media have already pegged Hillary a frontrunner, which means they're condemning America's anti-war majority, once again, to a campaign season without a presidential candidate who represents their ardent hopes.

This is intolerable. This is why I support and heartily endorse what is, in fact, a global movement to raise awareness by challenging the blood-myths of the nation-state and the inevitability of war, and the geopolitical canard extraordinaire that high-tech, high-kill, earth-poisoning modern wars have any chance of achieving controllable ends and do not spew incalculable suffering and future wars in their wake.

"What we seek," write Bhaneja and Arbess, "is a world in which peaceful relations between states are a systematically pursued norm and that the numerous non-aggression pacts between states become treaties of mutual support and collaboration. We envision a world in which a positive peace prevails as projected most recently in the U.N. International Decade for a Culture of Peace (2001-2010) Programme of Action."

The establishment of a peace academy, the training of peace workers, the promotion of nonviolent conflict resolution at every level of human interaction — there's no reason why such projects should be nothing more than the flickering dreams of protestors at candlelight vigils. There's no reason why they should not be the business of government. I have no doubt whatsoever that the public is ready to move beyond the barbarism history has bequeathed us, and would do so in an eye blink if enough respected voices said, "Now is the time."

And respected voices are saying this, if only we could hear them.

"What is quite clear — and would become clear as you go along with this campaign — is that you are trying, and I consider myself with you on this in every way . . . (to create) not only a massive but a basic change in our culture, in our entire approach to our relationships with other human beings. . . . It's not a matter of simply getting another department of government. You're speaking of an entire philosophical revolution."

This is Walter Cronkite, in conversation with Kucinich last September at a Department of Peace conference in Washington, D.C. Kucinich, the hero of this movement, first introduced Department of Peace legislation in 2001. The bill now has some 60 sponsors in the House and, in September, was introduced in the Senate (S. 1756) by Mark Dayton of Minnesota.

The architects of the war on terror have minds stuck in old paradigms of domination and conquest. Their enemy is always the same: Evil Incarnate. Today's jihadist was yesterday's Communist, playing the same game of dominos.

This war is doomed to create nothing but losers, and more and more people — including many who are in or close to the military, such as Jack Murtha — are grasping this. As they wake up, the Department of Peace will be waiting for them.

*December 2005*

*UPDATE: Dennis Kucinich introduced Department of Peace legislation into the 111th Congress on Feb. 9, 2009. All references to the legislation will use the bill's current House number, H.R. 808.*

**THE PEACE MAJORITY**

Tony Blair told it like it was the other day — well, almost. What he did was demonstrate that the echo of truth often drowns out even its most shameless evasions.

"There's a deliberate strategy," he told David Frost, ". . . to create a situation in which the will of the majority for peace is displaced by the will of the minority for war."

Of course, he was talking about Iraq, where "al-Qaida with Sunni insurgents on one hand, Iranian-backed elements with Shia militias on the other," were strangling democracy in its cradle, turning a nice invasion ugly. He wasn't talking about Great Britain or the United States, where a cabal of liars and fanatics (including Blair himself, of course) fobbed off a high-tech war on a public that assented only because they believed it would be easy and cheap. But he could have been.

The Bush administration, despite its repudiation in the midterm elections, is now preparing to ask Congress for another $127 billion or so to feed that failed war. And they'll probably get it, even as the opposition tepidly debates timetables for withdrawal and agonizes over the fate of our "mission."

The acknowledged cost of the war is now pushing $600 billion, making it, according to USA Today, our most expensive conflict since World War II. And that figure, of course, doesn't reflect the war's true costs, such as lifetime care for brain-injured, psychologically shattered and immune-system-compromised vets. A year ago, economists Joseph Stiglitz and Linda Bilmes estimated that such hidden costs could push the price tag for Bush's folly up to $2 trillion.

And even that estimate doesn't look at costs from the Iraqi point of view. Not only has that country's infrastructure been destroyed and its economy wrecked, but its soil has been poisoned for generations by the toxic detritus of war, such as depleted uranium dust, which causes, among other health disasters, birth defects and cancer. We've unleashed a moral horror on Iraq, and ourselves, that benefits only the war profiteers. Yet we're stuck with it.

The problem, as I see it, is that we've been preparing for war for the past six thousand years or so. It's what humanity seems to know best — our default response to fear. The unlearned lesson of the 21st century is that we've gotten far too good at it. The structure of our society — government, industry, the media — can gear up for war at a moment's notice, on half a pretext, no matter how abhorrent the idea may be in the souls of ordinary men and women. "The will of the majority for peace is displaced by the will of the minority for war." History has bequeathed us a built-in suicide machine.

All of which brings me to last week's action by the Chicago City Council. My fair city recently joined communities large and small across the country — Detroit, Cleveland, Atlanta, Minneapolis and Oakland, along with Silver City, N.M., Sebastopol, Calif., Hamtramck, Mich., Fairmont, Minn., and many others — in passing a resolution urging Congress to implement a cabinet-level Department of Peace.

In the context of a pending war appropriations bill that will get consideration in Congress long before the Department of Peace legislation, cynics will see such non-binding resolutions in remote city councils as futility incarnate: the smallest of small potatoes.

I beg to differ, if only because these resolutions in themselves represent huge organizing efforts on behalf of peace. In Chicago, members of the City Council Resolution Action Committee, chaired by Jeannette Kravitz and Scott Roos, worked on the project for nearly a year before reaping success on Nov. 15, when the city's 50 aldermen passed the resolution unanimously. Such efforts inevitably create what one might call collateral benefits: They educate us and wake us up.

They also plant seeds. "We recognize that the world is interconnected and that everything influences the whole. As a consequence, there is no 'them and us.' There is only us, and the welfare of others, indeed of all life, is our own welfare."

So the Peace Alliance states on its website (peacealliancefound.org), articulating a principle that absolutely must find manifestation in our politics, economy and social infrastructure if we are to have a future. The proposed Department of Peace would be a work in progress: a center for the study and implementation of peaceful conflict-resolution techniques as well as a symbol that stands against the momentum of war.

In conservative Fairmont, Minn., an online poll conducted by the local paper, the Fairmont Sentinel, was running, as of a few days ago, approximately four-to-one in favor of the Department of Peace resolution. Such numbers belied the naysayers' colorful dismissals of the resolution, in the comment section, as "feel-good liberal crap," "increased promiscuity rights for all people" and "all about ramming the gay agenda down the throats of people."

Such flailing nonsense reflects the terror that herds a population into war. I believe we're witnessing its last gasp. If the majority of us begin actively working for what we want, peace will be inevitable.

*November 2006*


## THE CRY OF OUR INNER GANDHI

"While Republicans fight the War on Terror, grow our robust economy, and crack down on illegal immigration, House Democrats plot to establish a Department of Peace, raise your taxes, and minimize penalties for crack dealers. The difference couldn't be starker."

As a contribution to the general noise and ignorance, House Whip Roy Blunt's website politicking is nothing special. Boo! Scared yet? Fear-baiting at election time is standard GOP save-our-keister strategy, but the list of acceptable bogeymen that party leaders parade before the constituency, with inimitable cynicism, is always instructional.

Taxes, check. Crack dealers, check. Department of Peace . . . huh?

Heaping derision on this quiet but potent piece of legislation may be a miscalculation on Blunt's part, given that most Americans have lost patience with the carnage in Iraq, don't feel safer because of the war on terror and want the country to move in a new direction.

I can understand why Blunt himself would be scared of it — the establishment of a cabinet-level Department of Peace would signal a profound national direction change — but, sadly, I also understand why he sees it as a safe target to mock and misrepresent. The extraordinary notion that violence, like disease, may have causes that can be eradicated — that it is not embedded in human nature and therefore inevitable — isn't in wide circulation yet. It remains barely a pinprick in the national awareness, as manifested by the mainstream media and other outlets of popular culture.

The concept is also dangerous and upsets the powers that be. Violence is not only big business, it permeates the mythology that unites us as a nation. To suggest building a culture of peace, of which a Department of Peace would be one component, no doubt seems like a "plot" to the likes of Blunt — but I'm convinced there is a groundswell of hope for such a culture, indeed, a spiritual hunger for it.

A woman recently wrote to me: "I don't think I've ever felt a deeper level of frustration with the direction this country is going. Honestly though, what do you do? I give to the candidates and important causes, I've gone to marches and rallies, I write letters when necessary but I honestly don't know what to do with the anger, frustration, despair that I feel. I've had this conversation with friends and we talk about it but then agree that we don't 'Do' anything. But what is there to do? What is the best way to get involved?"

How many of us haven't felt such anguish ourselves? There's no simple fix for this sort of frustration, which, though it may be triggered by the Bush presidency, is far more spiritual in nature than it is political. For all the nation's vaunted self-aggrandizement as the world's oldest democracy, we are not encouraged by the mass media to participate in public life — certainly not at that level.

The Washington Post, for instance, in a story about House Minority Leader Nancy Pelosi (the story quotes Blunt's laundry list of bogeymen), describes how the California Democrat set about revitalizing her party after its defeat in '04. Did she reach out to the public, tap into the great desire for change afoot in the land or craft a relevant party platform? Well, actually, no.

Instead, the story matter-of-factly notes, "she reached out to advertising executives, Internet moguls and language specialists to ask how Democrats could rise from the ashes and challenge President Bush and the Republicans."

This is the kind of story that ruins my day. The word "participatory" seems to be so thoroughly atrophied at this point that no self-respecting journalist would seriously consider using it as a modifier — much less an amplifier — for "democracy." Yet my anguished letter-writer is groping for precisely this word. That vibrating imperative she expressed, to do something that matters, is nothing less, in my view, than the cry of our inner Gandhi to become the change we want to see happen in the world.

And this brings me back to the Department of Peace, the culture of peace, the idea of peace. If we don't break the cycles of violence that keep hatred and injustice at a constant simmer, our future is limited and stunted. "We need a partner in our government so that peace becomes an organizing principle in this society," said Dot Maver, executive director of The Peace Alliance. That's the value of the movement to establish a Department of Peace, and for those of you, like my correspondent, who want to know where to put your energy, this may be the place.

Peace, as defined by Johan Galtung at transcend.org, is "the capacity to handle conflicts with empathy, nonviolence and creativity." Far from being a "plot" hatched by a cabal of Democrats led by Nancy Pelosi, as Rep. Blunt seems to think it is (if only he were right), peace is a principle, an array of social technologies and, above all, a life commitment demanding every ounce of our strength.

*October 2006*

## THE CONSCIENCE OF LOS ALAMOS

I looked up when Ed pointed to the butte that loomed suddenly in the bend of the mountain road and said, "See. That's where they should go, right there."

And for an instant I imagined them towering against the big sky over Los Alamos, N.M.: two white granite "peace obelisks" 30 feet high, signaling to everyone entering or leaving the Atomic City, birthplace of The Bomb and home for 60-plus years of the national weapons lab that bears its name, that a counter-consciousness has staked its claim in the heart of the nuclear weapons industry. Their inscription begins:

"Welcome to Los Alamos, New Mexico, the United States of America, the city of fire. Our fires are brighter than a thousand suns. It was once believed that only God could destroy the world, but scientists working in Los Alamos first harnessed the power of the atom. The power released through fission and fusion gives many men the ability to commence the destruction of all life on earth. . . ."

This is the vision and nightmare of Ed Grothus, for 20 years a machinist in that very weapons lab, and for almost twice as long since then a much different sort of presence in town — peace activist, clown prince, self-proclaimed cardinal of the First Church of High Technology and, as proprietor of the Black Hole (dubbed "the most unusual place in the universe" by former astronaut Don Pettit), a dealer in old bomb casings and dented file cabinets and other, occasionally mind-bogglingly exotic discarded equipment from the lab, or what he calls "nuclear waste."

A lot of people call their visit to the Black Hole a pilgrimage, and there is indeed something awe-inspiring, if not hallowed, about the place — an acre or so of junk and history, much of it crammed into the shell of a former Piggly-Wiggly grocery store, all of it animated by Ed himself. The 84-year-old man, weathered and craggy, with a shock of white hair, gives tours to dozens of people each day; each tour is a combination history lesson and peace lecture, and both are personal.

For instance, at the requisite stop at a certain high-speed camera, once exquisitely state-of-the-art, with a complex revolving mirror, but which is now obsolete — lab junk, out the back door with it — Ed will tell you with a fierce mixture of pride, bitterness and gallows humor that when he worked at the lab he wielded this baby.

"It takes a picture of the exact moment of the blast," he said. "I worked in the weapons group to develop 'better' atomic bombs." As he talks he hugs the camera — it was his, and it still is. And he shakes his head at the waste: a $2 billion annual budget at the lab allows scientists to discard what they're done with after a year or maybe after a single experiment.

Ed buys the stuff at auctions and sells it to people with a wide variety of interests. A lot of artists frequent the Black Hole and poke around for inspiration. Ed also supplies movie props, beginning with "Silkwood" in 1983. It's nuts, of course, but in such an American way — that part of the residue of weapons production winds up in anti-nuke and other movies. But Ed doesn't linger too long on the oddness or irony.

As a machinist at R Site, "We did the hydrodynamics of implosions," he told me. "We reduced the size of a bomb by 30 times while we increased the yield by 30 times."

It was during the Vietnam War that his own conscience imploded. While watching war coverage on TV, he lost his protective illusion that this was honorable work, ultimately bringing good to the world. He started getting involved in anti-war activities. Before too long, the schism between work and conscience became untenable and, in late 1969, he left the lab. But he had no interest in leaving Los Alamos.

Ed prospered as a businessman, selling turquoise and silver jewelry and dealing "nuclear waste" on the side. Now he just does the latter, but his real occupation is staring down the true believers of the nuclear establishment.

"Everyone from Einstein on down failed," he said. Failed, that is, to curb that establishment or even spread the alarm sufficiently, so that most of the human race grasped the danger they were in. "It's terrible to have a conceit like mine," he conceded, "to think that everything depends on me." But he added, "Failure is not an option for us."

And this brings me back to those obelisks, which are real. They were quarried and carved in China — a project of considerable undertaking that Ed conceived in a flash some years ago, shortly after he had acquired, at auction, two three-ton blocks of black granite from the lab, which he dubbed the "Doomsday Stones." Inspired by a book he was reading on ancient Egypt, he decided to turn them into modern-day Rosetta Stones, which would bear an inscription in 15 languages, including, if he ever finds a translator, hieroglyphics. The obelisks, which he shipped back from China last fall and are currently in storage in a trailer on the lot of the Black Hole, would be mounted atop the Doomsday Stones . . . maybe on that butte overlooking Los Alamos.

And maybe not, of course. And maybe no matter what happens to them, it will be too late for humanity. But the proprietor of the Black Hole won't stop trying to sound his message until it is.

*June 2007*

*UPDATE: Ed died quietly at home, of cancer, on Feb. 12, 2009. He was 85.*

## NAKED AND AFRAID

What blessings, what outrage.

The Amish child said, "Shoot me first." The survivors counseled forgiveness and prayed for the soul of the murderer. This was all too solemn and too real to be purveyed by the mainstream media as nothing more than picturesque curiosity, horse-and-buggy morality in the age of the Hummer.

The Amish modeled courage and healing for the rest of America. They modeled a peace built not on intimidation and conquest but on respect and forgiveness. They shut down the cynics for almost a week. They grieved, they buried their dead and they reached out to the killer's widow.

Kneel with them, mourn with them, rise up angry.

The body count in our nation's schools over a period of barely a week was eight innocents: students, a teacher, a principal, shot point-blank by psycho-terrorists with easy access to personal arsenals. Another eight were injured and at least one of them, an Amish girl, is in grave condition. More than 400 people have died in school violence in the last dozen years, many hundreds of others have been wounded, and uncounted close calls — like the one this past Monday morning — have been averted.

On Monday, a 13-year-old boy in a black trench coat walked into his school in Joplin, Mo., with a Mac-90 assault rifle and fired it into the ceiling. No one was injured, but "it was a very close call," the superintendent said. Let me repeat: 13-year-old boy, Mac-90. An officer interviewed by the Associated Press said, "Police believe they know where the student got the weapon but would not disclose those details. He said it was not uncommon for people in the area to own high-power firearms."

We're stalled in the pretense of not knowing. "Experts can only speculate . . ." Who the hell are these experts the media invoke in the wake of every slaughter, to blink and shrug through their fog of innocence and tell us nothing? We know, I submit, more than we think we know. We know that the path to begin addressing this horror lies in the direction we most fear: the path of disarmament.

"This is imitation of Christ at its most naked," author Tom Shachtman told the New York Times, speaking of the Amish practice of nonviolence (I came across the quote in a fine column by Rod Dreher in the Dallas Morning News). Who of us dares to stand naked in the presence of our deepest fears? Yet this is what we must do. What a leap we'll have to make if we are to save our children — if we are to survive.

This is not about having the right religion. This is not about being Amish. This is about living our lives with a calm courage that understands that survival lies in reaching out, not striking back. Even more so, it is about renouncing the culture of heavily armed fear that surrounds us. Look where it's gotten us.

Consider: "But the enduring tragedy of Bush's 'mother of all presidential miscalculations,'" writes Robert Parry for Consortium News, "is that his underlying theory for addressing the problem of Islamic militancy hasn't changed. It is still a strategy of 'kill, kill, kill' — get revenge for 9/11 even against Muslims who had nothing to do with it — and that is likely to continue, if not expand, after the Nov. 7 elections."

Milk-truck driver Charlie Roberts, who was angry with God, had pretty much the same policy. So did the Columbine killers and all the other lost souls who have yielded to the ultimate temptation of our times. What if this kind of behavior were not role-modeled from the top?

A week after the murder of the schoolgirls in Lancaster County, Pa., and the day after the 13-year-old boy loosed a round of Mac-90 ammo at a water pipe on the ceiling of his school in Joplin, the Bush administration convened a summit on school violence in Maryland. It was led by, of all people, Attorney General Alberto Gonzales, the guy who called the Geneva Conventions "quaint" and asserted that torture was legal.

The highlight of the summit seems to have been a rebuke of Bush administration policy by the manager of the Center for the Prevention of School Violence in Raleigh, N.C. He wanted to know why the administration attempted to cut the $347 million allotted for school-safety grants for states this year.

In the context of what the administration actually stands for — bloated militarism, niggardly incompetence in the social sphere and, of course, a president who's above the law — the platitudes the first lady and others mouthed at the summit were particularly painful. "I urge all adults across the country to take their responsibility to children — their own children, and their community's children — seriously," Laura Bush said.

Responsibility this vague has a way of being passed along to someone else. I fear Marian Fisher won't be the last child to have to say, "Shoot me first."

*October 2006*

## THE VIOLENCE INTERRUPTERS CeaseFire

A dozen of us stood around a dead flower and a piece of bare sidewalk. There may have been more ho-hum in my heart than grief, at least at first, but slowly something started to break.

"Oh God, have mercy." This is what we chanted.

I paw at hope as I write about this — hope for Chicago, where I live, hope for this country and hope for peace. I say those last words with humility and skepticism, aware of how small I felt as I stood in this group, but knowing I was only there because a large turning is in motion.

"Oh God, we come before you today, crying out for the shooting initiated by Anthony Morgan, which led to his death on this corner of our neighborhood Tuesday night."

In the annals of homicide, this is a three-paragraph story on page 8. A 21-year-old man/boy was walking along Pratt Boulevard on Chicago's Far North Side — my neighborhood, Rogers Park — one balmy evening last week. A police car drove past, he started walking the other way, the cops thought this was suspicious and stopped, Morgan started running, an officer started chasing him, then — according to police — Morgan fired three shots at the officer. The officer fired back and killed him. Morgan fell into the parkway, where neighbors had planted flowers, landing on one of them as he died.

I live about four blocks away and was walking home from my train stop as Morgan was in the process of running, shooting and dying. I saw the flashing blue lights on Pratt, a few blocks ahead of me, but I'm a big city boy, used to sirens, cops and commotion. I didn't think anything of it and continued on my way, learning only the next day that I'd almost walked into a shooting in progress.

Here's where I ponder my own calloused heart — my diminished sense of community, my protective withdrawal into "me and mine" mentality. I could, upon hearing the story, have reduced the dead young man to "probably a gangbanger" status and given the incident no more thought, by which I mean, consign my fleeting awareness of another pointless shooting to some generic hell in my imagination and pretend I've forgotten about it. Life goes on, etc.

What happened instead is that I ran into my neighbor, Sally Youngquist, a minister who, it turns out, is linked up with CeaseFire, a citywide organization — part of the Chicago Project for Violence Prevention — that for the past dozen years has quietly been dealing with violence as a public-health issue and building coalitions in high-risk Chicago neighborhoods (including my own!) for the purpose of interrupting predictable cycles of violence and lowering the horrific kill count in those neighborhoods.

There are reasons to believe the program, which is a project of the University of Illinois/Chicago Department of Public Health, is having a significant effect. According to the organization's website, shootings and killings have dropped substantially in neighborhoods where CeaseFire has been active. For example: "Beat 1413 in Logan Square went from worst beat in (Chicago) in 2003 with seven killings to no killings in 2004, which coincides with more than a doubling of CeaseFire effort."

These efforts include public education, mediation and other forms of direct violence intervention by street-savvy, courageous staff members and volunteers, possibly after a shooting has occurred and the likelihood of a retaliatory shooting is high. These folks — called "violence interrupters" — will get out of bed in the middle of the night, if necessary, to visit a trouble spot and talk sense to the armed and aggrieved.

"When someone gets shot, or sometimes beaten or stabbed, and the hospital chaplains or trauma team members believe there is potential for retaliation, they call me," writes Elena Quintana at ceasefirechicago.org. "Sometimes they call me in the middle of a meeting, or during dinner, but often I'm called late at night. It is not uncommon to be called two or three times a day. I was called six times in the last 24 hours. It's July, and this is the killing season."

Quintana, who manages a violence-intervention partnership between CeaseFire and Advocate Christ Medical Center in the Chicago neighborhood of Oak Lawn, goes on to explain that, when she learns of a dangerous situation, she taps her community resources — the violence interrupters — who visit the site and do what they can to defuse whatever is going on. Where such programs are active, violence rates drop.

I write about this in wonder. This is the "technology of peace" — almost as invisible as the headlines it prevents.

CeaseFire's coalition-building efforts are extensive, and its efforts aren't limited to intervention. Not every shooting, in our volatile society, can be prevented, but the tear in the social fabric from each bullet hole must be repaired. Thus two days after Anthony Morgan's shooting, Sally led a brief, nondenominational service at the spot of his death that hallowed and reclaimed an ordinary stretch of sidewalk and made me — a resident of this neighborhood for 30 years — feel a deeper connection to it than I ever have before.

*June 2007*

## PRESENCE OF MIND

MYTH g redemptive violence

"I knew the situation was serious. I was shaking all over. But I was amazed by the complexity of my mind — the most clear part was just the speed and agility of my mind. I immediately began talking to him in a calm voice and engaged in eye contact. But he was not in his eyes. He was in his own world — pointing a gun at me."

Is this a good time to address the big lie? You know, the lie about our stark, raving helplessness in the face of armed danger and malevolence? Fortress Gun Nut has the whole country hostage to the big lie that a safe America is an armed America, and yet as our stockpile of weaponry, domestic and otherwise, increases, so does our fearfulness, and so does the danger.

And the heroes are often indistinguishable from the perps. We're all heroes in our own minds. We all watch the movies and imbibe the whack 'n' win culture. We all learn that real justice must be delivered at the point of a sword that is terrible and swift.

Christian theologian Walter Wink calls it the myth of redemptive violence, this self-evident conviction — as old as Mesopotamia, as current as the Saturday morning cartoons — that violence is effective and free of unwanted consequences. Six millennia of evidence to the contrary hasn't changed anything because myth is impervious to empirical data. It's born anew with every war, every special-effects extravaganza from Hollywood, every loner's sad plot for revenge. And so many people profit from it.

I think our only hope is to pierce the myth — this smug, self-satisfied myth that keeps luring us into foolish decisions. Maybe it will never go away; the appeal of clean and easy vengeance and the ultimate end run around obstacles is perennially appealing. But if we challenge the myth with an even more appealing truth — that we have extraordinary inner resources we can tap in a crisis — perhaps we can push the myth out of cultural dominance and, crucially, disarm it.

The place to start is where we're the most desperate. How do we defend ourselves? Whether or not you're armed, you need presence of mind, and if you have that you may not need anything else.

"I remember clearly continuing to talk to him and keeping eye contact," my friend Shelly, who is quoted above, told me. One night some years ago, shortly after she had left her husband, he showed up at her house and pulled a gun on her. Their 2-year-old son Seth was asleep in the next room.

Shelly's is a story of courage and quick thinking, which are the basic tools of self-defense. As soon as her vacant-eyed ex pulled out his handgun, her mind went into high gear, evaluating possible actions. She realized instantly that trying to run or grabbing for the phone would lead to disaster. She simply maintained eye contact.

"I had a very calm tone of voice. It wasn't fearful," she said. "It was very clear there was a narrow window here. That's where it felt almost like something else taking over me. I was aware I was shaking. But I was fully present to the situation, totally alert.

"At some point I said, if you shoot me you'll wake up Seth. Then what will happen? That's when he came back. I saw him come back into his eyes. He started swinging his gun around."

She continued talking with hyper-calmness, as though addressing a child, reminding him: "You don't want to wake up Seth." Finally she said, "'Well, I have to go to work tomorrow.' I turned around and walked into the bathroom and started brushing my teeth."

He put his gun away. The crisis was over. He eventually left and got on with his life.

"Most assailants work from a definite set of expectations about how the victim will respond, and they need the victim to act like a victim," writes Wink in *The Powers That Be*. And the best way not to "act like a victim" is to respond to a threat from outside the expectations of the attacker — not with flailing fear or paralyzed surrender but, sheerly, with presence of mind. In such a state, your self-defense options multiply.

My friend Leigh's mother once confronted every woman's worst nightmare. "She woke up and heard the window slide open and someone prying open the screen," he told me. "She looked up and saw a man climbing in through the window. He announced he'd been looking forward to this for a long time and described what he intended to do to her.

"Mom — I hate to say it — wore black plastic horn-rim glasses, like the women in Far Side cartoons," Leigh went on. "She reached under her nightstand, grabbed her glasses, let one arm fall down and held it out as if it were a handgun. She yelled at the guy to get back or she'd fire. And he left."

I relay these stories in the hopes of getting more. The point is not that horn-rimmed glasses are a reliable defense against rape but that people who maintain their presence of mind under dire threat will think of something to do. I'd like to start a clearinghouse of such testimony. Please e-mail me if you have yourself or know someone who has defused a threat with unarmed presence of mind. Perhaps the sum total of a thousand or a million unique stories is a myth-busting truth that could transform a culture.

*August 2007*

## THE PREREQUISITE FOR SALVATION

The poster exploits the howling demons of our culture. It's my morning smack-in-the-eye, bright gold, four feet high, dominated by a female in stark silhouette striding resolutely into the wreckage of post-apocalypse Las Vegas. She wields a wicked-looking blaster in each hand.

The ad, for the movie *Resident Evil: Extinction*, occupies the spot on the elevated train platform where I await the start of my daily commute to work.

This is not a movie I'm going to see, but I can't avoid feeling the impact of its throbbing message: Justice cometh, and she has a nice butt, and she's armed.

Wow. The gears mesh — yet again! — on the perfect delusion. For entertainment, we hop ourselves up on sex and road rage, and fantasy bleeds into reality. The result is an armed, frightened society and a high-tech war on terror that promises to cut a terrible swath of destruction across the planet before it runs out of, so to speak, gas.

Last week I wrote a column about what theologian Walter Wink called "the myth of redemptive violence" — the ancient and all-purpose justification for war, conquest and exploitation that permeates our belief system at both the macro and micro levels. Over and over again, we mobilize around the illusion of consequence-free, violent eradication of threats and annoyances and, in the process, run roughshod over a more complex view of human interaction and effective problem-solving.

In the spirit of challenging the cultural dominance of the myth of redemptive violence, I invited readers to e-mail stories to me of their own or a friend's use of unarmed presence of mind to defuse a dangerous situation. The invitation is still open. The idea is to establish a clearinghouse on the effectiveness of unarmed conflict resolution.

The stories I've received so far vary widely, of course, but have a few common threads, the most significant of which was summed up by Barry Stevens, who wrote: "I really believe in that power of locking in the humanity through the eyes."

Eye contact! This is the prerequisite for salvation.

Some of the correspondents wrote of breaking an assailant's resolve by piercing through to his humanity; others did so with a convincing threat or contemptuous dismissal of the assailant's ability to do harm. But in every case, the "victim" held eye contact and refused to surrender his or her power in the moment, just because the person making the threat A) had a weapon, or B) was physically intimidating.

"I am a psychiatrist," said a writer who requested anonymity. "I was treating a combat survivor for PTSD-related issues. He had an argument with his wife and had gone into 'combat mode.' I was sitting in my study when he broke into my house, Marine K-bar in his hand, ready for violence. I also went into the hyperalert, engage-the-attacker mode.

"I was unable to distract the man from his violent intent," the writer continued, "until I thought to say, 'You know, I'm going to have to call your wife and tell her you're here at nine o'clock at night.' At this he immediately sat down on one of my chairs and started crying. His wife eventually came and got him, and the episode was over.

"The next day, I went out to the garage and saw that the man had taken the axe used to split wood and slammed it so hard into the chopping block that no one could extract it. THEN I got scared, really scared. It took a while before I settled down again."

My friend B.C., who lives in Arizona, wrote of encountering a different sort of threat, twice in the same day. The first time, she panicked when she saw a three-foot rattlesnake in her back yard. "I ran like hell, falling headlong into the gravel." She made it to her deck with a bleeding knee and arm.

"Later that day, it began to thunder outside," she wrote. "After about a half-hour, I decided I'd better go out and turn off my fountain since lightning was likely in the area. To my surprise, when I opened the back door, a beautiful bobcat was stationed at the other water dish, drinking. I was mesmerized and knew if I went in to get the camera, it would likely leave. I talked to it very quietly, telling it it was OK and to drink all it wanted. Its green eyes never left my face and once it had its fill, it walked down the stairs, out into my back yard and down the ravine.

"I guess I didn't have presence of mind in the first instance — just fear — but in the second episode, presence of mind took over and I just talked calmly to something that was a wild and beautiful creature."

This is the truth of redemptive connection. We connect primarily through the eyes. And when we connect thus, it's with a nakedness and honesty that makes me think of nothing so much as the words of philosopher-priest Pierre Teilhard de Chardin: "Someday, after we have mastered the wind, the waves, the tides, and gravity, we shall harness for God the energies of Love. Then, for the second time in the history of the world, we will have discovered fire."

*September 2007*


## A WORLD THAT WORKS FOR EVERYBODY

Peace is a chant, a vibration, a leap of the human spirit into the 21st century and beyond. It's also H.R. 808 — radical common sense crafted into a bill and introduced this week into the new Congress by Dennis Kucinich.

Let me describe for you, as best I can in this brief space, the heave of emotion this piece of legislation and the campaign to support it have set off in me the past few days. For this I thank and blame the Peace Alliance, which held a conference in D.C. over the weekend in support of the bill — well, it was half conference, fact-dense and nitty-gritty, brimming with info on bullying and suicide and war; and half revival, alive with music and global religion, full of God and Buddha and the spirit of the Founding Fathers and Gandhi and Martin Luther King and Jane Addams and Susan B. Anthony and many others.

By the time the Rev. Michael Beckwith — this was on Sunday morning, a day and a half into it — invoked the idea of "a world that works for everybody," I felt an unbearable cry from the private depths of my heart: I believe! I believe! The cry pushed ferociously against an almost equal disbelief and I felt split in two — but maybe giving birth is always like that.

That morning, the main headline in the Washington Post read: "At Least 125 Killed in Blast at Baghdad Market." This is so clearly not a world that works for everybody, and it's so clearly getting worse. "A suicide bomber detonated more than a ton of explosives in a market in central Baghdad late Saturday afternoon. . . . 'It's like a slaughterhouse. You can see blood everywhere. It's an unbelievable sight.'"

Peace is not a lull between bomb blasts. But to envision the world that Beckwith and others at the conference invoked — to compress hope into a rending certainty that such a world is possible as well as necessary — peels away the numbness and cynicism that lets us live in this one. No wonder so few people are embracing it.

And yet that's not true at all. A yearning for peace is at everyone's core, and the recognition of our complex, planetary interdependence is hardly controversial. Peace studies and nonviolent conflict resolution — the technology of peace — are gaining prominence in universities around the world.

"There are new ideas on the world's horizon, as different from the twentieth-century worldview as the twentieth century was different from the nineteenth century," writes Marianne Williamson, founder of the Peace Alliance, in her book Healing the Soul of America. "We are ready to apply principles of healing and recovery, not just to our bodies, not just to our relationships, but to every aspect of life."

Kucinich's legislation, which calls for the creation of a cabinet-level Department of Peace, is just a step in the process. It's not a fabrication out of whole cloth. It would fund and coordinate programs already in existence, in schools, prisons and elsewhere; link the concepts of domestic and international violence; and give the U.S. government access to the latest thought and research on everything from safe schools to international arms control.

Its implementation would acknowledge and further an awareness, a rationality, already taking hold. For instance: "It's a fraction of the cost to prevent a war than prosecute a war," Williamson pointed out at the conference. Somewhere in the corridors of power, a voice should be sounding, and advocating for, such common sense.

Similarly, while the state of California, Williamson noted, spends $150,000 per year per juvenile delinquent, violence-prevention programs are funded at the level of $150 per youth. It's nuts — such an allocation of resources is as foolish and wasteful and wrongheaded as a suicide bomber in the marketplace. "Nothing is so dangerous for our security," Williamson said, "as large groups of desperate people."

Yet the rationality of peace tends to just sit there — ho hum, what else is new? — while the headlines go off in our faces. Are we doomed to a violent politics, with all its news drama and illusion of instant transformation? Powerful interests, even government itself, seem locked into the mechanisms of war and human violence, however suicidal in the long, and now middle-distance, run.

The creation of a Department of Peace would by no means extricate us from our dilemma, but it would signal our collective interest in making a start. Yet the bill faces enormous obstacles just to come up for debate. In the last session of Congress, it had 74 co-sponsors; with its reintroduction, 41 legislators are so far back on board. Its advocates will need enormous passion to keep the interest in it growing.

This brings me back to that moment in the conference when a just, fair world — a world that works for everybody — flickered in my heart as more than an abstraction, and I felt myself clot with tears. Perhaps you'd cry too if you sensed how close we are to such a world, and how close we are to blowing it forever.

*February 2007*

## WHERE WAR MEETS PEACE

"I trained my weapon on him," Kristopher Goldsmith said. It was a little boy, 6 years old maybe, standing on a roof, menacing the soldiers with a stick. "I was thinking, I hate these Iraqis who throw rocks. I could kill this kid."

OK, America, let's look through the sights of Goldsmith's rifle for a long, long half-minute or so, draw a bead on the boy's heart, fondle the trigger — what to do? The soldier's decision is our decision.

This is occupied Iraq: the uncensored version, presented to us with relentless, at times unbearable honesty over four intense days last week in a historic gathering outside Washington, D.C., of returning vets, many of them broken and bitter about what they were forced to do, and what's been done to them, in sometimes two, three, four tours of duty in the biggest mistake in American history.

"These are the times that try men's souls," Thomas Paine wrote in 1776. "The summer soldier and sunshine patriot will, in this crisis, shrink from the service of his country; but he that stands it now, deserves the love and thanks of man and woman."

The vets who told their stories last week, in an event at the National Labor College in Silver Spring, Md., sponsored by Iraq Vets Against the War, are the "winter soldiers" of the war on terror, standing in service to their country by bearing the truth to it, just as Vietnam vets held the first Winter Soldier gathering 37 years ago in Detroit, in the wake of the My Lai massacre revelations, to let the American public know that that massacre wasn't an aberration but, rather, the logical result of our brutal, official policy there.

Once again, the crisis we are in is the result of an official policy that has dehumanized an entire country, an entire people. Once again, we are waging a war that can only be "won" when the American people themselves demand an end to it. The men and women who spoke last week brought not just the truth but an imperative as urgent as a live grenade:

Unconditional withdrawal of all troops and contractors from Iraq NOW; full benefits for all returning vets; reparations for the Iraqi people, so they can rebuild their country on their own terms.

I was able to attend two days of the Winter Soldier gathering. What I witnessed was a convergence of forces of historical significance, as angry, idealistic warriors, horrified by what they saw and were ordered to do during their time in the military, ashamed of what they sometimes did willingly within the context of racist arrogance that is the occupation of Iraq, reclaimed their humanity by declaring themselves peace warriors. I found myself at the heart of the American conscience: the place where war meets peace.

To experience the full impact of this event, you can listen to the testimony, among other places, at ivaw.org. In this column, I have space for the briefest of summaries, as GIs up to the rank of captain talked about the realities of the occupation of Iraq.

House raids: Over and over again, the speakers gave variations of these words of Jeffrey Smith: "We had everyone in house, including children, zip-tied on the front lawn (when we) realized we were in the wrong house. So we went to another house." Or these of Matthew Childers: "It seemed like we raided countless residences — 3 a.m., our semiautomatics out, screaming at them in a language they didn't understand. We rarely found anything."

Detainees: Common themes were the beatings, the sleep deprivation. Childers again: "They were beaten, humiliated, teased with food and water. These guys were in our custody for a week and I didn't see them eat the whole time. A Marine wiped his ass with an Iraqi's hat and tried to feed it to a blindfolded Iraqi — who was desperate for food and tried to eat it."

Racism and general disrespect: The Iraqis were "hadjis" — the equivalent, of course, of gooks or untermenschen. Speaker after speaker talked about receiving no cultural training in boot camp, but plenty of bayonet training. Matt Howard: "We treated Iraq like our own personal cesspool." Bryan Casler: "I saw the destruction of the Babylon ruins — people breaking off chunks to bring home; joyriding up walls. There was a complete lack of understanding."

With all this in mind — with an awareness that as many as a million Iraqis have died since the invasion, that 4 or 5 million have been displaced — let us peer once again at the little boy in the sights of Goldsmith's rifle.

"I was so close to killing a 6-year-old boy," he said. "I was put in that position by the occupation of Iraq." He could have taken the kid out, without consequence, but mastered the impulse, mastered his own drilled-in contempt for Iraqi life, and lowered his rifle.

He completed his tour, saw the horror, felt the death of his own youth, came home a severe alcoholic who got no help from the Army. Shortly before he was due to be discharged, his platoon was locked into an 18-month redeployment (part of the president's troop surge); instead of going back, he tried to kill himself with pills and vodka. He failed at that, was hospitalized and ultimately received a general discharge from the Army with a "misconduct, serious offense" notation. He lost his college benefits. His life is shattered. He delivers pizza on Wednesdays to get by.

As he finished his testimony, Goldsmith named his commanding officers and announced, "I have a message for you." He sprang to his feet, held his fingers in a V and cried: "Peace!"

*March 2008*

# Index

**Part Three:** *9/11 Revisited*

**Part Four:** *A Hole in God's Grace*

**Part Five:** *Einstein's Door*

**Part Six:** *Common Wonders*

## Part Seven: *Courage Grows Strong at the Wound*

LaVergne, TN USA
01 February 2011
214686LV00001B/8/P